THE LANGUAGE OF LITERATURE

THE ***InterActive*** READER™

McDougal Littell
A HOUGHTON MIFFLIN COMPANY
Evanston, Illinois • Boston • Dallas

Reading Consultant, *The InterActive Reader™*

Sharon Sicinski-Skeans, Ph.D. Assistant Professor of Reading, University of Houston-Clear Lake; former K-12 Language Arts Program Director, Spring Independent School District, Houston, Texas
The reading consultant guided the conceptual development of the *InterActive Reader.™* She participated in the development of prototype materials, the planning and writing of lessons, and the review of completed materials.

Senior Consultants, *The Language of Literature*

Arthur N. Applebee Professor of Education, State University of New York at Albany; Director, National Research Center on English Learning and Achievements; Senior Fellow, Center for Writing and Literacy

Andrea B. Bermúdez Professor of Studies in Language and Culture; Director, Research Center for Language and Culture; Chair, Foundations and Professional Studies, University of Houston-Clear Lake

Sheridan Blau Senior Lecturer in English and Education and former Director of Composition, University of California at Santa Barbara; Director, South Coast Writing Project; Director, Literature Institute for Teachers; Past President, National Council of Teachers of English

Rebekah Caplan Coordinator, English Language Arts K-12, Oakland Unified School District, Oakland, California; Teacher-Consultant, Bay Area Writing Project, University of California at Berkeley; served on the California State English Assessment Development Team for Language Arts

Peter Elbow Professor of English, University of Massachusetts at Amherst; Fellow, Bard Center for Writing and Thinking

Susan Hynds Professor and Director of English Education, Syracuse University, Syracuse, New York

Judith A. Langer Professor of Education, State University of New York at Albany; Director, National Research Center on English Learning and Achievements; Director, Albany Institute for Research on Education

James Marshall Professor of English and English Education, University of Iowa, Iowa City

Acknowledgments

Arte Público Press: "Legal Alien," from *Chants* by Pat Mora (Houston: Arte Público Press—University of Houston, 1985). Copyright © 1985 by Pat Mora. Reprinted by permission of the publisher.

Susan Bergholz Literary Services: "Straw into Gold: The Metamorphosis of the Everyday" by Sandra Cisneros. First published in *The Texas Observer,* 25 September 1987. Copyright © 1987 by Sandra Cisneros. Reprinted by permission of Susan Bergholz Literary Services, New York. All rights reserved.

Chronicle Books: "Mexicans Begin Jogging" by Gary Soto, from *Gary Soto: New & Selected Poems,* published by Chronicle Books, San Francisco. Copyright © 1995 by Gary Soto. Reprinted by permission of Chronicle Books.

(Continued on page 356)

ISBN 0-618-00792-X

Contents

	The InterActive Reader™		iv
	User's Guide		vi
	Student Model		xii
William Bradford	*from* **Of Plymouth Plantation**	CHRONICLE	2
Jonathan Edwards	*from* **Sinners in the Hands of an Angry God**	SERMON	13
Arthur Miller	*from* **The Crucible**	DRAMA	21
Patrick Henry	**Speech in the Virginia Convention**	SPEECH	48
Michel-Guillaume Jean de Crèvecoeur	**What Is An American?**	ESSAY	59
Ralph Waldo Emerson	*from* **Self-Reliance**	ESSAY	66
Henry David Thoreau	*from* **Civil Disobedience**	ESSAY	76
Walt Whitman	**I Hear America Singing** **I Sit and Look Out** *from* **Song of Myself**	POETRY	96
Edgar Allan Poe	**The Masque of the Red Death**	SHORT STORY	112
Nathaniel Hawthorne	**Dr. Heidegger's Experiment**	SHORT STORY	132
William Faulkner	**A Rose for Emily**	SHORT STORY	157
Ambrose Bierce	**An Occurrence at Owl Creek Bridge**	SHORT STORY	172
Mark Twain	*from* **Life on the Mississippi**	MEMOIR	187
Willa Cather	**A Wagner Matinee**	SHORT STORY	197
Emily Dickinson	**"Hope" is the thing with feathers—** **My life closed twice before its close—** **I Heard a Fly Buzz—when I died—** **Because I could not stop for Death—**	POETRY	210
Charlotte Perkins Gilman	**The Yellow Wallpaper**	SHORT STORY	219
Paul Laurence Dunbar	**We Wear the Mask** **Sympathy**	POETRY	241
Langston Hughes	**I, Too** **Harlem** **The Weary Blues**	POETRY	247
Zora Neale Hurston	**How It Feels to Be Colored Me**	ESSAY	254
Robert Frost	**The Death of the Hired Man**	POETRY	263
Ernest Hemingway	**The End of Something**	SHORT STORY	274
T. S. Eliot	**The Love Song of J. Alfred Prufrock**	POETRY	282
Katherine Anne Porter	**The Jilting of Granny Weatherall**	SHORT STORY	297
Martin Luther King, Jr.	*from* **Letter from Birmingham Jail**	LETTER	312
Gary Soto	**Mexicans Begin Jogging**	POETRY	330
Pat Mora	**Legal Alien**	POETRY	330
Sandra Cisneros	**Straw into Gold**	ESSAY	335
	Personal Word List		344

Introducing *The InterActive Reader*™

The InterActive Reader™ is a new kind of literature book. As you will see, this book encourages your involvement at every stage of your reading. It's a book to mark on, write on, and make your own.

An Easy-to-Carry Literature Text

This book won't weigh you down—it can fit comfortably in your backpack. Yet it contains many of the best-known authors and most popular selections in high school classes, such as the following:

Edgar Allan Poe's classic tale of terror "The Masque of the Red Death"

William Faulkner's unforgettable story "A Rose for Emily"

Four memorable poems by **Emily Dickinson**, one of America's greatest poets

Martin Luther King's eloquent "Letter from Birmingham Jail"

All major types of literature are represented—fiction, nonfiction, poetry, and drama. *The InterActive Reader*™ is your "take home" book, so that you can study these classic works on your own. The book is also ideal for in-class work.

Help for Reading

Many works of literature are challenging, especially when you're reading them for the first time. *The InterActive Reader*™ gives you the help you need to make sense of these works. Here's just a sampling of what you'll find:

Reading Tips Simple and effective reading strategies are provided for each selection.

Preview A preview is given at the beginning of each selection so that you'll know what to expect.

Focus Each work is divided into sections, with a focus at the beginning of each section. It tells you what to look for as you read.

Pause and Reflect At the end of each section, you'll find questions that will help you check your understanding.

Read Aloud Special passages are marked for oral interpretation. Reading aloud will increase your understanding—and enjoyment.

A Book to Write In

Finally! Here's a book that you're supposed to write in! You can mark up this book in a number of different ways. By reading with a pen or a pencil in hand, you'll become a more active reader and a better reader. Look for the MARK IT UP symbol in the following places:

Keep Track This feature suggests an easy marking system—a check, question mark, and exclamation mark—to track your understanding. This system is illustrated on pages vi and x.

Focus Here, you will often be asked to underline or circle passages as you read—or to take notes in the margins.

Pause and Reflect At these stopping points, you will often be asked to go back into the text to mark up key passages.

Challenge This feature occurs at the end of each selection. Often, you will be asked to mark up the text as a way of supporting your judgment.

Also, the **Notes** column in the side margin gives you space to write down reactions, make connections, and explore your thoughts.

Vocabulary Support

Words to Know In most selections, you'll find Words to Know. These words are underlined in the text and defined at the bottom of the page. To practice your knowledge of these words, use the Words to Know SkillBuilder page at the end of the selection.

Personal Word List You'll also have frequent chances to build your own personal vocabulary. You can mark new words as you come across them in the selections, then add them to your Personal Word List, which begins on page 344.

SkillBuilder Pages

After each selection, you'll usually find these SkillBuilder pages:
Active Reading SkillBuilder
Literary Analysis SkillBuilder
Words to Know SkillBuilder (for most selections)
These pages will help you practice and apply important skills.

Links to *The Language of Literature*

If you are using McDougal Littell's *The Language of Literature,* you will find *The InterActive Reader™* to be a perfect companion. The selections in the *Reader* can all be found in that book, which gives you additional background information and a wide range of follow-up activities. *The InterActive Reader™* gives you an opportunity to read certain core selections from *The Language of Literature* in greater depth.

Read on to learn more!

User's Guide

The InterActive Reader™ has an easy-to-follow organization, illustrated by these sample pages from Of Plymouth Plantation.

Before You Read

1 If you are using *The Language of Literature*, this section will help you use features from that book.

Reading Tips

2 These practical strategies will help you gain more from your reading.

PREVIEW

3 This feature tells you what the selection is about, so that you'll know what to expect.

FOCUS

4 Every literary work is broken into sections. Each section is introduced by a Focus that tells you what to look for as you read.

MARK IT UP

5 This feature often appears in the Focus. It may ask you to underline or circle key passages in the text or to take notes in the margin as you read.

MARK IT UP KEEP TRACK

6 This easy-to-use marking system will help you track your understanding. Turn to page xii to see how a model of the system can be used.

CHRONICLE

1 Before You Read

If you are using **The Language of Literature . . .**

* Use the information on page 81 to prepare for reading.
* Look at the art on pages 84 and 87. It will help you **visualize** the Pilgrims and their settlement.

2 Reading Tips

A **chronicle** is a work of **nonfiction**, a historical account of important events. William Bradford actually witnessed the events he describes in this firsthand account.

Bradford wrote this chronicle more than 300 years ago. Some of the sentences are long, and some of the words may look strange. Try these strategies to help your understanding:

* Use the heading for each section as a guide to the content.
* Read at a steady pace and just keep moving. Try to take in big chunks of meaning. Look for main ideas and don't get lost in the details.

6 MARK IT UP **KEEP TRACK**

As you read, you can use these marks to keep track of your understanding.

✔ ..... I understand.

? ..... I don't understand this.

! ..... Interesting or surprising idea

2 The InterActive Reader

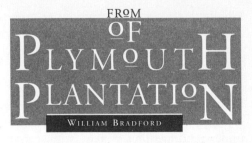

FROM
OF PLYMOUTH PLANTATION

WILLIAM BRADFORD

3 PREVIEW These excerpts tell about the Pilgrims' survival in America in the early 1600s. William Bradford, the first governor of Plymouth colony, describes the Pilgrims' many hardships, their strength of character, and their faith in God. He also explains how some Native Americans helped the colonists to survive.

4 FOCUS

Bradford describes the Pilgrims' arrival at Cape Cod in November of 1620. The Pilgrims faced the frightening wilderness of an unknown world.

5 MARK IT UP As you read, circle any details that help you understand the Pilgrims' situation. An example is highlighted.

THEIR SAFE ARRIVAL AT CAPE COD

But to omit other things (that I may be brief) after long beating at sea they[1] fell with that land which is called Cape Cod; the which being made and certainly known to be it, they were not a little joyful. . . .

Being thus arrived in a good harbor, and brought safe to land, they fell upon their knees and blessed the God of Heaven who had brought them over the vast and furious ocean, and delivered them from all the perils and miseries thereof, again to set their feet on the firm and stable earth, their proper element. . . .

But here I cannot but stay and make a pause, and stand half amazed at this poor people's present condition; and so I

---

1. **they:** Bradford refers to the Pilgrims in the third person even though he is one of them.

think will the reader, too, when he well considers the same.
Being thus passed the vast ocean, and a sea of troubles before
in their preparation (as may be remembered by that which
went before), they had now no friends to welcome them nor
20 inns to entertain or refresh their weatherbeaten bodies; no
houses or much less towns to repair to, to seek for succor.[2] It
is recorded in Scripture as a mercy to the Apostle and his
shipwrecked company, that the barbarians showed them no
small kindness in refreshing them,[3] but these savage
barbarians, when they met with them (as after will appear)
were readier to fill their sides full of arrows than otherwise.
And for the season it was winter, and they that know the
winters of that country know them to be sharp and violent,
and subject to cruel and fierce storms, dangerous to travel to
30 known places, much more to search an unknown coast.
Besides, what could they see but a hideous and <u>desolate</u>
wilderness, full of wild beasts and wild men—and what
multitudes there might be of them they knew not. Neither
could they, as it were, go up to the top of Pisgah[4] to view
from this wilderness a more goodly country to feed their
hopes; for which way soever they turned their eyes (save
upward to the heavens) they could have little <u>solace</u> or
content in respect of any outward objects. For summer being
done, all things stand upon them with a weatherbeaten face,
40 and the whole country, full of woods and thickets, represented
a wild and savage <u>hue</u>. If they looked behind them, there was
the mighty ocean which they had passed and was now as a
main bar and gulf to separate them from all the civil parts of
the world. . . .

 9 *Pause* **&** *Reflect*

---

2. **succor** (sŭk′ər): help; relief.

3. **It is . . . refreshing them:** a reference to the biblical account of the
   courteous reception of Paul and his companions by the inhabitants of
   Malta (Acts 27:41–28:2).

4. **Pisgah** (pĭz′gə): the mountain from whose peak Moses saw the Promised
   Land (Deuteronomy 34:1–4).

7 WORDS
TO
KNOW
    desolate (dĕs′ə-lĭt) *adj.* without inhabitants; barren
    solace (sŏl′ĭs) *n.* comfort in sorrow or distress
    hue (hyōō) *n.* appearance; color

MARK IT UP WORD POWER

8 Mark words that you'd like to
add to your **Personal Word List.**
After reading, you can record
the words and their meanings
beginning on page 344.

Pause **&** *Reflect*

10 1. Review the details you circled as
you read. Then write a sentence
or two to **summarize** the
Pilgrims' situation after landing
at Cape Cod.

_____

_____

_____

2. Imagine you are one of the
Pilgrims who have just set foot
on land. What do you think is the
greatest challenge that awaits
you and the other Pilgrims in the
New World? **(Evaluate)**

_____

_____

_____

_____

Of Plymouth Plantation 3

MARK IT UP WORD POWER

8 This feature will remind you
to mark words that you'd
like to add to your **Personal
Word List**. After reading,
you can look up the definitions and record information
about each word. The
Personal Word List begins
on page 344.

Pause **&** *Reflect*

9 Whenever you see these
words in a selection,
stop reading. Go to the side
column and answer the
questions. Then move
ahead to the next Focus and
continue your reading.

10 These questions appear at
the end of every section.
They provide a follow-up to
the Focus activity that
begins each section, and
they give you a quick way to
check your understanding.

---

7 WORDS
TO
KNOW
    Important **Words to Know** are
underlined in each selection.
Definitions are given at the bottom
of the page.

And there's more

11 NOTES

afterwards profitable unto them; as also of the people here, of their names, number and strength, of their situation and distance from this place, and who was chief amongst them. His name was Samoset. He told them also of another Indian whose name was Squanto, a native of this place, who had been in England and could speak better English than himself.

Being, after some time of entertainment and gifts dismissed, a while after he came again, and five more with him, and they brought again all the tools that were stolen away before, and made way for the coming of their great Sachem,[12] called Massasoit. Who, about four or five days after, came with the chief of his friends and other attendance, with the aforesaid Squanto. With whom, after friendly entertainment and some gifts given him, they made a peace with him (which hath now continued this 24 years) in these terms:

> 1. That neither he nor any of his should injure or do hurt to any of their people.
> 2. That if any of his did hurt to any of theirs, he should send the offender, that they might punish him.
> 3. That if anything were taken away from any of theirs, he should cause it to be restored; and they should do the like to his.
> 4. If any did unjustly war against him, they would aid him; if any did war against them, he should aid them.
> 5. He should send to his neighbors confederates to certify them of this, that they might not wrong them, but might be likewise comprised in the conditions of peace.[13]
> 6. That when their men came to them, they should leave their bows and arrows behind them.

After these things he returned to his place called Sowams,[14] some 40 miles from this place, but Squanto continued with them and was their interpreter and was a special instrument sent of God for their good beyond their expectation. He directed them how to set their corn, where to take fish, and to <u>procure</u> other <u>commodities</u>, and was also their pilot to bring them to unknown places for their profit, and never left them till he died.

Pause **&** *Reflect*

Pause **&** *Reflect*

READ ALOUD

12 1. Read aloud the terms in the peace treaty between the Pilgrims and Massasoit's people (the boxed passage). Then cross out the one phrase below that does *not* apply to the treaty. **(Infer)**

promotes safety

discourages theft

sets up an alliance

protects the Indian languages

2. Review the details you underlined as you read. What did the Pilgrims learn from Samoset and Squanto? **(Summarize)**

_____

_____

_____

_____

13
12. **Sachem** (sā′chəm): chief.
13. **He should . . . peace:** Massasoit was to inform other tribes about the compact so that they might also keep peace with the Pilgrims.
14. **Sowams** (sō′ämz): near the site of present-day Barrington, Rhode Island.

WORDS TO KNOW	
procure (prō-kyoor′) *v.* to get by special effort; obtain
commodity (kə-mŏd′ĭ-tē) *n.* something useful; an article of commerce

MARK IT UP

14 Some questions have a Mark It Up. This will direct you to go back into the selection to find and mark important details.

CHALLENGE

15 This question or activity occurs at the end of the selection. It challenges you to think about issues, ideas, or literary techniques that are important to the selection. Usually, you will be asked to go back into the text to mark key details or passages.

Wrapping Up

16 This appears at the end of each selection. If you are using *The Language of Literature*, this will direct you to the appropriate follow-up activities in that book.

FOCUS

Read to find out how the Pilgrims prepare for their second winter in America.

FIRST THANKSGIVING

They began now to gather in the small harvest they had, and to fit up their houses and dwellings against winter, being all well recovered in health and strength and had all things in good plenty. For as some were thus employed in affairs abroad, others were exercised in fishing, about cod and bass and other fish, of which they took good store, of which every family had their portion. All the summer there was no want; and now began to come in store of fowl, as winter approached, of which this place did abound when they came first (but afterward decreased by degrees). And besides waterfowl there was great store of wild turkeys, of which they took many, besides venison, etc. Besides they had about a peck[15] a meal a week to a person, or now since harvest, Indian corn to that proportion. Which made many afterwards write so largely of their plenty here to their friends in England, which were not <u>feigned</u> but true reports.

Pause & *Reflect*

15. peck: a unit of measurement equal to eight dry quarts.

WORDS
TO
KNOW

feigned (fānd) *adj.* not real; pretended

Pause & *Reflect*

MARK IT UP

14 1. Circle the types of food that the Pilgrims store for the winter. **(Clarify)**

2. What is your impression of the Pilgrims after reading these excerpts from *Of Plymouth Plantation?* **(Connect)**

_____
_____
_____
_____

CHALLENGE

15 At the beginning of this selection, Bradford says that the Pilgrims "fell upon their knees and blessed the God of Heaven who had brought them over the vast and furious ocean." Mark other passages in which Bradford mentions God. Then imagine that these passages were not included in the **chronicle**. How would your impression of the Pilgrims be different? **(Evaluate)**

Wrapping Up

16 If you are using *The Language of Literature*, you can now move to the questions and activities on pages 88–90 of that book.

Of Plymouth Plantation **9**

User's Guide continued

For especially challenging selections, extra help is provided. Here are sample pages from "The Masque of the Red Death."

SHORT STORY

Before You Read

If you are using *The Language of Literature* . . .

- Use the information on page 454 to prepare for reading.
- The art on page 455 will help you **visualize** some of the dancers at the masked ball.

Reading Tips

In his **short stories**, Poe creates an eerie world beyond everyday life. When you read a Poe story, let your imagination run wild. Feel the terror of the unknown.

- Use Poe's **details** to help you **visualize** the **setting** and the **characters**. Picture the rooms in the abbey, the prince, and the masqueraders.
- Use the Guide for Reading to help you understand unfamiliar words and difficult lines and passages.

The following selections in this book have a Guide for Reading

Patrick Henry, Speech in the Virginia Convention

Ralph Waldo Emerson, *from* Self Reliance

Henry David Thoreau, *from* Civil Disobedience

Walt Whitman, I Sit and Look Out *and from* Song of Myself

Edgar Allan Poe, The Masque of the Red Death

Nathaniel Hawthorne, Dr. Heidegger's Experiment

T. S. Eliot, The Love Song of J. Alfred Prufock

The Masque of the Red Death

EDGAR ALLAN POE

PREVIEW Edgar Allan Poe was a master of the horror story. His tale "The Masque of the Red Death" is set during the Middle Ages. It tells about a prince who locks his friends and himself inside an abbey, walling it shut, to escape a deadly disease. For several months, all goes well. Then one night, the prince holds a masked ball. On the stroke of midnight, a strange figure suddenly appears.

FOCUS
The "Red Death" threatens the country. Read to find out about the disease and what Prospero does to try to escape it.

MARK IT UP As you read, circle details that help you understand how life outside Prospero's abbey is different from life inside. An example is highlighted on page 114.

The "Red Death" had long devastated the country. No pestilence had ever been so fatal, or so hideous. Blood was its Avatar and its seal—the redness and horror of blood. There were sharp pains, and sudden dizziness, and then profuse bleeding at the pores, with dissolution. The scarlet stains upon the body, and especially upon the face of the victim, were the pest ban which shut him out from the aid and from the sympathy of his fellow men. And the whole seizure, progress, and termination of the disease were the incidents of half an hour.

But the Prince Prospero was happy and <u>dauntless</u> and <u>sagacious</u>. When his dominions were half depopulated, he

| WORDS TO KNOW | **dauntless** (dônt'lĭs) *adj.* fearless |
| | **sagacious** (sə-gā'shəs) *adj.* wise |

① **GUIDE FOR READING**

Use this guide for help with unfamiliar words and difficult passages.

NOTES

✎ **MARK IT UP** WORD POWER

Mark words that you'd like to add to your **Personal Word List.** After reading, you can record the words and their meanings beginning on page 344.

② 1 **devastated** (dĕv'ə-stā'tĭd): laid waste to.
2 **pestilence** (pĕs'tə-ləns): a very destructive infectious disease.
4 **Avatar** (ăv'ə-tär'): an appearance in physical form of an unseen force.

8 **dissolution:** death.

10 **pest ban:** a proclamation announcing that a person is sick with the plague.

✎ **JOT IT DOWN** Reread Lines 8–12

③ Why do people show no pity for the victims of the Red Death? **(Clarify)**

_____
_____
_____

The Masque of the Red Death 113

GUIDE FOR READING

① This guide gives you help with unfamiliar words and difficult passages.

② Note that these definitions and explanations are directly across from the selection.

✎ **JOT IT DOWN**

③ This feature calls attention to important passages. It asks you to reread the passage and answer a question. Note that the passage is boxed so that you can easily find it in the text. You'll also find Read Aloud and Mark It Up features that also call attention to key passages.

Student Model

These pages show you how one student made use of
The InterActive Reader™ for the selection *Of Plymouth Plantation*.

Pause & Reflect

▶ **MARK IT UP**   **1.** What did the Pilgrims take from the Indians' houses? Circle the items mentioned on page 4. Star the item that kept the Pilgrims from starving. **(Clarify)**

2. What did the Pilgrims do to drive off the attacking Indians? **(Cause and Effect)**

They ran at them wearing armor, holding swords. They also fired muskets at them.

3. What do you think will happen at the next encounter between the Pilgrims and the Indians? **(Predict)**

I think the Indians now realize that the Pilgrims will defend themselves, so maybe both sides will try to get along.

Note how this student used the following symbols:

✓ marks a place where something is made clear or understandable

? marks where something is not understood or is confusing

! marks a surprising or interesting place in the text

Also notice how two words are circled, *providence* and *sundry*. These are words that the student marked for her Personal Word List.

---

of their rendezvous[9] but were commanded not to shoot till they could take full aim at them. And the other two charged
120 again with all speed, for there were only four had arms there, and defended the barricado, which was first assaulted. The cry of the Indians was dreadful, especially when they [the Indians] saw their men [the English] run out of the rendezvous toward the shallop to recover their arms, the Indians wheeling about upon them. But some running out with coats of mail on, and cutlasses[10] in their hands, they [the English] soon got their arms and let fly amongst them [the Indians] and quickly stopped their violence. . . .

Thus it pleased God to vanquish their enemies and give
130 them deliverance; and by His special providence so to dispose that not any one of them were either hurt or hit, though their arrows came close by them and on every side [of] them; and sundry of their coats, which hung up in the barricado, were shot through and through. Afterwards they gave God solemn thanks and praise for their deliverance, and gathered up a bundle of their arrows and sent them into England afterward by the master of the ship, and called that place the First Encounter. . . .

Pause & Reflect

FOCUS
Read to find out about the Pilgrims' first
140 winter at Cape Cod.

THE STARVING TIME
But that which was most sad and lamentable was, that in two or three months' time half of their company died, especially in January and February, being the depth of winter, and wanting houses and other comforts; being infected with the scurvy[11] and other diseases which this long voyage and their inaccommodate condition had brought upon them. So as there died some times two or three of a day in the foresaid time, that of 100 and odd persons, scarce fifty

---

9. **rendezvous** (rän′dā-vōō′): a gathering place; here used to denote the Pilgrims' encampment.
10. **coats of mail . . . and cutlasses:** armor made of joined metal links, and short curved swords.
11. **scurvy** (skûr′vē): a disease caused by lack of vitamin C.

WORDS
TO   **vanquish** (văng′kwĭsh) *v.* to defeat in battle
KNOW

remained. And of these, in the time of most distress, there was but six or seven sound persons who to their great commendations, be it spoken, spared no pains night nor day, but with abundance of toil and hazard of their own health fetched them wood, made them fires, dressed them meat, made their beds, washed their loathsome clothes, clothed and unclothed them. . . . In a word, did all the homely and necessary offices for them which dainty and queasy stomachs cannot endure to hear named; and all this willingly and cheerfully, without any grudging in the least, showing herein their true love unto their friends and brethren; a rare example and worthy to be remembered. Two of these seven were Mr. William Brewster, their reverend Elder, and Myles Standish, their Captain and military commander, unto whom myself and many others were much beholden in our low and sick condition. And yet the Lord so upheld these persons as in this general calamity they were not at all infected either with sickness or lameness. . . .

Pause **&** *Reflect*

INDIAN RELATIONS

All this while the Indians came skulking about them, and would sometimes show themselves <u>aloof</u> off, but when any approached near them, they would run away; and once they [the Indians] stole away their [the colonists'] tools where they had been at work and were gone to dinner. But about the 16th of March, a certain Indian came boldly amongst them and spoke to them in broken English, which they could well understand but marveled at it. At length they understood by discourse with him, that he was not of these parts, but belonged to the eastern parts where some English ships came to fish, with whom he was acquainted and could name (sundry) of them by their names, amongst whom he had got his language. He became profitable to them in acquainting them with many things concerning the state of the country in the east parts where he lived, which was

WORDS
TO
KNOW

aloof (ə-lōōf′) *adj.* distant

They died of disease and exposure to the cold of winter.

The people who were healthy fed and cleaned the sick and kept them warm by tending the fires.

Why did they take the tools?

?

✓

Of Plymouth Plantation 7

Before You Read
If you are using **The Language of Literature** . . .

- Use the information on page 81 to prepare for reading.

- Look at the art on pages 84 and 87. It will help you **visualize** the Pilgrims and their settlement.

Reading Tips
A **chronicle** is a work of **nonfiction,** a historical account of important events. William Bradford actually witnessed the events he describes in this firsthand account.

Bradford wrote this chronicle more than 300 years ago. Some of the sentences are long, and some of the words may look strange. Try these strategies to help your understanding:

- Use the heading for each section as a guide to the content.

- Read at a steady pace and just keep moving. Try to take in big chunks of meaning. Look for main ideas and don't get lost in the details.

◢MARK IT UP KEEP TRACK

As you read, you can use these marks to keep track of your understanding.

✔ ..... I understand.

? ..... I don't understand this.

! ..... Interesting or surprising idea

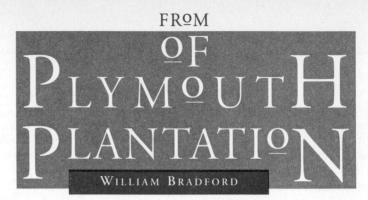

FR**O**M
OF PLYMO**UTH PLANTATI**O**N**
WILLIAM BRADFORD

PREVIEW These excerpts tell about the Pilgrims' survival in America in the early 1600s. William Bradford, the first governor of Plymouth colony, describes the Pilgrims' many hardships, their strength of character, and their faith in God. He also explains how some Native Americans helped the colonists to survive.

FOCUS
Bradford describes the Pilgrims' arrival at Cape Cod in November of 1620. The Pilgrims faced the frightening wilderness of an unknown world.

◢MARK IT UP As you read, circle any details that help you understand the Pilgrims' situation. An example is highlighted.

THEIR SAFE ARRIVAL AT CAPE COD
But to omit other things (that I may be brief) after long beating at sea they[1] fell with that land which is called Cape Cod; the which being made and certainly known to be it, they were not a little joyful. . . .

Being thus arrived in a good harbor, and brought safe to land, they fell upon their knees and blessed the God of Heaven who had brought them over the vast and furious ocean, and delivered them from all the perils and miseries thereof, again to set their feet on the firm and stable earth, their proper element. . . .

But here I cannot but stay and make a pause, and stand half amazed at this poor people's present condition; and so I

---

1. **they:** Bradford refers to the Pilgrims in the third person even though he is one of them.

think will the reader, too, when he well considers the same. Being thus passed the vast ocean, and a sea of troubles before in their preparation (as may be remembered by that which went before), they had now no friends to welcome them nor inns to entertain or refresh their weatherbeaten bodies; no houses or much less towns to repair to, to seek for succor.[2] It is recorded in Scripture as a mercy to the Apostle and his shipwrecked company, that the barbarians showed them no small kindness in refreshing them,[3] but these savage barbarians, when they met with them (as after will appear) were readier to fill their sides full of arrows than otherwise. And for the season it was winter, and they that know the winters of that country know them to be sharp and violent, and subject to cruel and fierce storms, dangerous to travel to known places, much more to search an unknown coast. Besides, what could they see but a hideous and desolate wilderness, full of wild beasts and wild men—and what multitudes there might be of them they knew not. Neither could they, as it were, go up to the top of Pisgah[4] to view from this wilderness a more goodly country to feed their hopes; for which way soever they turned their eyes (save upward to the heavens) they could have little solace or content in respect of any outward objects. For summer being done, all things stand upon them with a weatherbeaten face, and the whole country, full of woods and thickets, represented a wild and savage hue. If they looked behind them, there was the mighty ocean which they had passed and was now as a main bar and gulf to separate them from all the civil parts of the world. . . .

Pause & Reflect

---

2. **succor** (sŭk′ər): help; relief.

3. **It is . . . refreshing them:** a reference to the biblical account of the courteous reception of Paul and his companions by the inhabitants of Malta (Acts 27:41–28:2).

4. **Pisgah** (pĭz′gə): the mountain from whose peak Moses saw the Promised Land (Deuteronomy 34:1–4).

WORDS	**desolate** (dĕs′ə-lĭt) *adj.* without inhabitants; barren
TO	**solace** (sŏl′ĭs) *n.* comfort in sorrow or distress
KNOW	**hue** (hyo͞o) *n.* appearance; color

✎ **MARK IT UP** WORD POWER

Mark words that you'd like to add to your **Personal Word List.** After reading, you can record the words and their meanings beginning on page 344.

Pause & Reflect

1. Review the details you circled as you read. Then write a sentence or two to **summarize** the Pilgrims' situation after landing at Cape Cod.

_____

_____

_____

_____

2. Imagine you are one of the Pilgrims who have just set foot on land. What do you think is the greatest challenge that awaits you and the other Pilgrims in the New World? **(Evaluate)**

_____

_____

_____

_____

After the Pilgrims landed, they discovered food and supplies in the deserted houses of Indians. Later, the Pilgrims were attacked. Read to find out about their first experiences on shore.

THE FIRST ENCOUNTER

Being thus arrived at Cape Cod the 11th of November, and necessity calling them to look out a place for habitation (as well as the master's and mariners' importunity); they having brought a large shallop[5] with them out of England, stowed in quarters in the ship, they now got her out and set their carpenters to work to trim her up; but being much bruised and shattered in the ship with foul weather, they saw she would be long in mending. Whereupon a few of them tendered themselves to go by land and discover those nearest places, whilst the shallop was in mending; . . .

After this, the shallop being got ready, they set out again for the better discovery of this place, and the master of the ship desired to go himself. So there went some thirty men but found it to be no harbor for ships but only for boats. There was also found two of their [the Indians'] houses covered with mats, and sundry of their implements in them, but the people were run away and could not be seen. Also there was found more of their corn and of their beans of various colors; the corn and beans they [the English] brought away, purposing to give them [the Indians] full satisfaction when they should meet with any of them as, about some six months afterward they did, to their good content.[6]

And here is to be noted a special providence of God, and a great mercy to this poor people, that here they got seed to plant them corn the next year, or else they might have starved, for they had none nor any likelihood to get any till the season had been past, as the sequel did manifest. Neither is it likely they had had this, if the first voyage had not been made, for the ground was now all covered with snow and hard frozen; but the Lord is never wanting unto His in their greatest needs; let His holy name have all the praise.

The month of November being spent in these affairs, and

---

5. **shallop** (shăl′əp): an open boat usually used in shallow waters.

6. **purposing . . . content:** intending to repay the Nauset Indians whose corn and beans they took, as they in fact did, to the Indians' satisfaction, six months later.

WORDS TO KNOW
providence (prŏv′ĭ-dəns) *n.* an instance of divine care or guidance

80 much foul weather falling in, the 6th of December they sent out their shallop again with ten of their principal men and some seamen, upon further discovery, intending to circulate that deep bay of Cape Cod. The weather was very cold and it froze so hard as the spray of the sea lighting on their coats, they were as if they had been glazed. . . . [The next night they landed and] made them a barricado[7] as usually they did every night, with logs, stakes, and thick pine boughs, the height of a man, leaving it open to leeward,[8] partly to shelter them from the cold and wind (making their fire in the middle and lying

90 round about it) and partly to defend them from any sudden assaults of the savages, if they should surround them; so being very weary, they betook them to rest. But about midnight they heard a hideous and great cry, and their <u>sentinel</u> called "Arm! arm!" So they bestirred them and stood to their arms and shot off a couple of muskets, and then the noise ceased. They concluded it was a company of wolves or such like wild beasts, for one of the seamen told them he had often heard such a noise in Newfoundland.

So they rested till about five of the clock in the morning; for
100 the tide, and their purpose to go from thence, made them be stirring betimes. So after prayer they prepared for breakfast, and it being day dawning it was thought best to be carrying things down to the boat. But some said it was not best to carry the arms down, others said they would be the readier, for they had lapped them up in their coats from the dew; but some three or four would not carry theirs till they went themselves. Yet as it fell out, the water being not high enough, they laid them down on the bank side and came up to breakfast.

But presently, all on the sudden, they heard a great and
110 strange cry, which they knew to be the same voices they heard in the night, though they varied their notes; and one of their company being abroad came running in and cried, "Men, Indians! Indians!" And withal, their arrows came flying amongst them. Their men ran with all speed to recover their arms, as by the good providence of God they did. In the meantime, of those that were there ready, two muskets were discharged at them, and two more stood ready in the entrance

> **READ ALOUD** Lines 109–115
>
> Notice how this passage reflects the Puritan devotion to God.

---

7. **barricado** (băr′ĭ-kā′dō): a barrier for defense.
8. **to leeward** (lē′wərd): on the side sheltered from the wind.

sentinel (sĕn′tə-nəl) *n.* a guard

MARK IT UP **1.** What did
the Pilgrims take from the
Indians' houses? Circle the items
mentioned on page 4. Star the
item that kept the Pilgrims from
starving. **(Clarify)**

2. What did the Pilgrims do to drive
off the attacking Indians? **(Cause
and Effect)**

_____

_____

_____

_____

3. What do you think will happen at
the next encounter between the
Pilgrims and the Indians?
(Predict)

_____

_____

_____

_____

of their rendezvous[9] but were commanded not to shoot till
they could take full aim at them. And the other two charged
120 again with all speed, for there were only four had arms there,
and defended the barricado, which was first assaulted. The cry
of the Indians was dreadful, especially when they [the Indians]
saw their men [the English] run out of the rendezvous toward
the shallop to recover their arms, the Indians wheeling about
upon them. But some running out with coats of mail on, and
cutlasses[10] in their hands, they [the English] soon got their
arms and let fly amongst them [the Indians] and quickly
stopped their violence. . . .

　　Thus it pleased God to <u>vanquish</u> their enemies and give
130 them deliverance; and by His special providence so to dispose
that not any one of them were either hurt or hit, though
their arrows came close by them and on every side [of] them;
and sundry of their coats, which hung up in the barricado,
were shot through and through. Afterwards they gave God
solemn thanks and praise for their deliverance, and gathered
up a bundle of their arrows and sent them into England
afterward by the master of the ship, and called that place
the First Encounter. . . .

Pause **&** **Reflect**

FOCUS
Read to find out about
the Pilgrims' first
140 winter at Cape Cod.

The Starving Time

But that which was most sad and
lamentable was, that in two or three
months' time half of their company
died, especially in January and February, being the depth of
winter, and wanting houses and other comforts; being infected
with the scurvy[11] and other diseases which this long voyage
and their inaccommodate condition had brought upon them.
So as there died some times two or three of a day in the
foresaid time, that of 100 and odd persons, scarce fifty

---

9. **rendezvous** (rän′dā-vōō′): a gathering place; here used to denote the
　 Pilgrims' encampment.
10. **coats of mail . . . and cutlasses:** armor made of joined metal links, and
　 short curved swords.
11. **scurvy** (skûr′vē): a disease caused by lack of vitamin C.

WORDS	
TO	**vanquish** (văng′kwĭsh) v. to defeat in battle
KNOW	

remained. And of these, in the time of most distress, there was but six or seven sound persons who to their great commendations, be it spoken, spared no pains night nor day, but with abundance of toil and hazard of their own health fetched them wood, made them fires, dressed them meat, made their beds, washed their loathsome clothes, clothed and unclothed them. . . . In a word, did all the homely and necessary offices for them which dainty and queasy stomachs cannot endure to hear named; and all this willingly and cheerfully, without any grudging in the least, showing herein their true love unto their friends and brethren; a rare example and worthy to be remembered. Two of these seven were Mr. William Brewster, their reverend Elder, and Myles Standish, their Captain and military commander, unto whom myself and many others were much beholden in our low and sick condition. And yet the Lord so upheld these persons as in this general calamity they were not at all infected either with sickness or lameness. . . .

Pause & Reflect

Pause & Reflect

✎ MARK IT UP **1.** Why do almost half of the Pilgrims die the first winter? Write the answer below. Then circle details on page 6 that support your answer. **(Cause and Effect)**

_____

_____

_____

_____

2. Reread the boxed sentences on this page. Then write a sentence to **summarize** what the healthy few do to take care of the sick.

_____

_____

_____

_____

INDIAN RELATIONS

FOCUS
Read to find out about the relationship that develops between the Pilgrims and the Indians.

✎ MARK IT UP As you read, underline details that show what the Pilgrims learn from their Indian friends.

All this while the Indians came skulking about them, and would sometimes show themselves <u>aloof</u> off, but when any approached near them, they would run away; and once they [the Indians] stole away their [the colonists'] tools where they had been at work and were gone to dinner. But about the 16th of March, a certain Indian came boldly amongst them and spoke to them in broken English, which they could well understand but marveled at it. At length they understood by discourse with him, that he was not of these parts, but belonged to the eastern parts where some English ships came to fish, with whom he was acquainted and could name sundry of them by their names, amongst whom he had got his language. He became profitable to them in acquainting them with many things concerning the state of the country in the east parts where he lived, which was

WORDS
TO
KNOW

aloof (ə-lo͞of') *adj.* distant

afterwards profitable unto them; as also of the people here, of their names, number and strength, of their situation and distance from this place, and who was chief amongst them. His name was Samoset. He told them also of another Indian whose name was Squanto, a native of this place, who had been in England and could speak better English than himself.

Being, after some time of entertainment and gifts dismissed,
190 a while after he came again, and five more with him, and they brought again all the tools that were stolen away before, and made way for the coming of their great Sachem,[12] called Massasoit. Who, about four or five days after, came with the chief of his friends and other attendance, with the aforesaid Squanto. With whom, after friendly entertainment and some gifts given him, they made a peace with him (which hath now continued this 24 years) in these terms:

> 1. That neither he nor any of his should injure or do hurt to any of their people.
> 200 2. That if any of his did hurt to any of theirs, he should send the offender, that they might punish him.
> 3. That if anything were taken away from any of theirs, he should cause it to be restored; and they should do the like to his.
> 4. If any did unjustly war against him, they would aid him; if any did war against them, he should aid them.
> 5. He should send to his neighbors confederates to certify them of this, that they might not wrong them, but might be likewise comprised in the conditions of peace.[13]
> 6. That when their men came to them, they should leave
> 210 their bows and arrows behind them.

After these things he returned to his place called Sowams,[14] some 40 miles from this place, but Squanto continued with them and was their interpreter and was a special instrument sent of God for their good beyond their expectation. He directed them how to set their corn, where to take fish, and to <u>procure</u> other <u>commodities</u>, and was also their pilot to bring them to unknown places for their profit, and never left them till he died.

Pause & Reflect

12. **Sachem** (sā′chəm): chief.
13. **He should . . . peace:** Massasoit was to inform other tribes about the compact so that they might also keep peace with the Pilgrims.
14. **Sowams** (sō′ämz): near the site of present-day Barrington, Rhode Island.

WORDS TO KNOW	**procure** (prō-kyŏŏr′) v. to get by special effort; obtain **commodity** (kə-mŏd′ĭ-tē) n. something useful; an article of commerce

---

Pause & Reflect

READ ALOUD **1.** Read aloud the terms in the peace treaty between the Pilgrims and Massasoit's people (the boxed passage). Then cross out the one phrase below that does *not* apply to the treaty. **(Infer)**

promotes safety

discourages theft

sets up an alliance

protects the Indian languages

2. Review the details you underlined as you read. What did the Pilgrims learn from Samoset and Squanto? **(Summarize)**

FIRST THANKSGIVING

They began now to gather in the small harvest they had, and to fit up their houses and dwellings against winter, being all well recovered in health and strength and had all things in good plenty. For as some were thus employed in affairs abroad, others were exercised in fishing, about cod and bass and other fish, of which they took good store, of which every family had their portion. All the summer there was no want; and now began to come in store of fowl, as winter approached, of which this place did abound when they came first (but afterward decreased by degrees). And besides waterfowl there was great store of wild turkeys, of which they took many, besides venison, etc. Besides they had about a peck[15] a meal a week to a person, or now since harvest, Indian corn to that proportion. Which made many afterwards write so largely of their plenty here to their friends in England, which were not <u>feigned</u> but true reports.

Pause **&** *Reflect*

---

15. **peck:** a unit of measurement equal to eight dry quarts.

WORDS
TO
KNOW

feigned (fānd) *adj.* not real; pretended

Pause **&** *Reflect*

MARK IT UP **1.** Circle the types of food that the Pilgrims store for the winter. **(Clarify)**

2. What is your impression of the Pilgrims after reading these excerpts from *Of Plymouth Plantation?* **(Connect)**

_____

_____

_____

_____

CHALLENGE
At the beginning of this selection, Bradford says that the Pilgrims "fell upon their knees and blessed the God of Heaven who had brought them over the vast and furious ocean." Mark other passages in which Bradford mentions God. Then imagine that these passages were not included in the **chronicle.** How would your impression of the Pilgrims be different? **(Evaluate)**

Wrapping Up

If you are using **The Language of Literature,** you can now move to the questions and activities on pages 88–90 of that book.

Active Reading SkillBuilder

Summarizing

Summarizing means condensing a work into fewer words, restating only the main ideas and important details. Summarizing a complex selection, like the historical narrative from *Of Plymouth Plantation,* helps readers clarify their understanding of key information. In the chart below write a one- or two-sentence summary of each section listed. An example is shown.

Section	Summary
Their Safe Arrival at Cape Cod	*After reaching land, the Pilgrims thanked God. With no friends to help them, the Pilgrims faced the wilderness in the dead of winter.*
The First Encounter	
The Starving Time	
Indian Relations	
First Thanksgiving	

Literary Analysis SkillBuilder

Primary Sources

Primary sources are written or created by people who observed or participated in a historical event. Primary sources include letters, wills, diaries, tape recordings, photographs, speeches, and eyewitness accounts. Primary sources often reveal the writer's or speaker's personal opinions, beliefs, motives, assumptions—or preconceived ideas—and biases. Fill in the following chart to analyze *Of Plymouth Plantation* as a primary source. An example is shown.

Source	*Of Plymouth Plantation*
Purpose (reason for writing)	*to show how the Pilgrims survived in the new world*
Point of View (perspective from which events are told)	
Assumptions (preconceived ideas)	
Biases (personal prejudices)	

Words to Know SkillBuilder

Words to Know

aloof	desolate	hue	providence	solace
commodity	feigned	procure	sentinel	vanquish

A. Fill in each set of blanks with the correct word from the word list.

1. This is what the admirals and generals on *our* side
   hope to do to admirals and generals on *their* side.

   _ _ _ _ _ _ ☐ _

2. If you close your eyes, you'll miss this completely,
   because your other senses won't help.

   _ _ ☐

3. This is like *get* or *obtain* but suggests that the getting
   is not easy.

   ☐ _ _ _ _ _ _

4. If *our* admirals and generals succeed in their efforts,
   their admirals and generals may need this.

   _ _ _ ☐ _ _

5. This might be anything from a big, impressive
   miracle to a small, still voice inside.

   _ ☐ _ _ _ _ _ _ _

6. Although this can mean "emotionally distant,"
   Bradford uses it to mean just "far away."

   ☐ _ _ _ _

7. This could be a car, a shirt, a steel beam,
   a bushel of corn, or—yech!—a pork belly.

   _ _ _ _ _ _ _ ☐ _

8. When an employee calls in sick and then goes
   fishing, he or she has this kind of sickness.

   _ _ ☐ _ _ _ _

9. The Dead Sea, abandoned houses,
   ghost towns, and the moon are all this.

   _ _ ☐ _ _ _ ☐ _

10. You might see this at the White House, Buckingham
    Palace, or outside your kid brother's fort.

    ☐ _ _ _ _ _ _ _

Complete the following sentence with the word that the boxed letters spell out.

In England, the 41 Puritans on the *Mayflower* were known as _____.

B. Imagine that you are a Pilgrim at Plymouth in 1621. Write about the first fall
harvest as you might describe it in a letter to a friend back in England. Use at least
four of the Words to Know in your description.

from Sinners

in the Hands of an Angry God

JONATHAN EDWARDS

PREVIEW "Sinners in the Hands of an Angry God" is a **sermon** about the punishment in store for the wicked after death. Jonathan Edwards, a Puritan minister, preached this sermon in 1741. He wanted his listeners to turn to God and save their souls. As this excerpt shows, he used the power of words to trigger a basic emotion—fear.

FOCUS
Edwards divides his listeners into two groups: those who have accepted Christ in their hearts and those who have not ("the unconverted," or unchanged). God is angry at the unconverted. Read to find out what God has planned for them.

We find it easy to tread on and crush a worm that we see crawling on the earth; so it is easy for us to cut or singe a slender thread that any thing hangs by; thus easy is it for God when he pleases to cast his enemies down to hell. . . .

They[1] are now the objects of that very same *anger* and <u>wrath</u> of God, that is expressed in the torments of hell. And the reason why they do not go down to hell at each moment, is not because God, in whose power they are, is not then very angry with them; as angry as he is with many miserable creatures now tormented in hell, who there feel and bear the fierceness of his wrath. Yea, God is a great deal more angry with great numbers

---

1. **they:** Earlier in the sermon, Edwards refers to "unconverted men." They are people who have not been "born again," meaning that they have not accepted Christ.

WORDS
TO
KNOW

wrath (răth) *n.* fierce anger, or punishment resulting from such anger

Before You Read

If you are using *The Language of Literature . . .*

- Use the information on page 152 to prepare for reading.

- The art on pages 155 and 157 will help you picture some of the **images** used in this sermon.

Reading Tips

This **sermon** contains long sentences and some words and phrases no longer in common use.

- Keep in mind that you don't have to understand every word in a sentence to get at the overall meaning.

- When you come upon long sentences, look for the verbs. They will help you to follow the action.

- Use the author's **images** to help visualize his descriptions of hell and God's anger.

- Try reading some sentences aloud to increase your understanding and to feel the emotional force.

MARK IT UP **KEEP TRACK**

As you read, you can use these marks to keep track of your understanding.

✔ ..... I understand.

? ..... I don't understand this.

! ..... Interesting or surprising idea

that are now on earth; yea, doubtless, with many that are now in this congregation,[2] who it may be are at ease, than he is with many of those who are now in the flames of hell.

So that it is not because God is unmindful of their wickedness, and does not resent it, that he does not let loose his hand and cut them off. God is not altogether such an one as themselves, though they may imagine him to be so. The wrath of God burns against them, their damnation does not slumber; the pit is prepared, the fire is made ready, the furnace is now hot, ready to receive them; the flames do now rage and glow. The glittering sword is whet,[3] and held over them, and the pit hath opened its mouth under them. . . .

Unconverted men walk over the pit of hell on a rotten covering, and there are innumerable places in this covering so weak that they will not bear their weight, and these places are not seen. The arrows of death fly unseen at noonday; the sharpest sight cannot discern them. God has so many different unsearchable ways of taking wicked men out of the world and sending them to hell, that there is nothing to make it appear, that God had need to be at the expense of a miracle, or go out of the ordinary course of his providence, to destroy any wicked man, at any moment. . . .

Pause & Reflect

FOCUS
Read to find out more about the terrible danger that sinners (here, called "natural men") are in.

✎ **MARK IT UP** As you read, circle the details that help you understand this danger. An example is highlighted.

So that, thus it is that natural men[4] are held in the hand of God, over the pit of hell; they have deserved the fiery pit, and are already sentenced to it; and God is dreadfully provoked, his anger is as great towards them as to those that are actually suffering the executions of the fierceness of his wrath in hell; and they have done nothing in the least to <u>appease</u> or abate that anger, neither is God in the least bound by any promise to hold them up one moment; the devil is waiting for them, hell is gaping for them, the flames

---

2. **this congregation:** the Puritans listening to Edwards.
3. **whet:** sharpened.
4. **natural men:** people who have not been "born again."

Pause & Reflect

1. God is angry at the wicked in hell. He is even more angry at the unconverted. What does he have planned for these people? **(Main Idea)**

_____

_____

_____

✎ **MARK IT UP** **2.** Imagine you are in the audience, listening to Edwards's description of hell. In the boxed passage on this page, circle the words and phrases that might make you afraid. **(Emotional/Loaded Language)**

WORDS
TO
KNOW

appease (ə-pēz′) v. to bring peace, quiet, or calm to; soothe

⑤⓪ gather and flash about them, and would fain⁵ lay hold on them, and swallow them up; the fire pent up in their own hearts is struggling to break out: and they have no interest in any Mediator,⁶ there are no means within reach that can be any security to them. In short, they have no refuge, nothing to take hold of. . . .

The bow of God's wrath is bent, and the arrow made ready on the string, and justice bends the arrow at your heart, and strains the bow, and it is nothing but the mere pleasure of God, and that of an angry God, without any promise or obligation at all, that ⑥⓪ keeps the arrow one moment from being made drunk with your blood. Thus all you that never passed under a great change of heart, by the mighty power of the Spirit of God upon your souls; all you that were never born again, and made new creatures, and raised from being dead in sin, to a state of new, and before altogether unexperienced light and life, are in the hands of an angry God. However you may have reformed your life in many things, and may have had religious affections,⁷ and may keep up a form of religion in your families and closets,⁸ and in the house of God, it is nothing but his mere pleasure that keeps you from ⑦⓪ being this moment swallowed up in everlasting destruction. . . .

The God that holds you over the pit of hell, much as one holds a spider, or some <u>loathsome</u> insect over the fire, <u>abhors</u> you, and is dreadfully provoked: his wrath towards you burns like fire; he looks upon you as worthy of nothing else, but to be cast into the fire; he is of purer eyes than to bear to have you in his sight; you are ten thousand times more <u>abominable</u> in his eyes, than the most hateful venomous serpent is in ours. You have offended him infinitely more than ever a stubborn rebel did his prince; and yet it is nothing but his hand that holds you from falling into the fire ⑧⓪ every moment. It is to be <u>ascribed</u> to nothing else, that you did not go to hell the last night; that you was suffered⁹ to awake again in this world, after you closed your eyes to sleep. And there is no other reason to be given, why you have not dropped into hell since you arose in the morning, but that God's hand has held you

---

5. **fain:** rather.
6. **Mediator:** Christ, who mediates, or helps bring about, salvation.
7. **affections:** feelings or emotions.
8. **closets:** private rooms for meditation.
9. **suffered:** permitted.

WORDS TO KNOW	**loathsome** (lōth′səm) *adj.* arousing great dislike
	abhor (ăb-hôr′) *v.* to regard with disgust
	abominable (ə-bŏm′ə-nə-bəl) *adj.* thoroughly detestable
	ascribe (ə-skrīb′) *v.* to attribute to a specified cause or source

MARK IT UP WORD POWER

Mark words that you'd like to add to your **Personal Word List**. After reading, you can record the words and their meanings beginning on page 344.

READ ALOUD **Lines 71–77**

Read aloud the boxed sentences on this page. How would you describe the way God views sinners? **(Infer)**

_____

_____

_____

_____

up. There is no other reason to be given why you have not gone to hell, since you have sat here in the house of God, provoking his pure eyes by your sinful wicked manner of attending his solemn worship. Yea, there is nothing else that is to be given as a reason why you do not this very moment drop down into hell.

90 O sinner! Consider the fearful danger you are in: it is a great furnace of wrath, a wide and bottomless pit, full of the fire of wrath, that you are held over in the hand of that God, whose wrath is provoked and incensed as much against you, as against many of the damned in hell. You hang by a slender thread, with the flames of divine wrath flashing about it, and ready every moment to singe it, and burn it asunder;[10] and you have no interest in any Mediator, and nothing to lay hold of to save yourself, nothing to keep off the flames of wrath, nothing of your own, nothing that you ever have done, nothing that you

100 can do, to induce God to spare you one moment. . . .

It is *everlasting* wrath. It would be dreadful to suffer this fierceness and wrath of Almighty God one moment; but you must suffer it to all eternity. There will be no end to this exquisite[11] horrible misery. When you look forward, you shall see a long forever, a boundless duration before you, which will swallow up your thoughts, and amaze your soul; and you will absolutely despair of ever having any deliverance, any end, any mitigation, any rest at all. You will know certainly that you must wear out long ages, millions of millions of ages, in wrestling

110 and conflicting with this almighty merciless vengeance; and then when you have so done, when so many ages have actually been spent by you in this manner, you will know that all is but a point to what remains. So that your punishment will indeed be infinite. Oh, who can express what the state of a soul in such circumstances is! All that we can possibly say about it, gives but a very feeble, faint representation of it; it is inexpressible and inconceivable: For "who knows the power of God's anger?"[12]

How dreadful is the state of those that are daily and hourly in the danger of this great wrath and infinite misery! But this is

120 the dismal case of every soul in this congregation that has not been born again, however moral and strict, sober and religious, they may otherwise be. . . .

Pause & Reflect

1. Review the details you circled as you read. Then write a sentence to **summarize** the danger facing sinners.

   _____
   _____
   _____
   _____

2. Circle the four words below that are true to Edwards's idea of God. **(Clarify)**

calm	furious
stern	loving
disgusted	tender
frightening	forgetful

---

10. **asunder** (ə-sŭn'dər): into separate parts or pieces.

11. **exquisite** (ĕk'skwĭ-zĭt): sharply intense.

12. **"who knows . . . anger?"**: a reference to Psalm 90:11, "Who knoweth the power of thine anger?"

_____

_____

_____

_____

And now you have an extraordinary opportunity, a day wherein Christ has thrown the door of mercy wide open, and stands in the door calling and crying with a loud voice to poor sinners; a day wherein many are flocking to him, and pressing into the kingdom of God. Many are daily coming[13] from the east, west, north, and south; many that were very lately in the same miserable condition that you are in, are now in a happy state, with their hearts filled with love to him who has loved them, and washed them from their sins in his own blood, and rejoicing in hope of the glory of God. How awful is it to be left behind at such a day! To see so many others feasting, while you are pining and perishing! To see so many rejoicing and singing for joy of heart, while you have cause to mourn for sorrow of heart, and howl for vexation of spirit! How can you rest one moment in such a condition? . . .

Therefore, let every one that is out of Christ, now awake and fly from the wrath to come. . . .

Pause & Reflect

2. Reread the last sentence of Edwards's sermon. Then restate his idea in your own words. **(Paraphase)**

_____

_____

_____

_____

....

....

....

....

....

....

....

....

CHALLENGE

Circle or highlight examples of powerful **images** in this sermon. What makes these images so powerful? How do they help Edwards accomplish his purpose? **(Evaluate)**

Wrapping Up

If you are using **The Language of Literature**, you can now move to the questions and activities on pages 158–159 of that book.

---

13. **Many . . . coming:** Edwards is referring to the hundreds of people who were being converted during the Great Awakening. The Great Awakening was a religious movement during the years 1734 to 1750. Edwards was one of the leaders.

Active Reading SkillBuilder

Analyzing Emotional Language

Persuasive writing often contains **loaded language—**words or phrases with strong connotations, or emotional associations. As you read this sermon, use the chart to list three examples of specific words, phrases, and images that Edwards uses to achieve the greatest emotional effect. Then describe the emotional impact that this loaded language might have had on his audience.

Example	Emotional Impact
1. The furnace is now hot.	terror, guilt
2.	
3.	

Literary Analysis SkillBuilder

Persuasive Writing

The goal of **persuasive writing** is to convince readers to adopt a particular opinion or perform a certain action. Persuasive writing uses both logical and emotional appeals. Emotional appeals sometimes contain very little factual information. Instead, they rely on highly charged language that triggers intense feelings. On the diagram that follows, record three examples of emotional appeals that you find in Edwards's sermon.

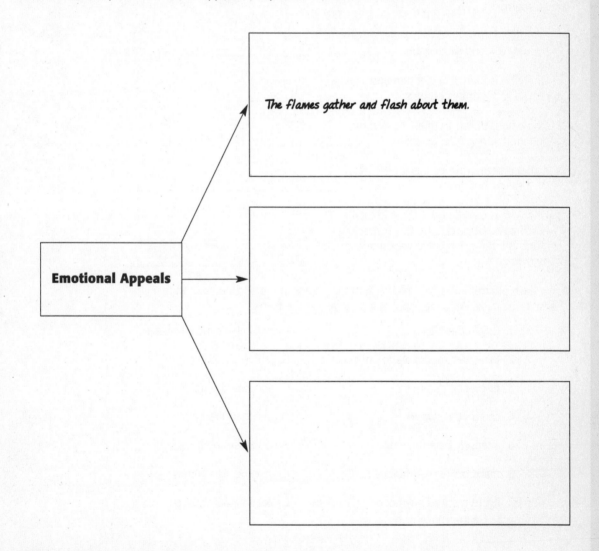

The flames gather and flash about them.

Emotional Appeals

Follow Up: Discuss whether Edwards's use of emotional appeals is justified, considering that his goal is to frighten people away from hell.

Words to Know SkillBuilder

Words to Know

abhor	appease	deliverance	inconceivable	mitigation
abominable	ascribe	incense	loathsome	wrath

A. Fill in each set of blanks with the correct word from the word list. The boxed letters will spell out something that Edwards claims is not automatically given to church members.

1. One might try to do this to a crying baby by rocking it and singing to it.

   __ __ __ __ __ ☐ __

2. One who is mad as a wet hen and seeing red is filled with this emotion.

   __ __ ☐ __ __

3. One who is pulled from an icy river or a burning building receives this.

   __ __ ☐ __ ☐ __ __ ☐ __ __ __

4. A cool breeze provides this for the heat on a stifling hot day.

   __ __ ☐ __ __ __ __ ☐ __ __

5. One who is completely awful and totally horrid could be said to be this (especially if one is a huge, furry, and very smelly "snowman").

   __ __ ☐ __ __ ☐ __ __ __ __

B. For each phrase in the first column, find the phrase in the second column that is closest in meaning. Write the letter of that phrase in the blank.

1. fury in the tub	A. believe it's inconceivable
2. think it is impossible to understand	B. abhor the chore
3. disgusting duds	C. incense the gents
4. soothe the swarm	D. wrath in the bath
5. intensely hate the work	E. appease the bees
6. make polite men furious	F. ascribe it to bribery
7. figure crooked payments to be the cause	G. loathsome clothing

C. How do your own views compare to Edwards's? Write a brief description of the agreement or disagreement between your views and his, using at least **five** of the Words to Know.

from

The CRUCIBLE

ARTHUR MILLER

PREVIEW This lesson includes the opening scenes in Act One of *The Crucible,* one of the most powerful plays of this century. The play is about the fear of witchcraft that gripped Salem, Massachusetts, in 1692. Many innocent people were tried as witches, or agents of the devil. Those who were accused of witchcraft faced a painful choice. They could tell a lie to save their lives, or they could tell the truth and die for honor.

Cast of Characters (order of appearance)

Reverend Samuel Parris	**Giles Corey**
Betty Parris	**Reverend John Hale**
Tituba	**Francis Nurse**
Abigail Williams	**Ezekiel Cheever**
John Proctor	**Marshal Herrick**
Elizabeth Proctor	**Judge Hathorne**
Susanna Walcott	**Martha Corey**
Mrs. Ann Putnam	**Deputy Governor Danforth**
Thomas Putnam	**Girls of Salem**
Mercy Lewis	**Sarah Good**
Mary Warren	
Rebecca Nurse	

Before You Read

If you are using *The Language of Literature* . . .

- Use the information on page 163 to prepare for reading.

- Examine the art on pages 164–176. It will help you visualize the **characters** and the **setting.**

Reading Tips

Like most plays, the script of this **drama** includes **stage directions** and **dialogue.** It also includes the author's commentaries. These commentaries look like "mini-essays." The author uses them to inform his readers about the Puritans and, sometimes, to share his views about American society in the 1950s.

- Treat these commentaries as pieces of nonfiction. Look for **main ideas.** Don't let the details bog you down.

- When you read the **dialogue,** use a different strategy. Read some of the lines aloud—by yourself or with a partner. Try to imagine yourself saying these lines on stage. What words would you stress? What gestures would you use?

Act One: An Overture

(A small upper bedroom in the home of Reverend Samuel Parris, Salem, Massachusetts, in the spring of the year 1692.) (There is a narrow window at the left. Through its leaded panes the morning sunlight streams. A candle still burns near the bed, which is at the right. A chest, a chair, and a small table are the other furnishings. At the back a door opens on the landing of the stairway to the ground floor. The room gives off an air of clean spareness. The roof rafters are exposed, and the wood colors are raw and unmellowed.)

10 *(As the curtain rises, Reverend Parris is discovered kneeling beside the bed, evidently in prayer. His daughter, Betty Parris, aged ten, is lying on the bed, inert.)*

At the time of these events Parris was in his middle forties. In history he cut a villainous path, and there is very little good to be said for him. He believed he was being persecuted wherever he went, despite his best efforts to win people and God to his side. In meeting, he felt insulted if someone rose to shut the door without first asking his permission. He was a widower with no interest in children, or talent with them. He 20 regarded them as young adults, and until this strange crisis he, like the rest of Salem, never conceived that the children were anything but thankful for being permitted to walk straight, eyes slightly lowered, arms at the sides, and mouths shut until bidden to speak.

His house stood in the "town"—but we today would hardly call it a village. The meeting house[1] was nearby, and from this point outward—toward the bay or inland—there were a few small-windowed, dark houses snuggling against the raw Massachusetts winter. Salem had been established 30 hardly forty years before. To the European world the whole

---

1. **meeting house:** the most important building in a Puritan community, used both for worship and for meetings.

province was a barbaric frontier inhabited by a sect of <u>fanatics</u> who, nevertheless, were shipping out products of slowly increasing quantity and value.

No one can really know what their lives were like. They had no novelists—and would not have permitted anyone to read a novel if one were handy. Their creed forbade anything resembling a theater or "vain enjoyment." They did not celebrate Christmas, and a holiday from work meant only that they must concentrate even more upon prayer.

40 Which is not to say that nothing broke into this strict and somber way of life. When a new farmhouse was built, friends assembled to "raise the roof," and there would be special foods cooked and probably some potent cider passed around. There was a good supply of ne'er-do-wells in Salem, who dallied at the shovelboard[2] in Bridget Bishop's tavern. Probably more than the creed, hard work kept the morals of the place from spoiling, for the people were forced to fight the land like heroes for every grain of corn, and no man had very much time for fooling around.

50 That there were some jokers, however, is indicated by the practice of appointing a two-man patrol whose duty was to "walk forth in the time of God's worship to take notice of such as either lye about the meeting house, without attending to the word and ordinances, or that lye at home or in the fields without giving good account thereof, and to take the names of such persons, and to present them to the magistrates, whereby they may be accordingly proceeded against." This <u>predilection</u> for minding other people's business was time-honored among the people of Salem, and it undoubtedly created many of the
60 suspicions which were to feed the coming madness. It was also, in my opinion, one of the things that a John Proctor would rebel against, for the time of the armed camp had almost passed, and since the country was reasonably—although not wholly—safe, the old disciplines were beginning to rankle. But, as in all such matters, the issue was not clear-cut, for danger was still a possibility, and in unity still lay the best promise of safety.

Pause ② Reflect

2. **shovelboard:** a game in which a coin or disc is shoved across a board by hand.

WORDS TO KNOW	**fanatic** (fə-năt′ĭk) *n.* a person possessed by an excessive and irrational zeal, especially for a religious or political cause **predilection** (prĕd′l-ĕk′shən) *n.* a personal preference

MARK IT UP WORD POWER
Mark words that you'd like to add to your **Personal Word List**. After reading, you can record the words and their meanings beginning on page 344.

Pause ② Reflect

1. What is Reverend Parris's attitude toward children? **(Clarify)**

_____

_____

_____

_____

MARK IT UP 2. Review the details you circled as you read. In your opinion, what are the most interesting or unusual details about Puritan life? Star those details. **(Make Judgments)**

3. Reread the boxed sentence on this page. Then **summarize** what the "two-man patrol" did.

_____

_____

_____

_____

FOCUS

The Puritan settlement was close to the forest. Read to find out how the Puritans viewed the forest.

The edge of the wilderness was close by. The American continent stretched endlessly west, and it was full of mystery for them. It stood, dark and threatening, over their shoulders night and day, for out of it Indian tribes marauded[3] from time to time, and Reverend Parris had parishioners who had lost relatives to these heathen.

The parochial snobbery of these people was partly responsible for their failure to convert the Indians. Probably they also preferred to take land from heathens rather than from fellow Christians. At any rate, very few Indians were converted, and the Salem folk believed that the virgin forest was the Devil's last preserve, his home base and the citadel of his final stand. To the best of their knowledge the American forest was the last place on earth that was not paying homage to God.

For these reasons, among others, they carried about an air of innate resistance, even of persecution. Their fathers had, of course, been persecuted in England. So now they and their church found it necessary to deny any other sect its freedom, lest their New Jerusalem[4] be defiled and corrupted by wrong ways and deceitful ideas.

They believed, in short, that they held in their steady hands the candle that would light the world. We have inherited this belief, and it has helped and hurt us. It helped them with the discipline it gave them. They were a dedicated folk, by and large, and they had to be to survive the life they had chosen or been born into in this country.

Pause *Reflect*

Pause & Reflect

1. Which of the following phrases are true to the Puritans' view of the forest? Circle or check two of them. **(Clarify)**

   a source of peace and beauty

   a place of mystery and fear

   the home of the Devil

   a place for worshipping God

READ ALOUD 2. Read aloud the boxed sentence on this page. How would you state this idea in your own words? **(Paraphrase)**

_____

_____

_____

_____

---

3. **marauded** (mə-rôd′ĭd): attacked and raided.

4. **New Jerusalem:** in Christianity, a heavenly city and the last resting place of the souls saved by Jesus. It was considered the ideal city, and Puritans modeled their communities after it.

FOCUS
Read to find out how the Puritans were able to survive in Massachusetts and how their society changed over time.

The proof of their belief's value to them may be taken from the opposite character of the first Jamestown settlement, farther south, in Virginia. The Englishmen who landed there were motivated mainly by a hunt for profit. They had thought to pick off the wealth of the new country and then return rich to England. They were a band of individualists, and a much more ingratiating[5] group than the Massachusetts men. But Virginia destroyed them. Massachusetts tried to kill off the Puritans, but they combined; they set up a communal society which, in the beginning, was little more than an armed camp with an autocratic and very devoted leadership. It was, however, an autocracy[6] by consent, for they were united from top to bottom by a commonly held ideology[7] whose perpetuation was the reason and justification for all their sufferings. So their self-denial, their purposefulness, their suspicion of all vain pursuits, their hardhanded justice, were altogether perfect instruments for the conquest of this space so antagonistic to man.

But the people of Salem in 1692 were not quite the dedicated folk that arrived on the Mayflower. A vast differentiation had taken place, and in their own time a revolution had unseated the royal government and substituted a junta[8] which was at this moment in power. The times, to their eyes, must have been out of joint, and to the common folk must have seemed as insoluble and complicated as do ours today. It is not hard to see how easily many could have been led to believe that the time of confusion had been brought upon them by deep and darkling forces. No hint of such speculation appears on the court record, but social disorder in any age breeds such mystical suspicions, and when, as in Salem, wonders are brought forth from below the social surface, it is too much to expect people to hold back very long from laying on the victims with all the force of their frustrations.

JOT IT DOWN Lines 101–104

Reread the boxed sentence. What enabled the Puritans to survive in Massachusetts? **(Cause and Effect)**

_____

_____

_____

_____

---

5. **ingratiating** (ĭn-grā′shē-ā′tĭng): pleasing.

6. **autocracy** (ô-tŏk′rə-sē): a government by one person.

7. **ideology** (ī′dē-ŏl′ə-jē): political beliefs.

8. **junta** (hŏŏn′tə): a Spanish term meaning a small, elite ruling council; in this case the group that led England's Glorious Revolution of 1688–1689.

1. Insert the words *freedom* and *order* in the right slots in the following sentence: When the Puritans settled in America, they set up a government that preserved

   _____

   at the expense of

   _____ .

   (Main Idea)

2. As Puritan society changed over time, many Puritans feared that the cause of social problems was "deep and darkling forces." What do these forces refer to? Circle the correct answer below. **(Clarify)**

   greedy citizens

   supernatural powers of evil

   Indian warriors

   British spies

   The Salem tragedy, which is about to begin in these pages, developed from a paradox.⁹ It is a paradox in whose grip we still live, and there is no prospect yet that we will discover its resolution. Simply, it was this: for good purposes, even high purposes, the people of Salem developed a theocracy,¹⁰ a combine of state and religious power whose function was to keep the community together, and to prevent any kind of disunity that might open it to destruction by material or ideological enemies. It was forged for a necessary purpose and accomplished that purpose. But all organization is and must be grounded on the idea of exclusion and prohibition, just as two objects cannot occupy the same space. Evidently the time came in New England when the repressions of order were heavier than seemed warranted by the dangers against which the order was organized. The witch-hunt was a perverse manifestation of the panic which set in among all classes when the balance began to turn toward greater individual freedom.

   When one rises above the individual villainy displayed, one can only pity them all, just as we shall be pitied someday. It is still impossible for man to organize his social life without repressions, and the balance has yet to be struck between order and freedom.

Pause Reflect

> **FOCUS**
>
> By searching for witches, the people of Salem hoped to root out evil. Read to find out how some Puritans used the witch-hunt for their own advantage.

The witch-hunt was not, however, a mere repression. It was also, and as importantly, a long overdue opportunity for everyone so inclined to express publicly his guilt and sins, under the cover of accusations against the victims. It suddenly became possible—and patriotic and holy—for a man to say that Martha Corey had come into his bedroom at night, and

---

9. **paradox:** a seemingly contradictory statement that is in fact true.

10. **theocracy** (thē-ŏk′rə-sē): a government ruled by religious authority.

that, while his wife was sleeping at his side, Martha laid herself down on his chest and "nearly suffocated him." Of course it was her spirit only, but his satisfaction at confessing himself was no lighter than if it had been Martha herself. One could not ordinarily speak such things in public.

160 Long-held hatreds of neighbors could now be openly expressed, and vengeance taken, despite the Bible's charitable injunctions.[11] Land-lust which had been expressed before by constant bickering over boundaries and deeds, could now be elevated to the arena of morality; one could cry witch against one's neighbor and feel perfectly justified in the bargain. Old scores could be settled on a plane of heavenly combat between Lucifer and the Lord; suspicions and the envy of the miserable toward the happy could and did burst out in the general revenge.

Pause & Reflect

> **FOCUS**
> Reverend Parris is worried about his sick daughter, Betty. He tries to find out from Abigail, his niece, what she, Betty, and the other girls did in the forest the previous night.
> **MARK IT UP** As you read, circle details that help you understand what the girls did.

170 (Reverend Parris *is praying now, and, though we cannot hear his words, a sense of his confusion hangs about him. He mumbles, then seems about to weep; then he weeps, then prays again; but his daughter does not stir on the bed.*)

(*The door opens, and his Negro slave enters.* Tituba *is in her forties.* Parris *brought her with him from Barbados,[12] where he spent some years as a merchant before entering the ministry. She enters as one does who can no longer bear to be barred from the sight of*
180 *her beloved, but she is also very frightened because her*

---

11. **injunctions** (ĭn-jŭngk′shənz): commands; orders.
12. **Barbados** (bär-bā′dōs′): an island in the West Indies under British rule until 1966.

Pause & Reflect

1. Which of the following phrases describe the advantages some Puritans found in the witch-hunt? Circle or check two of them. **(Clarify)**

   to get back at hated neighbors

   to reveal hidden sins

   to protect their neighbors' property rights

   to attack Indians near the settlement

2. Based on what you have learned about the witch-hunt, what do you **predict** will happen in this play?

   _____

   _____

   _____

slave sense has warned her that, as always, trouble in this house eventually lands on her back.)

Tituba (*already taking a step backward*). My Betty be hearty soon?

Parris. Out of here!

Tituba (*backing to the door*). My Betty not goin' die . . .

Parris (*scrambling to his feet in a fury*). Out of my sight! (*She is gone.*) Out of my—(*He is overcome with sobs. He clamps his teeth against them and closes the door and leans against it, exhausted.*) Oh, my God! God help me! (*Quaking with fear, mumbling to himself through his sobs, he goes to the bed and gently takes Betty's hand.*) Betty. Child. Dear child. Will you wake, will you open up your eyes! Betty, little one . . .

(*He is bending to kneel again when his niece,* Abigail Williams, *seventeen, enters—a strikingly beautiful girl, an orphan, with an endless capacity for dissembling.*[13] *Now she is all worry and apprehension and propriety.*)

Abigail. Uncle? (*He looks to her.*) Susanna Walcott's here from Doctor Griggs.

Parris. Oh? Let her come, let her come.

Abigail (*leaning out the door to call to Susanna, who is down the hall a few steps*). Come in, Susanna.
(Susanna Walcott, *a little younger than* Abigail, *a nervous, hurried girl, enters.*)

Parris (*eagerly*). What does the doctor say, child?

Susanna (*craning around Parris to get a look at Betty*). He bid me come and tell you, reverend sir, that he cannot discover no medicine for it in his books.

Parris. Then he must search on.

Susanna. Aye, sir, he have been searchin' his books since he left you, sir. But he bid me tell you, that you might look to unnatural things for the cause of it.

Parris (*his eyes going wide*). No—no. There be no unnatural cause here. Tell him I have sent for Reverend Hale of Beverly, and Mr. Hale will surely confirm that. Let him look to medicine and put out all thought of unnatural causes here. There be none.

---

13. **dissembling:** disguising the truth about something.

Susanna. Aye, sir. He bid me tell you. (*She turns to go.*)

Abigail. Speak nothin' of it in the village, Susanna.

Parris. Go directly home and speak nothing of unnatural causes.

Susanna. Aye, sir. I pray for her. (*She goes out.*)

Abigail. Uncle, the rumor of witchcraft is all about; I think you'd best go down and deny it yourself. The parlor's packed with people, sir. I'll sit with her.

Parris (*pressed, turns on her*). And what shall I say to them? That my daughter and my niece I discovered dancing like heathen in the forest?

Abigail. Uncle, we did dance; let you tell them I confessed it—and I'll be whipped if I must be. But they're speakin' of witchcraft. Betty's not witched.

Parris. Abigail, I cannot go before the congregation when I know you have not opened with me. What did you do with her in the forest?

Abigail. We did dance, uncle, and when you leaped out of the bush so suddenly, Betty was frightened and then she fainted. And there's the whole of it.

Parris. Child, sit you down.

Abigail (*quavering, as she sits*). I would never hurt Betty. I love her dearly.

Parris. Now look you, child, your punishment will come in its time. But if you trafficked with[14] spirits in the forest I must know it now, for surely my enemies will, and they will ruin me with it.

Abigail. But we never conjured spirits.

Parris. Then why can she not move herself since midnight? This child is desperate! (*Abigail lowers her eyes.*) It must come out—my enemies will bring it out. Let me know what you done there. Abigail, do you understand that I have many enemies?

Abigail. I have heard of it, uncle.

Parris. There is a faction that is sworn to drive me from my pulpit. Do you understand that?

READ ALOUD Lines 244–253

Do you think Parris is concerned more about his daughter or about his own reputation? (Draw Conclusions)

_____

_____

_____

14. **trafficked with:** met.

Abigail. I think so, sir.

Parris. Now then, in the midst of such disruption, my own household is discovered to be the very center of some obscene practice. Abominations[15] are done in the forest—

Abigail. It were sport, uncle!

Parris (*pointing at Betty*). You call this sport? (*She lowers her eyes. He pleads*). Abigail, if you know something that may help the doctor, for God's sake tell it to me. (*She is silent.*) I saw Tituba waving her arms over the fire when I came on you. Why was she doing that? And I heard a screeching and gibberish coming from her mouth. She were swaying like a dumb beast over that fire!

Abigail. She always sings her Barbados songs, and we dance.

Parris. I cannot blink what I saw, Abigail, for my enemies will not blink it. I saw a dress lying on the grass.

Abigail (*innocently*). A dress?

Parris (*it is very hard to say*). Aye, a dress. And I thought I saw—someone naked running through the trees!

Abigail (*in terror*). No one was naked! You mistake yourself, uncle!

Parris (*with anger*). I saw it! (*He moves from her. Then, resolved*). Now tell me true, Abigail. And I pray you feel the weight of truth upon you, for now my ministry's at stake, my ministry and perhaps your cousin's life. Whatever abomination you have done, give me all of it now, for I dare not be taken unaware when I go before them down there.

Abigail. There is nothin' more. I swear it, uncle.

Pause & Reflect

---

15. **abominations:** dreadful and evil things.

Pause & Reflect

1. What is the matter with Betty? (Clarify)

_____

_____

_____

_____

2. Review the details you circled as you read. What do you know so far about what the girls did in the forest? (Draw Conclusions)

_____

_____

_____

_____

290 **Parris** (*studies her, then nods, half convinced*). Abigail, I have fought here three long years to bend these stiff-necked people to me, and now, just now when some good respect is rising for me in the parish, you compromise my very character. I have given you a home, child, I have put clothes upon your back— now give me upright answer. Your name in the town—it is entirely white, is it not?

Abigail (*with an edge of resentment*). Why, I am sure it is, sir. There be no blush about my name.[16]

300 **Parris** (*to the point*). Abigail, is there any other cause than you have told me, for your being discharged from Goody[17] Proctor's service? I have heard it said, and I tell you as I heard it, that she comes so rarely to the church this year for she will not sit so close to something soiled. What signified that remark?

Abigail. She hates me, uncle, she must, for I would not be her slave. It's a bitter woman, a lying, cold, sniveling woman, and I will not work for such a woman!

Parris. She may be. And yet it has troubled me that you are now seven month out of their house, and in all this time no other family has ever called for your service.

310 **Abigail.** They want slaves, not such as I. Let them send to Barbados for that. I will not black my face for any of them! (*With ill-concealed resentment at him.*) Do you begrudge my bed, uncle?

Parris. No—no.

Abigail (*in a temper*). My name is good in the village! I will not have it said my name is soiled! Goody Proctor is a gossiping liar!

Pause & Reflect

---

16. **There be . . . my name:** there is nothing wrong with my reputation.
17. **Goody:** short for Goodwife, the Puritan equivalent of Mrs.

FOCUS

Mrs. Putnam and then her husband, Thomas, enter Betty's room. Read to find out what has happened to their daughter and how Thomas feels about Reverend Parris.

(*Enter* Mrs. Ann Putnam. *She is a twisted soul of forty-five, a death-ridden woman, haunted by dreams.*)

Parris (*as soon as the door begins to open*). No—no, I cannot have anyone. (*He sees her, and a certain deference springs into him, although his worry remains.*) Why, Goody Putnam, come in.

Mrs. Putnam (*full of breath, shiny-eyed*). It is a marvel. It is surely a stroke of hell upon you.

Parris. No, Goody Putnam, it is—

Mrs. Putnam (*glancing at* Betty). How high did she fly, how high?

Parris. No, no, she never flew—

Mrs. Putnam (*very pleased with it*). Why, it's sure she did. Mr. Collins saw her goin' over Ingersoll's barn, and come down light as bird, he says!

Parris. Now, look you, Goody Putnam, she never—(*Enter* Thomas Putnam, *a well-to-do, hardhanded landowner, near fifty.*) Oh, good morning, Mr. Putnam.

Putnam. It is a providence[18] the thing is out now! It is a providence. (*He goes directly to the bed.*)

Parris. What's out, sir, what's—?

(Mrs. Putnam *goes to the bed.*)

Putnam (*looking down at* Betty). Why, her eyes is closed! Look you, Ann.

Mrs. Putnam. Why, that's strange. (*To* Parris). Ours is open.

Parris (*shocked*). Your Ruth is sick?

Mrs. Putnam (*with vicious certainty*). I'd not call it sick; the Devil's touch is heavier than sick. It's death, y'know, it's death drivin' into them, forked and hoofed.

Parris. Oh, pray not! Why, how does Ruth ail?

---

18. **providence** (prŏv´ĭ-dəns): sign of good fortune.

Mrs. Putnam. She ails as she must—she never waked this morning, but her eyes open and she walks, and hears naught, sees naught, and cannot eat. Her soul is taken, surely.

(*Parris is struck.*)

Putnam (*as though for further details*). They say you've sent for Reverend Hale of Beverly?

Parris (*with dwindling conviction now*). A precaution only. He has much experience in all demonic arts, and I—

Mrs. Putnam. He has indeed; and found a witch in Beverly last year, and let you remember that.

Parris. Now, Goody Ann, they only thought that were a witch, and I am certain there be no element of witchcraft here.

Putnam. No witchcraft! Now look you, Mr. Parris—

Parris. Thomas, Thomas, I pray you, leap not to witchcraft. I know that you—you least of all, Thomas, would ever wish so disastrous a charge laid upon me. We cannot leap to witchcraft. They will howl me out of Salem for such corruption in my house.

A word about Thomas Putnam. He was a man with many grievances, at least one of which appears justified. Some time before, his wife's brother-in-law, James Bayley, had been turned down as minister of Salem. Bayley had all the qualifications, and a two-thirds vote into the bargain, but a faction stopped his acceptance, for reasons that are not clear.

Thomas Putnam was the eldest son of the richest man in the village. He had fought the Indians at Narragansett, and was deeply interested in parish affairs. He undoubtedly felt it poor payment that the village should so blatantly disregard his candidate for one of its more important offices, especially since he regarded himself as the intellectual superior of most of the people around him.

His vindictive[19] nature was demonstrated long before the witchcraft began. Another former Salem minister, George Burroughs, had had to borrow money to pay for his wife's funeral, and, since the parish was remiss in his salary, he was

> **JOT IT DOWN** **Lines 374–385**
>
> Reread the boxed passage. How do you think Mr. Putnam feels about Reverend Parris? **(Infer)**
>
> _____
> _____
> _____
> _____

---

19. **vindictive:** vengeful; eager to get even when wronged.

Pause & Reflect

✏ **MARK IT UP** **1.** What has happened to Ruth Putnam? Write the answer below. Then underline the details on pages 32 and 33 that support your answer. **(Clarify)**

_____

_____

_____

2. What is your opinion of Mr. and Mrs. Putnam? Give your reasons. **(Evaluate)**

_____

_____

_____

_____

soon bankrupt. Thomas and his brother John had Burroughs jailed for debts the man did not owe. The incident is important only in that Burroughs succeeded in becoming minister where Bayley, Thomas Putnam's brother-in-law, had been rejected; the motif of resentment is clear here. Thomas Putnam felt that his own name and the honor of his family had been smirched[20] by the village, and he meant to right matters however he could.

Another reason to believe him a deeply embittered man was his attempt to break his father's will, which left a disproportionate amount to a stepbrother. As with every other public cause in which he tried to force his way, he failed in this.

So it is not surprising to find that so many accusations against people are in the handwriting of Thomas Putnam, or that his name is so often found as a witness corroborating the supernatural testimony, or that his daughter led the crying-out at the most opportune junctures of the trials, especially when—But we'll speak of that when we come to it.

Pause & Reflect

FOCUS
The Putnams are convinced that a witch is responsible for recent events. Read to learn more about what the girls did in the forest.
✏ **MARK IT UP** As you read, underline details that reveal more about what happened.

Putnam (*at the moment he is intent upon getting* Parris, *for whom he has only contempt, to move toward the abyss*). Mr. Parris, I have taken your part in all contention here, and I would continue; but I cannot if you hold back in this. There are hurtful, vengeful spirits layin' hands on these children.

---

20. **smirched:** soiled; reduced in value.

WORDS TO KNOW **disproportionate** (dĭs'prə-pôr'shə-nĭt) *adj.* out of proportion; of an unequal size or amount

Parris. But, Thomas, you cannot—

Putnam. Ann! Tell Mr. Parris what you have done.

Mrs. Putnam. Reverend Parris, I have laid seven babies unbaptized in the earth. Believe me, sir, you never saw more hearty babies born. And yet, each would wither in my arms the very night of their birth. I have spoke nothin', but my heart has clamored intimations.[21] And now, this year, my Ruth, my only—I see her turning strange. A secret child she has become this year, and shrivels like a sucking mouth were pullin' on her life too. And so I thought to send her to your Tituba—

Parris. To Tituba! What may Tituba—?

Mrs. Putnam. Tituba knows how to speak to the dead, Mr. Parris.

Parris. Goody Ann, it is a formidable sin to conjure up the dead!

Mrs. Putnam. I take it on my soul, but who else may surely tell us what person murdered my babies?

Parris (*horrified*). Woman!

Mrs. Putnam. They were murdered, Mr. Parris! And mark this proof! Mark it! Last night my Ruth were ever so close to their little spirits; I know it, sir. For how else is she struck dumb now except some power of darkness would stop her mouth? It is a marvelous sign, Mr. Parris!

Putnam. Don't you understand it, sir? There is a murdering witch among us, bound to keep herself in the dark. (Parris *turns to* Betty, *a frantic terror rising in him.*) Let your enemies make of it what they will, you cannot blink it more.

Parris (*to* Abigail). Then you were conjuring spirits last night.

Abigail (*whispering*). Not I, sir—Tituba and Ruth.

Parris (*turns now, with new fear, and goes to* Betty, *looks down at her, and then, gazing off*). Oh, Abigail, what proper payment for my charity! Now I am undone.[22]

---

21. **clamored intimations** (klăm′ərd ĭn′tə-mā′shəns): nagging suspicions.
22. **undone**: ruined.

Putnam. You are not undone! Let you take hold here. Wait for no one to charge you—declare it yourself. You have discovered witchcraft—

Parris. In my house? In my house, Thomas? They will topple me with this! They will make of it a—

(*Enter* Mercy Lewis, *the Putnams' servant, a fat, sly, merciless girl of eighteen.*)

Mercy. Your pardons. I only thought to see how Betty is.

Putnam. Why aren't you home? Who's with Ruth?

Mercy. Her grandma come. She's improved a little, I think—she give a powerful sneeze before.

Mrs. Putnam. Ah, there's a sign of life!

Mercy. I'd fear no more, Goody Putnam. It were a grand sneeze; another like it will shake her wits together, I'm sure. (*She goes to the bed to look.*)

Parris. Will you leave me now, Thomas? I would pray a while alone.

Abigail. Uncle, you've prayed since midnight. Why do you not go down and—

Parris. No—no. (*To* Putnam). I have no answer for that crowd. I'll wait till Mr. Hale arrives. (*To get* Mrs. Putnam *to leave.*) If you will, Goody Ann . . .

Putnam. Now look you, sir. Let you strike out against the Devil, and the village will bless you for it! Come down, speak to them—pray with them. They're thirsting for your word, Mister! Surely you'll pray with them.

Parris (*swayed*). I'll lead them in a psalm, but let you say nothing of witchcraft yet. I will not discuss it. The cause is yet unknown. I have had enough contention since I came; I want no more.

Mrs. Putnam. Mercy, you go home to Ruth, d'y'hear?

Mercy. Aye, mum.

(Mrs. Putnam *goes out.*)

Parris (*to* Abigail). If she starts for the window, cry for me at once.

Abigail. I will, uncle.

Parris (*to* Putnam). There is a terrible power in her arms today. (*He goes out with* Putnam.)

Abigail (*with hushed trepidation*).[23] How is Ruth sick?

Mercy. It's weirdish, I know not—she seems to walk like a dead one since last night.

Abigail (*turns at once and goes to* Betty, *and now, with fear in her voice*). Betty? (Betty *doesn't move. She shakes her.*) Now stop this! Betty! Sit up now!

(Betty *doesn't stir.* Mercy *comes over.*)

Mercy. Have you tried beatin' her? I gave Ruth a good one and it waked her for a minute. Here, let me have her.

Abigail (*holding* Mercy *back*). No, he'll be comin' up. Listen, now; if they be questioning us, tell them we danced—I told him as much already.

Mercy. Aye. And what more?

Abigail. He knows Tituba conjured Ruth's sisters to come out of the grave.

Mercy. And what more?

Abigail. He saw you naked.

Mercy (*clapping her hands together with a frightened laugh*). Oh, Jesus!

(*Enter* Mary Warren, *breathless. She is seventeen, a subservient, naive, lonely girl.*)

Mary Warren. What'll we do? The village is out! I just come from the farm; the whole country's talkin' witchcraft! They'll be callin' us witches, Abby!

Mercy (*pointing and looking at* Mary Warren). She means to tell, I know it.

Mary Warren. Abby, we've got to tell. Witchery's a hangin' error, a hangin' like they done in Boston two year ago! We must tell the truth, Abby! You'll only be whipped for dancin', and the other things!

Abigail. Oh, we'll be whipped!

---

23. **trepidation** (trĕp′ĭ-dā′shən): alarm or dread.

WORDS TO KNOW **subservient** (səb-sûr′vē-ənt) *adj.* acting like a servant

Mary Warren. I never done none of it, Abby. I only looked!

Mercy (*moving menacingly toward* Mary). Oh, you're a great one for lookin', aren't you, Mary Warren? What a grand peeping courage you have!

(Betty, *on the bed, whimpers.* Abigail *turns to her at once.*)

Abigail. Betty? (*She goes to* Betty.) Now, Betty, dear, wake up now. It's Abigail. (*She sits* Betty *up and furiously shakes her.*) I'll beat you, Betty! (Betty *whimpers.*) My, you seem improving. I talked to your papa and I told him everything. So there's nothing to—

Betty (*darts off the bed, frightened of* Abigail, *and flattens herself against the wall*). I want my mama!

Abigail (*with alarm, as she cautiously approaches* Betty). What ails you, Betty? Your mama's dead and buried.

Betty. I'll fly to Mama. Let me fly! (*She raises her arms as though to fly, and streaks for the window, gets one leg out.*)

Abigail (*pulling her away from the window*). I told him everything; he knows now, he knows everything we—

Betty. You drank blood, Abby! You didn't tell him that!

Abigail. Betty, you never say that again! You will never—

Betty. You did, you did! You drank a charm to kill John Proctor's wife! You drank a charm to kill Goody Proctor!

Abigail (*smashes her across the face*). Shut it! Now shut it!

Betty (*collapsing on the bed*). Mama, Mama! (*She dissolves into sobs.*)

Abigail. Now look you. All of you. We danced. And Tituba conjured Ruth Putnam's dead sisters. And that is all. And mark this. Let either of you breathe a word, or the edge of a word, about the other things, and I will come to you in the black of some terrible night and I will bring a pointy reckoning that will shudder you.[24] And you know I can do it; I saw Indians smash my dear parents' heads on the pillow next to mine, and I have seen some reddish work done at night, and I can make you wish you had never seen the sun go down! (*She goes to* Betty *and roughly sits her up.*) Now, you—sit up and stop this! (*But* Betty *collapses in her hands and lies inert on the bed.*)

Mary Warren (*with hysterical fright*). What's got her? (Abigail *stares in fright at* Betty.) Abby, she's going to die! It's a sin to conjure, and we—

Abigail (*starting for* Mary). I say shut it, Mary Warren! (*Enter* John Proctor. *On seeing him,* Mary Warren *leaps in fright.*)

Pause & Reflect

FOCUS

Read to find out about Abigail's relationship with John Proctor.

MARK IT UP As you read, underline phrases in the dialogue and the stage directions that help you understand how they feel about each other.

Proctor was a farmer in his middle thirties. He need not have been a partisan of any faction in the town, but there is evidence to suggest that he had a sharp and biting way with hypocrites.[25] He was the kind of man—powerful of body, even-tempered, and not easily led—who cannot refuse support to partisans without drawing their deepest resentment. In Proctor's presence a fool felt his foolishness instantly—and a Proctor is always marked for calumny[26] therefore.

But as we shall see, the steady manner he displays does not spring from an untroubled soul. He is a sinner, a sinner not

24. **bring . . . shudder you:** inflict a terrifying punishment on you.

25. **hypocrites** (hĭp′ə-krĭts′): people who pretend to be what they are not.

26. **calumny** (kăl′əm-nē): slander; lies about someone.

Pause & Reflect

MARK IT UP **1.** Why did Mrs. Putnam send her daughter, Ruth, to Tituba? Write the answer below. Then underline the details on page 35 that support your answer. **(Cause and Effect)**

_____

_____

_____

READ ALOUD **2.** Read aloud the boxed passage on page 38. What did Abigail do in the forest? **(Clarify)**

_____

_____

_____

3. Review the details you underlined as you read. What would you say was the worst thing the girls did in the forest? **(Evaluate)**

_____

_____

_____

only against the moral fashion of the time, but against his own vision of decent conduct. These people had no ritual for the washing away of sins. It is another trait we inherited from them, and it has helped to discipline us as well as to breed hypocrisy among us. Proctor, respected and even feared in Salem, has come to regard himself as a kind of fraud. But no hint of this has yet appeared on the surface, and as he enters from the crowded parlor below it is a man in his prime we see, with a quiet confidence and an unexpressed, hidden force. Mary Warren, his servant, can barely speak for embarrassment and fear.

Mary Warren. Oh! I'm just going home, Mr. Proctor.

Proctor. Be you foolish, Mary Warren? Be you deaf? I forbid you leave the house, did I not? Why shall I pay you? I am looking for you more often than my cows!

Mary Warren. I only come to see the great doings in the world.

Proctor. I'll show you a great doin' on your arse one of these days. Now get you home; my wife is waitin' with your work! (*Trying to retain a shred of dignity, she goes slowly out.*)

Mercy Lewis (*both afraid of him and strangely titillated*). I'd best be off. I have my Ruth to watch. Good morning, Mr. Proctor.

(Mercy *sidles out. Since* Proctor's *entrance,* Abigail *has stood as though on tiptoe, absorbing his presence, wide-eyed. He glances at her, then goes to* Betty *on the bed.*)

Abigail. Gah! I'd almost forgot how strong you are, John Proctor!

Proctor (*looking at* Abigail *now, the faintest suggestion of a knowing smile on his face*). What's this mischief here?

Abigail (*with a nervous laugh*). Oh, she's only gone silly somehow.

Proctor. The road past my house is a pilgrimage[27] to Salem all morning. The town's mumblin witchcraft.

---

27. **pilgrimage:** a journey to a religious shrine, often made in groups.

Abigail. Oh, posh! (*Winningly she comes a little closer, with a confidential, wicked air.*) We were dancin' in the woods last night, and my uncle leaped in on us. She took fright, is all.

Proctor (*his smile widening*). Ah, you're wicked yet, aren't y'! (*A trill of expectant laughter escapes her, and she dares come closer, feverishly looking into his eyes.*) You'll be clapped in the stocks before you're twenty.

(*He takes a step to go, and she springs into his path.*)

Abigail. Give me a word, John. A soft word. (*Her concentrated desire destroys his smile.*)

Proctor. No, no, Abby. That's done with.

Abigail (*tauntingly*). You come five mile to see a silly girl fly? I know you better.

Proctor (*setting her firmly out of his path*). I come to see what mischief your uncle's brewin' now. (*With final emphasis.*) Put it out of mind, Abby.

Abigail (*grasping his hand before he can release her*). John—I am waitin' for you every night.

Proctor. Abby, I never give you hope to wait for me.

Abigail (*now beginning to anger—she can't believe it*). I have something better than hope, I think!

Proctor. Abby, you'll put it out of mind. I'll not be comin' for you more.

Abigail. You're surely sportin' with me.

Proctor. You know me better.

Abigail. I know how you clutched my back behind your house and sweated like a stallion whenever I come near! Or did I dream that? It's she put me out, you cannot pretend it were you. I saw your face when she put me out, and you loved me then and you do now!

Proctor. Abby, that's a wild thing to say—

Abigail. A wild thing may say wild things. But not so wild, I think. I have seen you since she put me out; I have seen you nights.

Proctor. I have hardly stepped off my farm this seven-month.

> **READ ALOUD** Lines 640–644
>
> What does Abigail imply is Proctor's real reason for coming to Salem? **(Infer)**
>
> _____
>
> _____
>
> _____

Abigail. I have a sense for heat, John, and yours has drawn me to my window, and I have seen you looking up, burning in your loneliness. Do you tell me you've never looked up at my window?

670 **Proctor.** I may have looked up.

Abigail (*now softening*). And you must. You are no wintry man. I know you, John. I know you. (*She is weeping.*) I cannot sleep for dreamin'; I cannot dream but I wake and walk about the house as though I'd find you comin' through some door. (*She clutches him desperately*).

Proctor (*gently pressing her from him, with great sympathy but firmly*). Child—

Abigail (*with a flash of anger*). How do you call me **680** child!

Proctor. Abby, I may think of you softly from time to time. But I will cut off my hand before I'll ever reach for you again. Wipe it out of mind. We never touched, Abby.

Abigail. Aye, but we did.

Proctor. Aye, but we did not.

Abigail (*with a bitter anger*). Oh, I marvel how such a strong man may let such a sickly wife be—

Proctor (*angered—at himself as well*). You'll speak **690** nothin' of Elizabeth!

Abigail. She is blackening my name in the village! She is telling lies about me! She is a cold, sniveling woman, and you bend to her! Let her turn you like a—

Proctor (*shaking her*). Do you look for whippin'?

(*A psalm is heard being sung below.*)

Abigail (*in tears*). I look for John Proctor that took me from my sleep and put knowledge in my heart! I never knew what pretense Salem was, I never knew **700** the lying lessons I was taught by all these Christian women and their covenanted[27] men! And now you bid me tear the light out of my eyes? I will not, I

---

27. **covenanted** (kŭv′ə-nən′tĭd): in Puritan religious practice, the men of a congregation would make an agreement, or a covenant, to govern the community.

cannot! You loved me, John Proctor, and whatever sin it is, you love me yet! (*He turns abruptly to go out. She rushes to him.*) John, pity me, pity me!

Pause & Reflect

FOCUS
Find out what Betty does that alarms the people in the parlor.

(*The words "going up to Jesus" are heard in the psalm, and* Betty *claps her ears suddenly and whines loudly.*)

Abigail. Betty? (*She hurries to* Betty, *who is now sitting up and screaming.* Proctor *goes to* Betty *as* Abigail *is trying to pull her hands down, calling* "Betty!")

710

Proctor (*growing unnerved*). What's she doing? Girl, what ails you? Stop that wailing!

(*The singing has stopped in the midst of this, and now* Parris *rushes in.*)

Parris. What happened? What are you doing to her? Betty! (*He rushes to the bed, crying,* "Betty, Betty!" Mrs. Putnam *enters, feverish with curiosity, and with her* Thomas Putnam *and* Mercy Lewis. Parris, *at the bed, keeps lightly slapping* Betty's *face, while she moans and tries to get up.*)

720

Abigail. She heard you singin' and suddenly she's up and screamin'.

Mrs. Putnam. The psalm! The psalm! She cannot bear to hear the Lord's name!

Parris. No. God forbid. Mercy, run to the doctor! Tell him what's happened here! (Mercy Lewis *rushes out.*)

Mrs. Putnam. Mark it for a sign, mark it!

(Rebecca Nurse, *seventy-two, enters. She is white-haired, leaning upon her walking-stick.*)

730

Putnam (*pointing at the whimpering* Betty). That is a notorious sign of witchcraft afoot, Goody Nurse, a prodigious[29] sign!

---

29. **prodigious** (prə-dĭj′əs): extraordinary.

Pause & Reflect

1. What happened between Abigail and John Proctor when she worked in the Proctor home? **(Infer)**

_____

_____

_____

_____

2. Review the phrases you underlined as you read. How does Abigail feel about John Proctor? **(Infer)**

_____

_____

_____

_____

3. Do you think Proctor will get back together again with Abigail? *Yes/No*, because _____

_____

_____

_____.

(Predict)

1. What does Betty do that alarms those in the parlor below? **(Clarify)**

_____

_____

2. How do Parris and the Putnams interpret her action? **(Infer)**

_____

_____

_____

3. What do you think will happen to Betty, Abigail, and the other girls later in this act? **(Predict)**

_____

_____

_____

_____

✎ **CHALLENGE**

Think about the **conflicts** that the author has set in motion so far in this play. What **external** and **internal conflicts** can you identify? Mark the lines that provide evidence of these conflicts. Which conflict do you think will be most important as the play goes on? **(Evaluate)**

Moving On

If you are using **_The Language of Literature,_** go to page 178 of that book to continue reading _The Crucible._ As you do so, continue to be an active reader. Ask yourself the kinds of questions you found in this excerpt from Act One.

Mrs. Putnam. My mother told me that! When they cannot bear to hear the name of—

Parris (_trembling_). Rebecca, Rebecca, go to her, we're lost. She suddenly cannot bear to hear the Lord's—
(Giles Corey, _eighty-three, enters. He is knotted with muscle, canny, inquisitive, and still powerful._)

Rebecca. There is hard sickness here, Giles Corey, so please to keep the quiet.

Giles. I've not said a word. No one here can testify I've said a word. Is she going to fly again? I hear she flies.

Putnam. Man, be quiet now!
(_Everything is quiet. Rebecca_ walks across the room to the bed. Gentleness exudes from her. Betty _is quietly whimpering, eyes shut._ Rebecca _simply stands over the child, who gradually quiets._)

Pause **&** **Reflect**

Active Reading SkillBuilder

Using a Graphic Organizer

A **graphic organizer** is a visual representation of information in a text. Graphic organizers include charts, diagrams, and time lines. Using a graphic organizer when reading can help the reader keep track of details and relationships. As you read *The Crucible,* fill in the chart below. Write one of John Proctor's character traits and the evidence that reveals this trait. The evidence may be from his actions, from his dialogue, or from the stage directions. An example is shown.

John Proctor

Trait: *self-doubt*	Trait:
Evidence: *still attracted to Abigail, but wants to forget her*	Evidence:

Follow Up: Create a similar chart for Abigail Williams, and fill it in as you continue to read the play.

Literary Analysis SkillBuilder

Stage Directions

The **stage directions** of a play are instructions for the director, actors, and stage crew. Stage directions may describe the props, scenery, costumes, and sound effects used during a performance and tell how characters look, move, speak, and feel. In *The Crucible* Arthur Miller also provides commentaries about the Puritans and American society. Fill in the chart below. In the first column list three details from the stage directions that help you imagine an important character in the play. In the second column, list three insights about Puritan life that Miller conveys in his commentaries. An example of each has been provided.

Character Details	Insights About Puritan Life
John Proctor has a quiet confidence.	Puritans liked to mind other people's business.

Words to Know SkillBuilder

Words to Know

arbitrate*	disproportionate	iniquity*	subservient
ascertain*	fanatic	predilection	

A. Decide which Word to Know best completes each sentence below. Write the word on the blank line on the right. Some words may be used more than once.

An atmosphere of fear can exist when a (1) ruthlessly pursues his or her goal.

_____
(1)

Mistreating those who are helpless is a special kind of (2).

_____
(2)

People who feel that they have no power sometimes assume a (3) attitude.

_____
(3)

Victims who have suffered serious financial losses may have to spend a (4) amount of money to resolve their situation.

_____
(4)

Outside observers who do not know if attacks are valid may find the truth hard to (5).

_____
(5)

Some people take their cases to court, where a judge will (6) and try to determine the truth.

_____
(6)

Generally, people respect justice and have a strong (7) for following the law.

_____
(7)

Respect for the law sometimes deters even someone who is overzealous, such as a (8).

_____
(8)

B. Find the Word to Know that best matches each clue below. Write the word in the blank.

1. inclined that way   _____

2. the need to know   _____

3. witch hunt person   _____

4. more than it should be   _____

5. settling an argument   _____

6. worthy of punishment or shame   _____

7. working hard without power or authority

* These words appear later in Act One of *The Crucible*. You can use a dictionary to check the definitions. The words are also defined in the lesson for *The Crucible,* found in **The Language of Literature.**

Before You Read

If you are using *The Language of Literature* . . .

- Use the information on page 262 of that book to prepare for reading.

- Look at the painting on page 265. What impression does it give of Patrick Henry? of his listeners?

Reading Tips

In this **persuasive speech,** Patrick Henry uses emotional and forceful language to try to convince his listeners to go to war with Great Britain. Some of the words and sentences may be difficult at first.

- As you read, imagine that you are a delegate at the Virginia Convention listening to Patrick Henry.

- Break up long, complicated sentences into smaller sections.

- Use the information in the Guide for Reading to help you with unfamiliar words and difficult passages.

✎ MARK IT UP KEEP TRACK

As you read, you can use these marks to keep track of your understanding.

✔ ..... I understand.

? ..... I don't understand this.

! ..... Interesting or surprising idea

SPEECH *in the*

VIRGINIA CONVENTION

PATRICK HENRY

PREVIEW In 1775, American colonists were divided about their relationship to Great Britain. Some were still hoping to work out disagreements and remain British subjects. Others, like the fiery Virginian Patrick Henry, believed that the only choice left was to go to war with Britain. In this speech to his fellow Virginia patriots, Henry makes a stirring plea for his cause.

FOCUS
Henry believes that the colonies are facing a critical moment in their struggle with Great Britain.

✎ **MARK IT UP** Underline at least two statements that show Henry's view of the situation. An example is highlighted.

March 23, 1775

Mr. President: No man thinks more highly than I do of the patriotism, as well as abilities, of the very worthy gentlemen who have just addressed the House. But different men often see the same subject in different lights; and, therefore, I hope that it will not be thought disrespectful to those gentlemen, if, entertaining as I do

10 opinions of a character very opposite to theirs, I shall speak forth my sentiments freely and without reserve. This is no time for ceremony. The question before the House is one of awful moment to this country. For my own part I consider it as nothing less than a question of freedom or slavery; and in proportion to the magnitude of the subject ought to be the freedom of the debate. It is only in this way that we can hope to arrive at truth, and fulfill the great responsibility which we

Use this guide for help with unfamiliar words and difficult passages.

1 Mr. President: the president of the Virginia Convention, Peyton Randolph.
1–5 Henry states his respect for the previous speakers.

9 entertaining: holding in mind.

12 The question before the House: The Virginia Convention must decide whether or not to prepare for war against Great Britain; **awful moment:** great importance.

> **MARK IT UP** WORD POWER
>
> Mark words that you'd like to add to your **Personal Word List.** After reading, you can record the words and their meanings beginning on page 344.

hold to God and our country. Should I keep back my opinions at such a time, through fear of giving offense, I should consider myself as guilty of treason towards my country, and of an act of disloyalty towards the majesty of heaven, which I revere above all earthly kings.

Mr. President, it is natural to man to indulge in the illusions of hope. We are apt to shut our eyes against a painful truth, and listen to the song of that siren, till she transforms us into beasts. Is this the part of wise men, engaged in a great and arduous struggle for liberty? Are we disposed to be of the number of those who, having eyes, see not, and having ears, hear not, the things which so nearly concern their temporal salvation? For my part, whatever anguish of spirit it may cost, I am willing to know the whole truth—to know the worst and to provide for it.

imagery
flattery
@ rhetorical question

Pause & Reflect

FOCUS
Henry explains why he thinks there is no hope for improving relations with Britain. As you read, look for the main reasons he gives for his position.

imagery

I have but one lamp by which my feet are guided; and that is the lamp of experience. I know of no way of judging of the future but by the past. And judging by the past, I wish to know what there has been in the conduct of the British ministry for the last ten years, to justify those hopes with which gentlemen have been pleased to solace themselves and the House? Is it that insidious smile with which our petition has been lately received? Trust it not, sir; it will prove a snare to your feet. Suffer not yourselves to be betrayed with a kiss.

@ rhetorical question

Ask yourselves how this gracious reception of our petition comports with these warlike preparations which cover our waters and darken our land. Are fleets and armies necessary to a work of love and reconciliation? Have we shown ourselves so unwilling to be reconciled that force must be called in to win back our love? Let us not deceive ourselves, sir. These are the implements of war and subjugation—the last arguments to which kings resort. I ask gentlemen, sir,

WORDS
TO
KNOW

insidious (ĭn-sĭd´ē-əs) *adj.* treacherous
subjugation (sŭb´jə-gā´shən) *n.* control by conquering

25–26 **song . . . beasts:** an allusion, or reference, to Homer's *Odyssey*. The sirens' tempting song lured sailors to their deaths. The goddess Circe lured men to her island and then magically turned them into pigs. Henry compares "the illusions of hope" to these dangerous mythical creatures.

28–29 **having eyes . . . hear not:** an allusion to a biblical passage (Ezekiel 12:2) that describes stubborn people who won't pay attention to important messages they receive.

30 **temporal:** worldly.

41 **solace** (sŏl′ĭs)**:** comfort.

43 **snare:** trap.

44 **betrayed with a kiss:** a biblical reference to the Apostle Judas, who betrayed Jesus. When soldiers came to arrest Jesus, Judas identified him by kissing him. Like Judas, the British government might betray the American colonists with friendly words that hide evil intentions.

Pause & Reflect

1. Look at the statements you underlined. How serious is the situation of the colonies in the eyes of Patrick Henry? **(Infer)**

_____
_____
_____

READ ALOUD 2. Read aloud the boxed passage on page 50. What does Henry say would be an act of treason for him? **(Analyze)**

_____
_____
_____

3. In lines 23–32, Henry warns his listeners against the "illusions of hope," or false hopes. What does he prefer instead, whatever the cost? **(Clarify)**

_____
_____
_____
_____

Rhetorical Q:

what means this <u>martial</u> array, if its purpose be not to force us to submission? Can gentlemen assign any other possible motives for it? Has Great Britain any enemy, in this quarter of the world, to call for all this accumulation of navies and armies? No, sir, she has none. They are meant for us; they can be meant for no other. They are sent over to bind and rivet upon us those chains which the British ministry have been so long forging.

60   And what have we to oppose to them? Shall we try argument? Sir, we have been trying that for the last ten years. Have we anything new to offer on the subject? Nothing. We have held the subject up in every light of which it is capable; but it has been all in vain. Shall we resort to entreaty and humble supplication? What terms shall we find which have not been already exhausted? Let us not, I beseech you, sir, deceive ourselves longer.

70   Sir, we have done everything that could be done to avert the storm which is now coming on. We have petitioned; we have remonstrated; we have supplicated; we have prostrated ourselves before the throne, and have implored its interposition to arrest the <u>tyrannical</u> hands of the ministry and Parliament. Our petitions have been slighted; our remonstrances have produced additional violence and insult; our supplications have been disregarded; and we have been <u>spurned</u>, with contempt, from the foot of the throne. In vain, after these things, may we indulge the fond hope of peace and reconciliation. There is no longer any room for hope.

Imagery

Pause & Reflect

80

FOCUS

Henry now focuses on convincing the Virginia patriots to go to war with Great Britain.

MARK IT UP Underline three of Henry's most powerful statements.

If we wish to be free—if we mean to preserve inviolate those inestimable privileges for which we have been so long contending—if we mean not basely to abandon the noble struggle in which we have been so long engaged, and which we have pledged ourselves never to abandon until the glorious object of our contest shall

---

WORDS
TO
KNOW

martial (mär′shəl) *adj.* warlike
tyrannical (tĭ-răn′ĭ-kəl) *adj.* harsh; oppressive
spurn (spûrn) *v.* to reject scornfully

52

61–67 Notice how Henry uses rhetorical questions—questions that don't need answers—to point out the arguments of his opponents.

65 entreaty (ĕn-trē'tē): earnest request; plea
66 supplication (sŭp'lĭ-kā'shən): the act of asking for something humbly or earnestly.

71 remonstrated (rĭ-mŏn'strā-tĭd): objected.
72–74 implored its interposition . . . of the ministry and Parliament: the colonists asked for help to stop the tyranny of the British government.

81 inviolate (ĭn-vī'ə-lĭt): not harmed; intact;
inestimable (ĭn-ĕs'tə-mə-bəl): extremely valuable.
84 basely (bās'lē): dishonorably.

▸ **MARK IT UP** Reread Lines 74–77

The colonists took action to avoid "the storm which is now coming on" (line 70). Circle the words that describe how Great Britain has responded. **(Clarify)**

Pause & Reflect

1. Circle two words below that describe methods the colonists used to protest Great Britain's treatment of them: **(Clarify)**

violence	petition
argument	war

2. In line 79, Henry says "there is no longer any room for hope." What main reasons does he give to support his position? **(Supporting Details)**

_____

_____

_____

_____

▸ **MARK IT UP** **3.** Henry gets the attention of his audience by asking many questions in his speech. Mark four questions that Henry asks. **(Rhetorical Questions/ Persuasion)**

Anaphora

be obtained, we must fight! I repeat it, sir, we must fight! An appeal to arms and to the God of Hosts is all that is left us!

90   They tell us, sir, that we are weak—unable to cope with so formidable an adversary. But when shall we be stronger? Will it be the next week, or the next year? Will it be when we are totally disarmed, and when a British guard shall be stationed in every house? Shall we gather strength by irresolution and inaction? Shall we acquire the means of effectual resistance, by lying supinely on our backs, and hugging the delusive phantom of hope, until our enemies shall have bound us hand and foot?

Rhetorical ①

Sir, we are not weak, if we make a proper use of those means which the God of nature hath placed in our power.
100   Three millions of people, armed in the holy cause of liberty, and in such a country as that which we possess, are invincible by any force which our enemy can send against us. Besides, sir, we shall not fight our battles alone. There is a just God who presides over the destinies of nations, and who will raise up friends to fight our battles for us. The battle, sir, is not to the strong alone; it is to the vigilant, the active, the brave. Besides, sir, we have no election. If we were base enough to desire it, it is now too late to retire from the contest. There is no retreat but in submission and slavery! Our chains are forged! Their
110   clanking may be heard on the plains of Boston! The war is inevitable—and let it come! I repeat it, sir, let it come!

Contrast

It is in vain, sir, to extenuate the matter. Gentlemen may cry, "Peace! peace!"—but there is no peace. The war is actually begun! The next gale that sweeps from the north will bring to our ears the clash of resounding arms! Our brethren are already in the field! Why stand we here idle? What is it that gentlemen wish? What would they have? Is life so dear, or peace so sweet, as to be purchased at the price of chains and slavery? Forbid it, Almighty God! I know not what course others may take; but as
120   for me, give me liberty, or give me death!

Pause & Reflect

WORDS
TO
KNOW

formidable (fôr′mĭ-də-bəl) *adj.* difficult to defeat
adversary (ăd′vər-sĕr′ē) *n.* an opponent
irresolution (ĭ-rĕz′ə-lōō′shən) *n.* uncertainty; indecision
invincible (ĭn-vĭn′sə-bəl) *adj.* unbeatable
vigilant (vĭj′ə-lənt) *adj.* alert; watchful

88–89 Henry has reached the climax, or emotional high point, of his speech—his call to arms.

105–106 battle . . . strong alone: an allusion, or reference, to Ecclesiastes 9:11— "the race is not to the swift, nor the battle to the strong."
107 election: choice.

112 extenuate (ĭk-stĕn′yoo-āt′)**:** to lessen the seriousness of, especially by providing partial excuses.
114 the next gale . . . north: Some colonists in Massachusetts had already shown open resistance to the British and were on the brink of war.

Pause & Reflect

1. Reread the statements you underlined. What do you think Henry sounded like and looked like when he was delivering the final part of his speech? **(Visualize)**

_____
_____
_____
_____

2. Henry believes the colonists will win a war against Britain because _____

_____
_____
_____ .

(Infer)

3. If you were a Virginian hearing Henry's speech, would you vote to go to war with Britain? *Yes/No,* because _____

_____
_____
_____ .

(Connect)

CHALLENGE

Do you think Henry appeals more to ideas or to emotions to convince his listeners? Mark passages that support your opinion. **(Persuasive Techniques)**

Wrapping Up

If you are using *The Language of Literature,* you can now move to the questions and activities on pages 267–269 of that book.

Active Reading SkillBuilder

Rhetorical Questions and Persuasion

A **rhetorical question** is a question to which no answer is expected because the answer is obvious. Writers often use rhetorical questions in persuasive writing to emphasize a point or create an emotional effect. As you read this speech, write in each block of the diagram below one rhetorical question that Henry uses to convince his audience to prepare for war with the British. Under each question, indicate what you think is the primary purpose of the question—emphasis or emotional effect. One box is filled in for you.

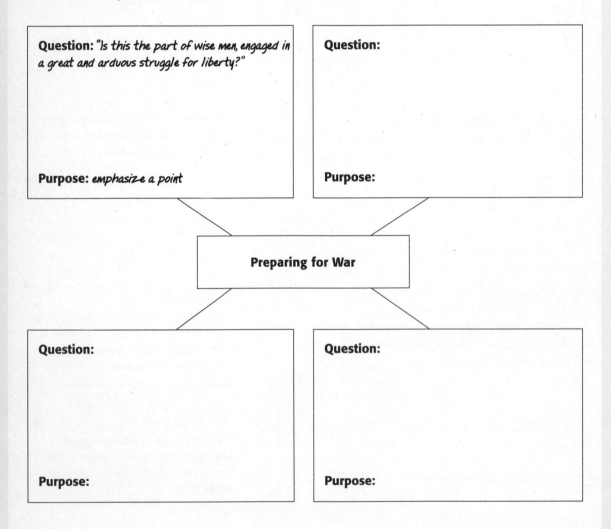

Question: *"Is this the part of wise men, engaged in a great and arduous struggle for liberty?"*

Purpose: *emphasize a point*

Question:

Purpose:

Preparing for War

Question:

Purpose:

Question:

Purpose:

Literary Analysis SkillBuilder

Allusion

An **allusion** is an indirect reference to a person, place, event, or literary work with which the author believes the reader will be familiar. By using allusions, writers draw on associations already in the reader's mind. On the chart below, list allusions from Henry's speech. Then identify the origin of each—according to the notes in the Guide for Reading—and describe the meaning that each allusion suggests to you. One example is given.

Allusion	Origin	Meaning
1. "listen to the song of that siren, till she transforms us into beasts"	Homer's <u>Odyssey</u>	If we let ourselves be deceived by false hopes, we may lose our freedom.
2.		
3.		
4.		

Follow Up: Which of the allusions that you listed on your chart do you think is most effective in the speech? Why?

Words to Know SkillBuilder

Words to Know

adversary	insidious	irresolution	spurn	tyrannical
formidable	invincible	martial	subjugation	vigilant

A. Decide which word from the word list belongs in each numbered blank. Then write the word on the blank line on the right.

My husband's a bully. He's as (1) as a dictator, and nobody can do a thing about it because he's so darn big. Oh, some brave souls have tried, but his size makes him pretty doggone (2). I'm not saying nobody could defeat him. I'm not saying the big oaf is (3), but it wouldn't be easy. He's always cutting the tops off candles with his sword and knocking chimneys off houses with karate kicks and generally practicing all his (4) skills.

One day this kid named Jack comes to the door. I'm afraid to let him in, seeing as how my husband's so mean, but I don't want to leave him standing out there either. My (5) about what to do keeps me hemming and hawing, but then I hear Mr. Big Shot coming, so I hustle the kid into a closet to hide him.

Well, in stomps Jumbo and gives a sniff. He prides himself on being observant and (6) for any sign of danger. Like everybody in town is hatching some (7) plot to overthrow him. Nobody could even lift him. Anyway, he starts carrying on about smelling the blood of an Englishman and how he's going to grind his bones to make bread. Give me a break. He can't make a TV dinner.

"Take a load off," I say, throwing a dozen hams on the table. "Sit down and eat." But he pushes the hams away, which is the first time I have ever seen Mr. Fee-Fi-Fo-Fum (8) anything edible, and tells me to get the chicken that lays the golden eggs.

"Ha!" I say. "You've got this territory subdued, conquered, and crushed. But I am not under your (9). Get the chicken yourself."

I hate that bird. We can't eat the eggs, and fowls don't belong in the house. We're giants, not slobs, for Pete's sake! Anyway, Mr. Huge finally eats his dinner and nods off. The kid hops out and grabs the chicken. I tip him a wink and off he goes. Then Mr. Sears Tower wakes up and blunders out after him.

"Hey," I yell. "Pick on an (10) your own size!" Of course, he ignores me. I don't know what happens to the kid. I guess nobody does. But, here's the good part. *The Big Guy never comes back!* Me? I'm packing for Florida!

(1) _____

(2) _____

(3) _____

(4) _____

(5) _____

(6) _____

(7) _____

(8) _____

(9) _____

(10) _____

B. Take the position of someone whose views oppose those of Patrick Henry. How might such a person respond to Henry's speech? Write a paragraph or two from such an opposing speech, using at least **five** of the Words to Know.

What Is an American?

Michel-Guillaume Jean de Crèvecoeur[1]

PREVIEW "What Is an American?" is part of an **essay** first published in 1782. It was written by a French immigrant to America. He described how immigrants improved their lives after settling in this country. He also created a famous definition of an American.

Before You Read

If you are using *The Language of Literature,* study the information on page 289 to prepare for reading.

Reading Tips

In this **essay**, the author states his **opinions** about European immigrants. He argues that they are better off in America than they were in Europe.

- As you read, keep in mind the basic **contrast** in this essay—between conditions in Europe and those in America.

- Look for **details** that convey how these conditions differ.

FOCUS

In this part, the author contrasts the immigrants' old life in Europe with their new one in America.

MARK IT UP As you read, circle any details that help you understand what the immigrants to America leave behind in Europe. An example is highlighted.

10

In this great American asylum,[2] the poor of Europe have by some means met together, and in consequence of various causes; to what purpose should they ask one another, what countrymen they are? Alas, two-thirds of them had no country. Can a wretch who wanders about, who works and starves, whose life is a continual scene of sore affliction or pinching penury[3]—can that man call England or any other kingdom his country? A country that had no bread for him, whose fields procured him no harvest, who met with

MARK IT UP KEEP TRACK

As you read, you can use these marks to keep track of your understanding.

✔ ..... I understand.

? ..... I don't understand this.

! ..... Interesting or surprising idea

---

1. **Michel-Guillaume Jean de Crèvecoeur** (mē-shĕl′ gē-yōm′ zhäɴ də-krĕv-kœr′)
2. **asylum** (ə-sī′ləm): a shelter.
3. **penury** (pĕn′yə-rē): extreme poverty.

1. Review the details you circled as you read. Then write a sentence to **summarize** what the immigrants to America leave behind in Europe.

_____

_____

_____

_____

2. What kind of life do the immigrants find in America? (Main Idea)

_____

_____

_____

_____

nothing but the frowns of the rich, the severity of the laws, with jails and punishments, who owned not a single foot of the extensive surface of this planet? No! urged by a variety of motives, here they came. Everything has tended to regenerate them: new laws, a new mode of living, a new social system. Here they are become men; in Europe they were as so many useless plants, wanting vegetative mold[4] and refreshing showers; they withered and were mowed down by want, hunger, and war. But now, by the power of transplantation, like all other plants, they have taken root and flourished! Formerly they were not numbered in any civil list of their country, except in those of the poor; here they rank as citizens. . . .

Pause & Reflect

FOCUS
Read to find out how de Crèvecoeur defines an American.

What attachment can a poor European emigrant have for a country where he had nothing? The knowledge of the language, the love of a few <u>kindred</u> as poor as himself were the only cords that tied him. His country is now that which gives him land, bread, protection, and consequence.[5] *Ubi panis ibi patria* [where my bread is earned, there is my country] is the motto of all emigrants. What then is the American, this new man? He is either a European or the descendant of a European; hence that strange mixture of blood which you will find in no other country. I could point out to you a man whose grandfather was an Englishman, whose wife was Dutch, whose son married a French woman, and whose present four sons have now four wives of different nations. *He* is an American who, leaving behind him all his ancient prejudices and manners, receives new ones from the new mode of life he has embraced, the new government he obeys, and the new

---

4. **vegetative mold:** loose, crumbly soil that is rich in nutrients and helps plants to grow.

5. **consequence:** importance.

WORDS
TO
KNOW

kindred (kĭn'drĭd) *n.* relatives or family

rank he holds. He becomes an American by being received in the broad lap of our great alma mater.[6]

Here individuals of all nations are melted into a new race of men, whose labors and posterity will one day cause great change in the world. Americans are the western pilgrims who are carrying along with them that great mass of arts, sciences, 50 vigor, and industry[7] which began long since in the east; they will finish the great circle. The Americans were once scattered all over Europe; here they are incorporated into one of the finest systems of population which has ever appeared, and which will hereafter become distinct by the power of the different climates they inhabit. The American ought, therefore, to love this country much better than that wherein either he or his forefathers were born. Here the rewards of his industry follow with equal steps the progress of his labor; his labor is founded on the basis of nature, self-interest. Can it want a 60 stronger <u>allurement</u>? Wives and children, who before in vain demanded of him a morsel of bread, now, fat and frolicsome, gladly help their father to clear those fields whence exuberant crops are to arise to feed and to clothe them all, without any part being claimed, either by a <u>despotic</u> prince, a rich abbot,[8] or a mighty lord. Here, religion demands but little of him; a small voluntary salary to the minister, and gratitude to God. Can he refuse these?

The American is a new man, who acts upon new principles; he must, therefore, entertain new ideas and form new 70 opinions. From involuntary idleness, <u>servile</u> dependence, penury, and useless labor he has passed to toils of a very different nature, rewarded by ample <u>subsistence</u>. This is an American.

 Pause & Reflect

---

6. **alma mater** (ăl′mə mä′tər): A Latin phrase that literally means "nourishing mother."

7. **industry:** energetic devotion to a task or endeavor; diligence.

8. **abbot** (ăb′ət): the head of a monastery.

WORDS TO KNOW	**allurement** (ə-lŏŏr′mənt) *n.* attraction; enticement **despotic** (dĭ-spŏt′ĭk) *adj.* like a dictator **servile** (sur′vəl) *adj.* humbly submissive; slavish **subsistence** (səb-sĭs′təns) *n.* livelihood

 Pause & Reflect

1. De Crèvecoeur defines an American. Which of the following phrases fit his definition? Circle or check three of them. **(Clarify / Infer)**

belongs to a new race

has little freedom

lives in poverty

owns land

has new ideas

pays high taxes

READ ALOUD 2. Read aloud the boxed passage on this page. What gets "melted" together in America? **(Clarify)**

_____

_____

_____

CHALLENGE

In the first paragraph, de Crèvecoeur uses **figurative language,** comparing immigrants to plants. Circle or highlight any words and phrases that are part of this comparison. How does the figurative language support the **main idea** of the paragraph?

Wrapping Up

If you are using *The Language of Literature,* you can now move to the questions and activities on pages 293–294 of that book.

Active Reading SkillBuilder

Analyzing Contrast

"What Is an American?" is structured as a series of contrasts: de Crèvecoeur contrasts
America and Americans with Europe and Europeans. To **contrast** two things is to
state or show how they are dissimilar. As you read de Crèvecoeur's essay, complete
the chart by noting the contrasts he makes. The first two contrasts have been noted
for you.

Category	Europe/European	America/American
Government	"despotic prince"	a new government
Work	no incentive to work hard	rewarded for working hard
Quality of Life		
Ethnic Background		
Religion		

Literary Analysis SkillBuilder

Theme

The **theme** of a literary work is the central idea the writer wishes to share with the reader. This idea may be a lesson about life or about people and their actions. Sometimes writers state the theme directly. Often, however, the reader must infer the central message. Review the contrasts between Americans and Europeans that you have already identified. Then use the categories on the diagram to list de Crèvecoeur's ideas about Americans. An example is shown.

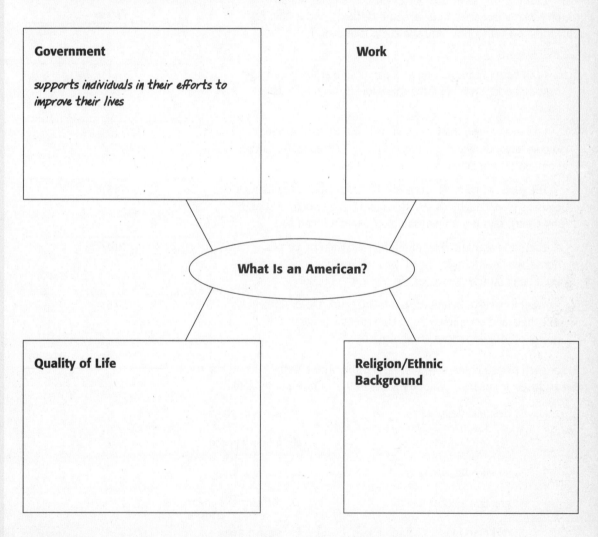

Government

supports individuals in their efforts to improve their lives

Work

What Is an American?

Quality of Life

Religion/Ethnic Background

Follow Up: Draw on the ideas you listed to write a statement that expresses de Crèvecoeur's theme. Share your statement with your classmates.

Words to Know SkillBuilder

Words to Know

allurement   despotic   kindred   servile   subsistence

A. Each of the following sentences suggests a word in the word list. The word itself is hidden in the sentence. Underline the hidden word and then write it on the line. An example, using another word from the story, has been done for you.

Example: My sister built an agricultural empire, starting only with a few acres of land, some chickens, and a calf. Arm Ernestine with a hoe, and she could take over the world.

_____farmer_____

I can barely make a living as a part-time teacher. When I get my paychecks, I wonder if the salary for subs is ten cents an hour!

(1) _____

I do every single thing my boss tells me to do. I've never known anyone meaner, cruder, or coarser. Vile as he is, though, I am always respectful, because I need the job.

(2) _____

For good nutrition, eat pumpkin. Dr. Edith Gourd, my father's cousin's granddaughter's second cousin once removed (that is, my sister), says it is a great source of vitamin A and fiber.

(3) _____

Dad's the absolute ruler in our house. When he comes home, we have to hide Spot. I can't tell you how much trouble we'd be in if he knew we let the dog in the house!

(4) _____

Want to snare a genius, date a brain? Study the dictionary! It's safe, free, and completely legal. Lure mental giants with the power of your enormous vocabulary!

(5) _____

B. For each phrase in the first column, find the phrase in the second column that is closest in meaning. Write the letter of that phrase in the blank.

_____ 1. despotic deputies

_____ 2. servile conduct

_____ 3. sportily dressed kindred

_____ 4. granting a subsistence

_____ 5. Old MacDonald's allurement

A. aunts in pants

B. a bossy posse

C. giving a living

D. the farmer's charm

E. slavish behavior

C. Does de Crèvecoeur's description of America seem appealing to you? Use at least **three** of the Words to Know in your answer.

Before You Read

If you are using **The Language of Literature,** study the information on page 363 of that book to prepare for reading.

Reading Tips

Sprinkled throughout this essay are short statements of general truth or wisdom called **aphorisms.** One way to get the main points of what Emerson is saying is to look for these kinds of statements.

• Identify the sentences that sound like aphorisms to you. They will usually be fairly short.

• Restate the **main idea** of each aphorism in your own words.

• Use the information in the Guide for Reading to help you with unfamiliar words and difficult passages.

✎ ▶ **MARK IT UP** **KEEP TRACK**

As you read, you can use these marks to keep track of your understanding.

✔ ..... I understand.

? ..... I don't understand this.

! ..... Interesting or surprising idea

FROM

Self-Reliance

Ralph Waldo Emerson

PREVIEW Ralph Waldo Emerson was a well-known writer and lecturer in the United States in the 19th century. He believed strongly in the need for every person to develop his or her potential as an individual. Emerson's essay "Self-Reliance" is a collection of his thoughts on the importance of the individual and the need to think independently.

FOCUS
In these paragraphs, Emerson explains what he means by an independent, or self-reliant, person.
✎ **MARK IT UP** Underline the passages that you think contain the **main ideas** in these paragraphs. An example is highlighted.

There is a time in every man's education when he arrives at the conviction that envy is ignorance; that imitation is suicide; that he must take himself for better for worse as his portion; that though the wide universe is full of good, no kernel of nourishing corn can come to him but through his toil bestowed on that plot of ground which is given to him to till. . . .

IMPLIED METAPHOR

Trust thyself: every heart vibrates to that iron string. Accept the place the divine providence has found for you, the society of your contemporaries, the connection of events. Great men have always done so, and confided themselves childlike to the genius of their age, betraying their perception that the absolutely trustworthy was seated at their heart, working through their hands, predominating in all their being. . .

Whoso would be a man, must be a nonconformist. He who

WORDS
TO
KNOW

bestowed (bǐ-stōd′) *adj.* applied; used **bestow** *v.*
predominating (prǐ-dŏm′ə-nāt′ing) *adj.* having controlling power or influence **predominate** *v.*
nonconformist (nŏn′kən-fôr′mǐst) *n.* one who does not follow generally accepted beliefs, customs, or practices

Use this guide for help with unfamiliar words
and difficult passages.

MARK IT UP WORD POWER

Mark words that you'd like to add to your
Personal Word List. After reading, you can
record the words and their meanings
beginning on page 344.

11 iron string: the divine nature that is part
of every person; self-knowledge.

12 the divine providence: God.

13–17 great men . . . being: Great men
have always recognized and made the most
of the particular strengths and unique
characteristics of the time period they were
born into. By doing so, they show their
understanding that God **(the absolutely
trustworthy)** is within them, working
through them and controlling all parts of their
lives.

MARK IT UP **Reread Lines 11–18**

Star one sentence that is an aphorism.

would gather immortal palms must not be hindered by the name of goodness, but must explore if it be goodness. Nothing is at last sacred but the integrity of your own mind. <u>Absolve</u> you to yourself, and you shall have the suffrage of the world. I remember an answer which when quite young I was prompted to make to a valued adviser who was wont to importune me with the dear old doctrines of the church. On my saying, "What have I to do with the sacredness of traditions, if I live wholly from within?" my friend suggested—"But these impulses may be from below, not from above." I replied, "They do not seem to me to be such; but if I am the Devil's child, I will live then from the Devil." No law can be sacred to me but that of my nature. Good and bad are but names very readily transferable to that or this; the only right is what is after my constitution; the only wrong what is against it. . . .

What I must do is all that concerns me, not what the people think. This rule, equally arduous in actual and in intellectual life, may serve for the whole distinction between greatness and meanness. It is the harder because you will always find those who think they know what is your duty better than you know it. It is easy in the world to live after the world's opinion; it is easy in solitude to live after our own; but the great man is he who in the midst of the crowd keeps with perfect sweetness the independence of solitude. . . .

Pause **&** **Reflect**

FOCUS

In this section, Emerson talks about obstacles facing the person who is trying to be self-reliant.

MARK IT UP Underline one obstacle that is created by other people and one that comes from within an individual.

For nonconformity the world whips you with its displeasure. And therefore a man must know how to estimate a sour face. The by-standers look askance on him in the public street or in the friend's parlor. If this <u>aversion</u> had its origin in contempt and resistance like his own he might well go home with a sad countenance; but

---

WORDS
TO
KNOW

absolve (əb-zŏlv′) *v.* to clear of guilt or blame
aversion (ə-vûr′zhən) *n.* a strong dislike

19 immortal palms: everlasting triumph and honor. In ancient times, people carried palm leaves as a symbol of victory, success, or joy.

22 suffrage: approval; support.

24 wont to importune me: accustomed to trouble me.

33 after my constitution: goes along with my physical and mental nature.

37 meanness: the state of being inferior in quality, character, or value.

39–42 Emerson says it is easy to go along with popular opinion when you are with other people. It is also easy to follow your own ideas when you are alone. A great person, however, remains independent even in a crowd.

43–48 Emerson notes that those who are nonconformists will meet with negative reactions from other people.

47 askance (ə-skăns′)**:** with disapproval, suspicion, or distrust.

Pause & Reflect

1. Look at the passages you underlined as you read. Two of Emerson's main ideas about self-reliance are

_____

_____

_____

and _____

_____

_____ .

(Main Idea)

READ ALOUD **2.** Read aloud the boxed passage on page 68. Star the statement below that Emerson would agree with. **(Infer)**

Right and wrong are the same for every person.

An individual must decide what is right or wrong for himself or herself.

3. According to Emerson, how much attention should we pay to other people's opinions of what we think and do? **(Infer)**

_____

_____

_____

_____

the sour faces of the multitude, like their sweet faces, have no deep cause, but are put on and off as the wind blows and a newspaper directs. . . .

The other terror that scares us from self-trust is our consistency; a reverence for our past act or word because the eyes of others have no other data for computing our orbit than our past acts, and we are loth to disappoint them. . . .

A foolish consistency is the hobgoblin of little minds, adored by little statesmen and philosophers and divines. With consistency a great soul has simply nothing to do. He may as well concern himself with his shadow on the wall. Speak what you think now in hard words and to-morrow speak what to-morrow thinks in hard words again, though it contradict every thing you said today.—"Ah, so you shall be sure to be misunderstood."— Is it so bad then to be misunderstood? Pythagoras was misunderstood, and Socrates, and Jesus, and Luther, and Copernicus, and Galileo, and Newton, and every pure and wise spirit that ever took flesh. To be great is to be misunderstood.

Pause & Reflect

58 **loth** (lōth): unwilling; reluctant.

59 **hobgoblin:** a source of fear or dread. Notice that Emerson does not criticize all consistency, only "foolish" consistency that does not allow for change or progress.

60 **divines:** religious leaders.

67–70 **Pythagoras . . . Newton:** great thinkers whose new theories and viewpoints caused controversy.

Pause & Reflect

1. Look back at the two obstacles that you underlined as you read. The obstacles are

_____

_____

and_____

_____.

(Clarify)

2. What does Emerson mean by the phrase "foolish consistency" (lines 59–60)?
(Infer/Summarize)

_____

_____

_____

_____

3. Emerson states that great thinkers may change their minds and seem to contradict themselves as they develop new ideas. According to Emerson, is such willingness to change a good or a bad trait? *Good/Bad,* because_____

_____

_____.

(Infer)

CHALLENGE

Do you think Emerson has an optimistic view of human nature or a pessimistic one? Mark passages that give you clues about his view. Then explain your judgments.
(Author's Perspective)

Wrapping Up

If you are using *The Language of Literature,* you can now move to the questions and activities on pages 367–368 of that book.

Active Reading SkillBuilder

Summarizing

To **summarize** a piece of writing is to state its main ideas briefly in one's own words, omitting less important details. Read the first paragraph in this essay, and then use the diagram below to record two important phrases or statements. Then write a sentence of your own to express the main idea of each statement you identified. The diagram has been started for you.

Paragraph 1	
Important Phrases and Statements	**Main Idea**
"imitation is suicide"	If you always imitate others, you will kill your own personality.

Follow Up: Use similar diagrams to identify and restate the main ideas of each paragraph in Emerson's essay. Then pull your sentences together to create a single summary.

Literary Analysis SkillBuilder

Aphorism

An **aphorism** is a brief statement, usually one sentence long, that expresses a general principle or truth about life. An example is Benjamin Franklin's aphorism "Honesty is the best policy." Using the diagram below, identify two aphorisms that you find in Emerson's essay. Then summarize the general principle or truth that he reveals in each one. An example is given.

Aphorism	General Principle or Truth
"Whoso would be a man, must be a nonconformist."	To be a fully developed person, you must follow your own ideas, not those of everybody else.

Follow Up: Discuss with groups of classmates the similarities and differences among the ideas that Emerson expresses in his aphorisms.

Words to Know SkillBuilder

Words to Know

absolve   aversion   bestowed   nonconformist   · predominate

A. Fill in each set of blanks with the correct word from the word list.

1. This is what accused people hope an
   alibi will do for them.

   __ __ __ __ __ __ ☐ ☐

2. The leader of the pack, the team's
   coach, and the boss all do this.

   __ __ __ __ __ __ __ __ __ ☐ __ __

3. Most people feel this for or toward
   dental work, vandals, and bullies.

   __ __ __ ☐ __ ☐ __ __

4. This can describe energy, money, or
   time—if it's devoted to a purpose.

   ☐ __ __ ☐ __ __ __ __

5. A maverick, an oddball, a rebel . . .
   anyone who doesn't follow the crowd
   is this.

   __ __ __ __ __ __ __ __ __ __ __ ☐

   __

Now, unscramble the boxed letters to make a synonym for quivers that will fill in the
blank in the following quotation.

"Trust thyself: every heart _____ to that iron string."

B. Fill in each blank with the correct word from the word list.

1. Jane was the only cheerleader who wore long underwear with her uniform. Who
   was warmest? The _____ .

2. The truck dumped gravel, which we spread over the muddy spots. We improved
   traction with the load _____ on the road.

3. "Someone else's fingerprints are on the weapon. You can't convict my client! The
   revolver will _____ her!"

4. In many elections, the real political power rests with those who select the candi-
   dates. They who nominate _____ .

5. I just want to sit in the hotel, read, play cards, and nap. I can't stand outings and
   tours, for I have an _____ to excursions.

C. A maxim is a concise rule of conduct. Write a maxim that reflects Emerson's phi-
losophy, using at least **one** of the Words to Know.

Before You Read

If you are using **The Language of Literature** . . .

- Use the information on page 369 to prepare for reading.

- Look at the photos and read the captions on pages 370 through 375. Think about what the subjects of the photos have in common.

Reading Tips

An **essay** is a short work of **nonfiction** in which a writer presents his or her personal views. Thoreau published this essay in 1847. At that time, writers typically used long sentences and paragraphs. Such a style makes this essay challenging for modern readers.

- Read the essay more than once. The first time, try to get the overall sense. Then reread it to deepen your understanding. During your second reading, answer the Pause and Reflect questions. Also use the Guide for Reading, beginning on page 77, for help with unfamiliar words and difficult passages.

- Look for the **main ideas.** After reading a paragraph, ask yourself, "What is Thoreau getting at here? What details support the main idea?"

from

Civil Disobedience
Henry David Thoreau

PREVIEW In this classic **essay**, Thoreau describes the highest duty of good citizens. They must do what they think is right, even at the cost of going to jail. Written more than a century ago, this essay still stirs the mind and the heart. Thoreau's message inspired Martin Luther King, Jr., who led the civil rights crusade in the 1950s and 1960s.

FOCUS

Thoreau begins his essay by explaining his views on government. Read to find out whether he favors more government or less.

I heartily accept the motto, "That government is best which governs least;" and I should like to see it acted up to more rapidly and systematically. Carried out, it finally amounts to this, which also I believe,—"That government is best which governs not at all;" and when men are prepared for it, that will be the kind of government which they will have. Government is at best but an expedient; but most governments are usually, and all governments are sometimes, <u>inexpedient</u>. The objections which have been brought against a standing army, and they are many and weighty, and deserve to prevail, may also at last be brought against a standing government. The standing army is only an arm of the standing government. The government itself, which is only the mode which the people have chosen to execute their will, is equally liable to be abused and perverted before the people can act

WORDS
TO
KNOW

inexpedient (ĭn′ĭk-spē′dē-ənt) *adj.* not useful for achieving a goal

Use this guide for help with unfamiliar words
and difficult passages.

MARK IT UP KEEP TRACK

As you read, you can use these marks to keep
track of your understanding.

✔ ..... I understand.

? ..... I don't understand this.

! ..... Interesting or surprising idea

6–7 "That government . . . not al all":
Thoreau is saying that it is best to have no
government at all. Someday, people will need
no government to make laws and enforce
them.

9 expedient (ĭk-spē′dē-ənt): a means to
an end.

13 standing army: a peace-time army, or
one in place even though the nation is not at
war. When Thoreau was writing, the United
States did not have a standing army.

18 perverted: turned away from what
is right.

MARK IT UP WORD POWER

Mark words that you'd like to add to your
Personal Word List. After reading, you can
record the words and their meanings
beginning on page 344.

through it. Witness the present Mexican war, the work of comparatively a few individuals using the standing government as their tool; for, in the outset, the people would not have consented to this measure. . . .

But, to speak practically and as a citizen, unlike those who call themselves no-government men, I ask for, not at once no government, but *at once* a better government. Let every man make known what kind of government would command his respect, and that will be one step toward obtaining it.

 Pause & Reflect

FOCUS

Thoreau wanted to limit the power of the majority so that individuals could follow their conscience. Read to find out why the individual conscience is so important to him.

After all, the practical reason why, when the power is once in the hands of the people, a majority are permitted, and for a long period continue, to rule is not because they are most likely to be in the right, nor because this seems fairest to the minority, but because they are physically the strongest. But a government in which the majority rule in all cases cannot be based on justice, even as far as men understand it. Can there not be a government in which majorities do not virtually decide right and wrong, but conscience?—in which majorities decide only those questions to which the rule of expediency is applicable? Must the citizen ever for a moment, or in the least degree, resign his conscience to the legislator? Why has every man a conscience, then? I think that we should be men first, and subjects afterward. It is not desirable to cultivate a respect for the law, so much as for the right. The only obligation which I have a right to assume is to do at any time what I think right. It is truly enough said, that a corporation has no conscience; but a corporation of <u>conscientious</u> men is a corporation *with* a conscience. Law never made men a whit more just; and, by means of their respect for it, even the well-disposed are daily made the agents of injustice.

WORDS
TO
KNOW

conscientious (kŏn′shē-ĕn′shəs) *adj.* guided by conscience; honest

19 the present Mexican war: the war between the United States and Mexico in 1846–1848. Thoreau strongly opposed this war.

28–37 Thoreau points out that a government based on the rule of the majority is based on power, not justice. The majority rule because they are the strongest class.

41–42 Must the citizen . . . legislator: To Thoreau, the answer to this question is "No." In other words, the citizen must always follow his or her conscience; **resign:** give up.

47 corporation: group.

49–51 Thoreau says that people can commit injustices by having too much respect for the law; **a whit:** the least bit.

Pause **&** *Reflect*

MARK IT UP **1.** Thoreau favors (circle one) *more / less* government. Circle details on page 76 that support your answer. **(Infer)**

2. A standing government is one that stays in power over time. Which phrase below is true to Thoreau's views about such a government? Circle or check it. **(Infer)**

always reflects the people's will

governs little or not at all

can be a tool of dishonest citizens

A common and natural result of an undue respect for law is, that you may see a file of soldiers, colonel, captain, corporal, privates, powder-monkeys, and all, marching in admirable order over hill and dale to the wars, against their wills, ay, against their common sense and consciences, which makes it very steep marching indeed, and produces a palpitation of the heart. They have no doubt that it is a damnable business in which they are concerned; they are all peaceably inclined. Now, what are they? Men at all? or small movable forts and magazines, at the service of some <u>unscrupulous</u> man in power? Visit the Navy-Yard, and behold a marine, such a man as an American government can make, or such as it can make a man with its black arts—a mere shadow and reminiscence of humanity, a man laid out alive and standing, and already, as one may say, buried under arms with funeral accompaniments, though it may be,—

"Not a drum was heard, not a funeral note,
    As his corse to the rampart we hurried;
Not a soldier discharged his farewell shot
    O'er the grave where our hero we buried."

Pause **&** **Reflect**

FOCUS
Thoreau describes three ways that citizens can serve the state: with their bodies, with their heads, and with their consciences. **MARK IT UP** As you read, circle details that explain these three ways. An example is highlighted.

The mass of men serve the state thus, not as men mainly, but as machines, with their bodies. They are the standing army, and the militia, jailers, constables, *posse comitatus,* etc. In most cases there is no free exercise whatever of the judgment or of the moral sense; but they put themselves on a level with wood and earth and stones; and wooden men can perhaps be manufactured that will serve the purpose as well. Such command no more respect than men of

WORDS
TO
KNOW

unscrupulous (ŭn-skrōō′pyə-ləs) *adj.* without principles; dishonorable

54 powder-monkeys: boys with the job of carrying gunpowder to artillery crews.

57 palpitation (păl′pĭ-tā′shən)**:** irregular, rapid beating.

61 magazines: places where ammunition is stored.

64 black arts: witchcraft.
65 a man . . . standing: a man who is dead as a human being because he does not obey his conscience.
68–71 "Not a drum . . . we buried": the opening lines of "The Burial of Sir John Moore After Corunna" by the Irish poet Charles Wolfe.

72 The mass of men: most people; **the state:** the nation or the government.

76 *posse comitatus* (pŏs′ē kŏm′ĭ-tŏt′əs) *Latin:* power of the county—a term used to refer to the group of people that can be called on by a sheriff to help enforce the law.

Pause & Reflect

1. Underline the phrase below that completes the following sentence correctly: According to Thoreau, his highest duty as a citizen is to _____ . **(Infer)**

follow majority rule

do what he thinks is right

obey the law

READ ALOUD **2.** Read aloud the boxed sentence on page 80. The soldiers marching off to war respect (circle one) *the law / their consciences* more than anything else. **(Main Idea)**

straw or a lump of dirt. They have the same sort of worth only as horses and dogs. Yet such as these even are commonly esteemed good citizens. Others—as most legislators, politicians, lawyers, ministers, and office-holders—serve the state chiefly with their heads; and, as they rarely make any moral distinctions, they are as likely to serve the Devil, without *intending* it, as God. A very few—as heroes, patriots, martyrs, reformers in the great sense, and *men*—serve the state with their consciences also, and so necessarily resist it for the most part; and they are commonly treated as enemies by it. . . .

Pause & Reflect

FOCUS
The government does not value reformers. Read to find out how the government treats reformers and how citizens should respond to unjust laws.

Unjust laws exist: shall we be content to obey them, or shall we <u>endeavor</u> to amend them, and obey them until we have succeeded or shall we transgress them at once? Men generally, under such a government as this, think that they ought to wait until they have persuaded the majority to alter them. They think that, if they should resist, the remedy would be worse than the evil. But it is the fault of the government itself that the remedy *is* worse than the evil. *It* makes it worse. Why is it not more apt to anticipate and provide for reform? Why does it not cherish its wise minority? Why does it cry and resist before it is hurt? Why does it not encourage its citizens to be on the alert to point out its faults, and *do* better than it would have them? Why does it always crucify Christ, and excommunicate Copernicus and Luther, and pronounce Washington and Franklin rebels? . . .

If the injustice is part of the necessary friction of the machine of government, let it go, let it go: perchance it will wear smooth, —certainly the machine will wear out. If the injustice

WORDS
TO
KNOW

endeavor (ĕn-dĕv′ər) *v.* to make an earnest effort; strive

90–93 Notice that those who serve the state in the highest way challenge or oppose it if their consciences tell them to do so.

97 transgress: to act in violation of the law.

110 Copernicus (kō-pûr′nə-kəs) **and Luther:** Nicolaus Copernicus (1473–1543), a Polish astronomer, theorized that the sun rather than the earth is the center of our planetary system. Martin Luther (1483–1546), a German theologian, was a leader in the Protestant Reformation. Both men were excommunicated (barred from participation in religious rites) by the Roman Catholic Church.

112–114 Thoreau compares injustice within government to friction in the workings of a machine. Both are often unavoidable byproducts of the workings of a complex system.

Pause & Reflect

1. Review the details you circled as you read. Thoreau favors serving the state with your (circle one) *body / mind / conscience* because

_____

_____

_____

_____ .

(Main Idea)

2. Imagine you are Thoreau. Which one of the following groups would you say is serving the state in the best way? Circle or check your answer. **(Evaluate)**

police officers who arrest dangerous criminals

students who protest against an unfair law

judges who sentence lawbreakers to jail

....

....

....

....

READ ALOUD Lines 103–111

Read aloud the boxed passage on page 82. Then write a sentence to **summarize** how the government treats those who resist injustice.

_____

_____

_____

_____

....

....

....

....

....

has a spring, or a pulley, or a rope, or a crank, exclusively for itself, then perhaps you may consider whether the remedy will not be worse than the evil; but if it is of such a nature that it requires you to be the agent of injustice to another, then, I say, break the law. Let your life be a counter-friction to stop the machine. What I have to do is to see, at any rate, that I do not lend myself to the wrong which I condemn. . . .

Pause **&** *Reflect*

FOCUS
A citizen can protest government policy by not paying taxes. Thoreau believes that citizens should be willing to go to jail to protest unjust policies. Read to find out why he believes such extremes are needed.

I meet this American government, or its representative, the state government, directly, and face to face, once a year— no more—in the person of its tax-gatherer; this is the only mode in which a man situated as I am necessarily meets it; and it then says distinctly, Recognize me; and the simplest, most effectual, and, in the present posture of affairs, the indispensablest mode of treating with it on this head, of expressing your little satisfaction with and love for it, is to deny it then. My civil neighbor, the tax-gatherer, is the very man I have to deal with,—for it is, after all, with men and not with parchment that I quarrel,—and he has voluntarily chosen to be an agent of the government. How shall he ever know well what he is and does as an officer of the government, or as a man, until he is obliged to consider whether he shall treat me, his neighbor, for whom he has respect, as a neighbor and well-disposed man, or as a maniac and disturber of the peace, and see if he can get over this obstruction to his neighborliness without a ruder and more impetuous thought or speech corresponding with his action. I know this well, that if one thousand, if one hundred, if ten men whom I could name,—if ten *honest* men only,—ay, if *one* HONEST man, in this State of Massachusetts, *ceasing to hold slaves,* were actually to withdraw from this copartnership, and be locked up in the county jail therefor, it would be the abolition of slavery in America. For it matters not how small

Pause & Reflect

MARK IT UP **1.** Thoreau says that if a certain condition applies, a citizen should break the law. Underline the words at the top of page 84 that identify that condition. **(Clarify)**

2. In Thoreau's time it was legal to own slaves. Can you think of other examples of laws that allow injustice? Name one example below and explain the injustice. **(Connect)**

_____

_____

_____

_____

130–131 posture of affairs: situation.

143 impetuous: filled with sudden emotion.
144–151 Thoreau says that the opponents of slavery should break the law and go to jail. Although most people in Thoreau's time did not act on his suggestion, civil rights leaders more than one hundred years later, in the 1960s, staged protests and went to jail to oppose unjust segregation laws and practices.

150 the beginning may seem to be: what is once well done is done forever. But we love better to talk about it: that we say is our mission. Reform keeps many scores of newspapers in its service, but not one man. . . .

Under a government which imprisons any unjustly, the true place for a just man is also a prison. The proper place today, the only place which Massachusetts has provided for her freer and less desponding spirits, is in her prisons, to be put out and locked out of the State by her own act, as they have already put themselves out by their principles. It is there that the
160 fugitive slave, and the Mexican prisoner on parole, and the Indian come to plead the wrongs of his race should find them; on that separate, but more free and honorable ground, where the State places those who are not *with* her, but *against* her,— the only house in a slave State in which a free man can abide with honor. If any think that their influence would be lost there, and their voices no longer afflict the ear of the State, that they would not be as an enemy within its walls, they do not know by how much truth is stronger than error, nor how much more eloquently and effectively he can combat injustice who
170 has experienced a little in his own person. Cast your whole vote, not a strip of paper merely, but your whole influence. A minority is powerless while it conforms to the majority; it is not even a minority then; but it is irresistible when it clogs by its whole weight. If the alternative is to keep all just men in prison, or give up war and slavery, the State will not hesitate which to choose. If a thousand men were not to pay their tax bills this year, that would not be a violent and bloody measure, as it would be to pay them, and enable the State to commit violence and shed innocent blood. This is, in fact, the definition
180 of a peaceable revolution, if any such is possible. If the tax-gatherer, or any other public officer, asks me, as one has done, "But what shall I do?" my answer is, "If you really wish to do anything, resign your office." When the subject has refused allegiance, and the officer has resigned his office, then the revolution is accomplished. But even suppose blood should flow. Is there not a sort of blood shed when the conscience is wounded? Through this wound a man's real manhood and immortality flow out, and he bleeds to an everlasting death. I see this blood flowing now. . . .

Pause & Reflect

152–153 Many newspapers print editorials calling for reform. No one,
however, has the courage to go to jail for the sake of justice; **score:** 20.

157 desponding: discouraging.

159–165 Thoreau was opposed to the government because it allowed slavery in the South and waged war against Mexico in the West. By not paying his taxes, Thoreau denied the government some of the revenue it needed to exist. The punishment for refusing to pay taxes was imprisonment. To Thoreau's way of thinking, however, a prison was not a place of shame. Instead, it was a place of honor set aside for those brave enough to act on their consciences.

171–174 A minority is powerless when it goes along with the majority. However, a minority can have great influence when it opposes the majority.
176–179 If a thousand . . . innocent blood. If a thousand men refused to pay taxes, such action would not be violent. Those who pay taxes to support a war, however, are guilty of violence.

Pause & Reflect

1. Thoreau says that he denies the government through its representative. Who is that representative? **(Clarify)**

_____

_____

◢ MARK IT UP 2. What would happen to slavery if even one honest person were to go to jail as a form of protest? Circle the sentence on page 84 that tells the answer. **(Cause and Effect)**

3. Reread the boxed sentence on page 86. How would you state Thoreau's idea in your own words? **(Paraphrase)**

_____

_____

_____

_____

4. Which two phrases below are true to Thoreau's views of a "peaceable revolution"? Circle or check them. **(Infer)**

involves breaking the law

never causes bloodshed

is led by the majority

is based on conscience

190

200

210

220

FOCUS

Read to find out about Thoreau's experience in jail.

MARK IT UP As you read, circle details that help you understand his attitude toward this experience.

I have paid no poll-tax for six years. I was put into a jail once on this account, for one night; and, as I stood considering the walls of solid stone, two or three feet thick, the door of wood and iron, a foot thick, and the iron grating which strained the light, I could not help being struck with the foolishness of that institution which treated me as if I were mere flesh and blood and bones, to be locked up. I wondered that it should have <u>concluded</u> at length that this was the best use it could put me to, and had never thought to avail itself of my services in some way. I saw that, if there was a wall of stone between me and my townsmen, there was a still more difficult one to climb or break through before they could get to be as free as I was. I did not for a moment feel confined, and the walls seemed a great waste of stone and mortar. I felt as if I alone of all my townsmen had paid my tax. They plainly did not know how to treat me, but behaved like persons who are underbred. In every threat and in every compliment there was a <u>blunder</u>; for they thought that my chief desire was to stand the other side of that stone wall. I could not but smile to see how industriously they locked the door on my <u>meditations</u>, which followed them out again without let or hindrance, and *they* were really all that was dangerous. As they could not reach me, they had resolved to punish my body; just as boys, if they cannot come at some person against whom they have a spite, will abuse his dog. I saw that the State was half-witted, that it was timid as a lone woman with her silver spoons, and that it did not know its friends from its foes, and I lost all my remaining respect for it, and pitied it.

Thus the State never intentionally <u>confronts</u> a man's sense, intellectual or moral, but only his body, his senses. It is not armed with superior wit or honesty, but with superior physical strength. I was not born to be forced. I will breathe

WORDS
TO
KNOW

conclude (kən-klōōd′) *v.* to arrive at a judgment or decision
blunder (blŭn′dər) *n.* a mistake
meditation (mĕd′ĭ-tā′shən) *n.* a thought or reflection
confront (kən-frŭnt′) *v.* to come up against; meet face to face

190 poll tax: a tax that one had to pay in order to vote.

209 underbred: ill-mannered.

211–215 I could not . . . that was dangerous: To Thoreau, his townspeople are fools. They locked him in jail to punish him. All they punished, however, was his body. They could not lock up their real enemies— Thoreau's mind and his conscience; **without let or hindrance** (hĭn'drəns)**:** without encountering obstacles.

217 spite: grudge.

READ ALOUD Lines 202–207

Notice the contradiction in these lines. Thoreau in jail is truly free. The townsmen outside the jail are not.

MARK IT UP WORD POWER

Remember to mark words that you'd like to add to your **Personal Word List**. Later, you can record the words and their meanings beginning on page 344.

after my own fashion. Let us see who is the strongest. What force has a <u>multitude</u>? They only can force me who obey a higher law than I. They force me to become like themselves. I do not hear of *men* being *forced* to live this way or that by masses of men. What sort of life were that to live? When I meet a government which says to me, "Your money or your life," why should I be in haste to give it my money? It may be in a great strait, and not know what to do: I cannot help that. It must help itself; do as I do. It is not worth the while to snivel about it. I am not responsible for the successful working of the machinery of society. I am not the son of the engineer. I perceive that, when an acorn and a chestnut fall side by side, the one does not remain inert to make way for the other, but both obey their own laws, and spring and grow and <u>flourish</u> as best they can, till one, perchance, overshadows and destroys the other. If a plant cannot live according to its nature, it dies; and so a man.

Pause Reflect

WORDS TO KNOW

multitude (mŭl′tĭ-tōōd′) *n.* a great number of people
flourish (flûr′ĭsh) *v.* to thrive

227–228 They only can force me who obey a higher law than I: Thoreau says that only those on a higher spiritual level can make him want to be like them.

235 snivel: whine or complain.

236 machinery of society: the government.

237 an acorn and a chestnut: An acorn is the fruit of an oak tree; a chestnut is the nut from a chestnut tree.

238 inert: unable to act.

Pause & Reflect

1. Thoreau was put in jail because _____ _____ .

(Clarify)

2. Review the details you circled as you read. Then write a sentence to **summarize** Thoreau's feelings about his experience in jail. **(Main Idea)**

_____

_____

_____

READ ALOUD 3. Read aloud the boxed sentences on page 90. Both the acorn and the chestnut obey the laws of nature. They fall to the ground, where each tries to take root, grow, and develop into a tree. What does this example suggest about Thoreau himself? **(Infer)**

_____

_____

_____

_____

CHALLENGE

The boxed sentences on page 90 conclude with an **aphorism:** "If a plant cannot live according to its nature, it dies; and so a man." Mark other aphorisms—brief statements that express a truth about life—in this essay. How does each aphorism support one of Thoreau's main ideas? Why does Thoreau use this technique in this **persuasive essay?**

Wrapping Up

If you are using *The Language of Literature,* you can now move to the questions and activities on pages 378–380 of that book.

Active Reading SkillBuilder

Strategies for Reading Essays

To get the most from this essay, use these **strategies for reading essays:** Keep in mind the historical context, continue reading even if a sentence is unclear, read the entire selection more than once, and keep track of the main ideas and supporting details. As you read, use the following chart to explore one of Thoreau's main ideas—how citizens serve the state. Identify the three ways indicated by Thoreau, then give examples of each. Circle the way that Thoreau believes is the best way. One example is given.

Ways to Serve the State

1. _with the body_	2. _____	3. _____
soldiers		

Literary Analysis SkillBuilder

Essay

An **essay** is a short work of nonfiction that deals with a single subject. The purpose of an essay may be to express ideas and feelings, to analyze, to inform, to entertain, or, as in the case of "Civil Disobedience," to persuade. Even when they discuss serious ideas, essays are often informal and highly personal. On the chart below, identify three passages in this essay in which Thoreau refers to himself–identifying his personal opinions or recounting personal experiences. Mark with an X the scale for each passage to show the degree to which Thoreau's personal opinions or experiences influence your acceptance of his arguments.

1. Passage:_____
_____

Very Influential |———|———|———|———|———|———|———|———|———| Not Influential

2. Passage:_____
_____

Very Influential |———|———|———|———|———|———|———|———|———| Not Influential

3. Passage:_____
_____

Very Influential |———|———|———|———|———|———|———|———|———| Not Influential

Follow Up: Discuss what effect omitting these passages would have on the essay.

Words to Know SkillBuilder

Words to Know

blunder	confront	endeavor	inexpedient	multitude
conclude	conscientious	flourish	meditation	unscrupulous

A. For each phrase in the first column, find the phrase in the second column that is closest in meaning. Write the letter of that phrase in the blank.

_____ 1. corrupt boss   A. a conscientious multitude

_____ 2. useless way to proceed   B. an unscrupulous manager

_____ 3. think it through   C. concede it's a blunder

_____ 4. many honest people   D. an inexpedient plan

_____ 5. admit a mistake   E. learn through meditation

B. Circle the word in each group that is a synonym for the capitalized word.

1. **inexpedient**	unnecessary	improper	useful	impractical
2. **meditation**	thinking	memory	peace	nature
3. **endeavor**	plan	regulate	attempt	promote
4. **flourish**	accomplish	predict	thrive	accept
5. **conscientious**	able	honest	careless	useful
6. **multitude**	meeting	reunion	crowd	conference
7. **unscrupulous**	unusual	disjointed	upset	dishonorable
8. **conclude**	decide	predict	reverse	alter
9. **confront**	manage	oppose	disappear	disagree
10. **blunder**	choice	decision	mistake	confusion

C. Write a letter to a representative in Congress suggesting one way the government might be improved. Use at least **four** Words to Know in the letter.

Before You Read

If you are using *The Language of Literature,* study the information on page 396 of that book to prepare for reading.

Reading Tips

Whitman wrote **free verse,** or poetry without regular patterns of rhyme and meter. His free verse rolls along like a song, echoing the rhythms of music and everyday speech.

• As you read each poem, keep moving and let the **images** form pictures in your imagination. Let the lines sweep you along. Note that each new line begins with a capital letter. Words that spill over from a line are indented.

• Read the poems once or twice for their overall sense. Then reread each poem to deepen your understanding. After you reread each poem, answer the Pause and Reflect questions.

• Also use the Guide for Reading, beginning on page 99, as you reread "I Sit and Look Out" and the excerpts from "Song of Myself."

MARK IT UP **KEEP TRACK**

As you read, you can use these marks to keep track of your understanding.

✔ ..... I understand.

? ..... I don't understand this.

! ..... Interesting or surprising idea

PREVIEW As a poet, Walt Whitman was a rebel. In 1855 he published *Leaves of Grass.* This collection of 12 poems broke new ground in content and style. Whitman treated subjects that often shocked his readers. He also made his own rhythms, rejecting typical verse forms and techniques. A spokesman for all that was American, he created a new poetry for a new age.

I Hear America Singing

WALT WHITMAN

FOCUS

This poem is one sentence long. The speaker names different kinds of workers, singing joyously. These workers reflect the spirit of America at the time.

MARK IT UP As you read, circle each kind of worker named in the poem. An example is highlighted.

I hear America singing, the varied carols I hear,
Those of mechanics,[1] each one singing his as it should
    be blithe[2] and strong,
The carpenter singing his as he measures his plank
    or beam,
The mason[3] singing his as he makes ready for work, or
    leaves off work,

---

1. **mechanics:** those who work with their hands.
2. **blithe** (blīth): carefree and lighthearted.
3. **mason:** one who works with bricks or stone.

5 The boatman singing what belongs to him in his boat,
   the deckhand singing on the steamboat deck,
The shoemaker singing as he sits on his bench, the
   hatter singing as he stands,
The wood-cutter's song, the ploughboy's on his way in
   the morning, or at noon intermission or at sundown,
The delicious singing of the mother, or of the young
   wife at work, or of the girl sewing or washing,
Each singing what belongs to him or her and to
   none else,
10 The day what belongs to the day—at night the party of
   young fellows, robust,[4] friendly,
Singing with open mouths their strong melodious songs.

Pause & *Reflect*

Pause & *Reflect*

1. Review the kinds of workers you circled as you read. How do these workers feel about their work? **(Infer)**

   _____

   _____

   _____

   _____

2. What does the workers' singing suggest about America? **(Draw Conclusions)**

   _____

   _____

   _____

   _____

4. **robust** (rō-bŭst′): full of health and strength.

I Sit and Look Out

WALT WHITMAN

FOCUS

Like the previous poem, this one is a single sentence in length. This time, though, the speaker describes the sorrows of life. Read to find out about these sorrows and the speaker's response to them.

I sit and look out upon all the sorrows of the world,
    and upon all oppression and shame,
I hear secret convulsive sobs from young men at
    anguish with themselves, remorseful after deeds done,
I see in low life the mother misused by her children,
    dying, neglected, gaunt, desperate,
I see the wife misused by her husband, I see the
    treacherous seducer of young women,
5 I mark the ranklings of jealousy and unrequited love
    attempted to be hid, I see these sights on the earth,
I see the workings of battle, pestilence, tyranny, I see
    martyrs and prisoners,
I observe a famine at sea, I observe the sailors casting
    lots who shall be kill'd to preserve the lives of the rest,
I observe the slights and degradations cast by arrogant persons
    upon laborers, the poor, and upon negroes, and the like;
All these—all the meanness and agony without end I
    sitting look out upon,
10 See, hear, and am silent.

Pause **&** *Reflect*

Use this guide for help with unfamiliar words and difficult passages.

1 oppression: cruel or unjust use of power. The first line states a general theme: "all the sorrows of the world." The speaker then gives examples of these sorrows.

2–5 In these lines, the speaker describes personal sorrows.

2 convulsive: intense and uncontrolled; **anguish:** extreme mental pain; **remorseful:** guilty.

3 low life: the life of the lower classes; **gaunt:** thin and bony.

4 seducer: a person who leads someone away from proper conduct.

5 ranklings: bitter feelings or resentments; **unrequited:** not returned.

6–8 In these lines the speaker lists social evils.

7 casting lots: deciding by means of a random choice of objects (as in drawing straws). The sailors draw lots to decide who will be thrown overboard so that the rest of them might live. There is not enough food to keep all the sailors alive.

8 degradations: insults; **arrogant:** very proud.

Pause & Reflect

MARK IT UP **1.** Reread lines 2–5. Underline three of the personal sorrows that the speaker observes. **(Clarify)**

2. List at least three of the social problems the speaker notices in lines 6–8. (Line 6 begins with the words "I see the workings.") **(Clarify)**

_____

_____

_____

_____

READ ALOUD **3.** Read aloud lines 9–10. In those lines the speaker describes his response to all this misery. Why do you think he responds in this way? **(Infer)**

_____

_____

_____

_____

from

Song of Myself

W A L T   W H I T M A N

FOCUS

Epic poems celebrate heroes of the past. The speaker of this poem celebrates an ordinary man—himself. Read to find out about his larger-than-life personality.

1

I celebrate myself, and sing myself,
And what I assume you shall assume,
For every atom belonging to me as good belongs to you.

I loaf and invite my soul,
5   I lean and loaf at my ease observing a spear of
      summer grass.

My tongue, every atom of my blood, form'd from this
      soil, this air,
Born here of parents born here from parents the same,
      and their parents the same,
I, now thirty seven years old in perfect health begin,
Hoping to cease not till death.

10   Creeds and schools in abeyance,
Retiring back a while sufficed at what they are, but never
      forgotten,
I harbor for good or bad, I permit to speak at every
      hazard,
Nature without check with original energy.

Pause & Reflect

1–3 The speaker relates to the reader from the beginning of the poem. He wants the reader to accept him as a spokesman for all.

5 **a spear of summer grass:** a blade or leaf of grass.

6–7 The speaker describes himself as a product of the soil and air of the United States.

10 **Creeds . . . in abeyance:** The speaker says that for now he will set aside time-honored beliefs and ways of thinking.
11 **sufficed at:** satisfied with.
12–13 The speaker says that he will take in **(harbor for)** good or bad experiences. He will allow Nature to speak freely and forcefully through him.

Pause & **Reflect**

1. Circle or check three phrases below that are true of the speaker. **(Infer)**

is self-confident

considers others his equal

celebrates the wisdom of books

praises city life

enjoys good health

2. Reread the boxed line on page 100. How would you restate this idea in your own words? **(Paraphrase)**

_____

_____

_____

MARK IT UP **3.** Which lines on page 100 suggest that the speaker is united with Nature? Circle these lines. **(Evaluate)**

FOCUS

Throughout Section 6, the speaker uses comparisons to suggest what the grass means to him. Each of these comparisons is highlighted. Read to find out what these comparisons suggest about the grass.

6

A child said *What is the grass?* fetching it to me with
full hands,
How could I answer the child? I do not know what it
is any more than he.
I guess it must be the flag of my disposition, out of
hopeful green stuff woven.

Or I guess it is the handkerchief of the Lord,
A scented gift and remembrancer designedly dropt,
Bearing the owner's name someway in the corners, that
we may see and remark, and say *Whose?*

Or I guess the grass is itself a child, the produced babe
of the vegetation.
Or I guess it is a uniform hieroglyphic,
And it means, Sprouting alike in broad zones and
narrow zones,
Growing among black folks as among white,
Kanuck, Tuckahoe, Congressman, Cuff, I give them the
same, I receive them the same.

Pause & *Reflect*

16 The speaker says that the grass is the sign **(flag)** of his usual mood **(disposition)**. The green color reminds the speaker that he usually looks on the bright side of things.

17–19 The speaker says that the grass is the token **(handkerchief)** that God **(the Lord)** uses to get people's attention. A lady's per-fumed **(scented)** handkerchief has her name or initials inscribed in one of its corners. The lady purposely drops this token of affection **(remembrancer designedly dropt)** to get someone to notice her. Similarly, the fragrance and freshness of the grass make people aware of God, who created it.

20 The speaker says that the grass is a child that the natural world **(the vegetation)** has given birth to **(produced)**.

21 The speaker says that the grass is a picture or symbol that represents something **(hieroglyphic)**. This picture looks the same wherever it is found **(uniform)**.

24 Kanuck, Tuckahoe, . . . Cuff: slang terms for various groups of people. A Kanuck (now spelled Canuck) is a Canadian, especially a French Canadian. A Tuckahoe is someone from the coast of Virginia. A Cuff is an African American.

Pause & Reflect

1. What does a child ask the speaker to define? **(Clarify)**

_____

_____

MARK IT UP **2.** Review the highlighted comparisons on page 102. Star the one you find most interesting and then tell why. **(Evaluate)**

_____

_____

_____

READ ALOUD **3.** Read aloud the boxed passage on page 102. At the end of line 24, the speaker imagines that the grass says, "I receive them [all humans] the same." What does this sentence mean? **(Infer)**

_____

_____

_____

_____

FOCUS
Read to find out the connection between
the grass and the dead.

25 And now it seems to me the beautiful uncut hair of graves.
Tenderly will I use you curling grass,
It may be you transpire from the breasts of young men,
It may be if I had known them I would have loved them,
It may be you are from old people, or from offspring
      taken soon out of their mothers' laps,
30 And here you are the mothers' laps.

This grass is very dark to be from the white heads of
      old mothers,
Darker than the colorless beards of old men,
Dark to come from under the faint red roofs of mouths.

O I perceive after all so many uttering tongues,
35 And I perceive they do not come from the roofs of
      mouths for nothing.

Pause & Reflect

FOCUS
The speaker tries to put into words the
message about dead people that the grass
reveals. Read to find out this message.

I wish I could translate the hints about the dead young
      men and women,
And the hints about old men and mothers, and the
      offspring taken soon out of their laps.

What do you think has become of the young and old men?
And what do you think has become of the women and
      children?
40 They are alive and well somewhere,
The smallest sprout shows there is really no death,

GUIDE FOR READING

25–29 The speaker says that the grass is "the beautiful uncut hair of graves." These lines suggest the cycle of decay and new growth. After death, the human body breaks down into basic chemical elements. These elements eventually become part of the soil and help form the grass.

27 transpire: emerge; ooze out.

29 offspring: babies.

34–35 The speaker compares the grass to "uttering tongues." Each blade of grass is like a tongue revealing **(uttering)** a message. These lines extend the idea of the life cycle in lines 25–29. The elements once were part of the "roofs of mouths" of those buried in the soil. These same elements now are part of the grass that grows on their graves.

41 sprout: young plant growth, such as a bud or shoot.

Pause & Reflect

READ ALOUD **1.** Read aloud the boxed passage on page 104. List the dead people the speaker imagines buried beneath the grass. **(Clarify)**

_____
_____
_____

MARK IT UP **2.** Circle details in lines 25–35 that help you understand how the speaker feels about these dead people. Then write a sentence to **summarize** his feelings. **(Infer)**

_____
_____
_____
_____

3. Reread lines 34–35 and the accompanying note in the Guide for Reading. The blades of grass are compared to "so many uttering tongues." What message about death might they reveal to the speaker? **(Draw Conclusions)**

_____
_____
_____
_____

_____
_____
_____
_____
_____
_____
_____
_____
_____

from **Song of Myself** **105**

And if ever there was it led forward life, and does not
    wait at the end to arrest it,
And ceas'd the moment life appear'd.

All goes onward and outward, nothing collapses,
And to die is different from what any one supposed,
    and luckier.

FOCUS

In the final section, the speaker suggests
what will happen to him.

MARK IT UP As you read, circle details
that help you understand what will become
of him.

52

The spotted hawk swoops by and accuses me, he
    complains of my gab and my loitering.

I too am not a bit tamed, I too am untranslatable,
I sound my barbaric yawp over the roofs of the world.

The last scud of day holds back for me,
It flings my likeness after the rest and true as any on
    the shadow'd wilds,
It coaxes me to the vapor and the dusk.

I depart as air, I shake my white locks at the
    runaway sun,
I effuse my flesh in eddies, and drift it in lacy jags.

Pause & Reflect

1. How would you restate line 41 on page 104 in your own words? (Paraphrase)

_____

_____

_____

_____

READ ALOUD 2. Read aloud the boxed line on page 106. The speaker says that to die is "luckier" than what people suppose. What do you think he means? (Infer)

_____

_____

_____

3. What message about the dead does the grass reveal to the speaker? (Infer)

_____

_____

_____

_____

48 **barbaric yawp:** A yawp is a sharp cry. This phrase may refer to Whitman's own poetry.
49 **scud:** wind-driven clouds.

52–58 The speaker describes his future physical changes.
52 **locks:** strands of hair.
53 **effuse** (ĭ-fyōōs): pour out;
eddies: currents, as of air or water.

I bequeath myself to the dirt to grow from the grass
    I love,
55 If you want me again look for me under your
    boot-soles.

You will hardly know who I am or what I mean,
But I shall be good health to you nevertheless,
And filter and fibre your blood.

Failing to fetch me at first keep encouraged,
60 Missing me one place search another,
I stop somewhere waiting for you.

 Pause **&** **Reflect**

54 bequeath (bĭ-kwē*th*)**:** leave (property) to another by a last will.

58 filter and fibre: clean and toughen.

59 The speaker may mean that if at first you don't get or understand his poetry **(fetch me)**, don't give up **(keep encouraged)**.

1. The speaker compares himself to a hawk in three ways (lines 47–48 on page 106). Describe one of these comparisons. **(Compare and Contrast)**

_____
_____
_____
_____

MARK IT UP **2.** Review the details you circled as you read. Star the ones that suggest that the speaker will become one with nature. **(Evaluate)**

3. At the end of the poem, the speaker says he's "waiting for you." What do you think he means? **(Infer)**

_____
_____
_____

CHALLENGE

"Song of Myself" begins with the word *I* and ends with the word *you*. The poem creates a special relationship between the **speaker** ("I") and the reader ("you"). Go back through the poem and mark the lines that help you understand this relationship. How would you describe it? **(Analyze)**

Wrapping Up

If you are using *The Language of Literature,* you can now move to the questions and activities on pages 404–405 of that book.

Active Reading SkillBuilder

Strategies for Reading Free Verse

Free verse is poetry without regular patterns of rhyme and meter. To better appreciate the rhythm—as well as the ideas—that Whitman creates in his free verse, use these **strategies for reading free verse:** Read the poems aloud; notice where Whitman uses the devices of catalog, repetition, and parallelism; appreciate the sweep of his images and ideas; build a mental image of the speaker. Then record your thoughts and impressions on the spider map below. Two examples are given.

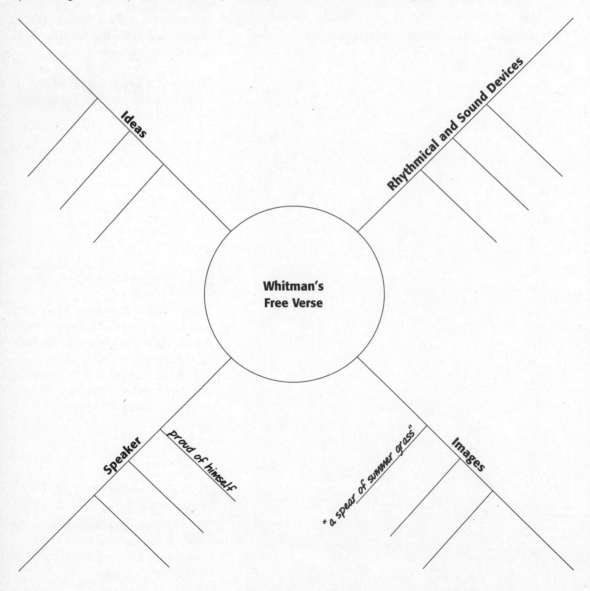

Ideas

Rhythmical and Sound Devices

**Whitman's
Free Verse**

Speaker

proud of himself

"a spear of summer grass"

Images

Literary Analysis SkillBuilder

Free Verse

Free verse is poetry without regular patterns of rhyme and meter. Lines in free verse often flow more naturally than do rhymed, metrical lines and therefore sound more like human speech. Although free verse lacks meter, it does exhibit a variety of rhythmical devices such as **repetition,** or recurring words, phrases, or lines; **parallelism,** or related ideas phrased in similar ways; and **catalog,** or lists of people, things, or attributes. Record on the chart below two examples of each of these devices found in "Song of Myself." An example of each device has been given.

Repetition	Parallelism	Catalog
"born here of parents born here from parents" (line 7)	this soil, this air (line 6)	Kenuck, Tuckahoe, Congressman, Cuff (line 24)

Before You Read

If you are using *The Language of Literature* . . .

- Use the information on page 454 to prepare for reading.
- The art on page 455 will help you **visualize** some of the dancers at the masked ball.

Reading Tips

In his **short stories,** Poe creates an eerie world beyond everyday life. When you read a Poe story, let your imagination run wild. Feel the terror of the unknown.

- Use Poe's **details** to help you **visualize** the **setting** and the **characters.** Picture the rooms in the abbey, the prince, and the masqueraders.
- Use the Guide for Reading to help you understand unfamiliar words and difficult lines and passages.

MARK IT UP **KEEP TRACK**

As you read, you can use these marks to keep track of your understanding.

✔ ..... I understand.

? ..... I don't understand this.

! ..... Interesting or surprising idea

The Masque of the Red Death

EDGAR ALLAN POE

PREVIEW Edgar Allan Poe was a master of the horror story. His tale "The Masque of the Red Death" is set during the Middle Ages. It tells about a prince who locks his friends and himself inside an abbey, walling it shut, to escape a deadly disease. For several months, all goes well. Then one night, the prince holds a masked ball. On the stroke of midnight, a strange figure suddenly appears.

FOCUS

The "Red Death" threatens the country. Read to find out about the disease and what Prospero does to try to escape it.

MARK IT UP As you read, circle details that help you understand how life outside Prospero's abbey is different from life inside. An example is highlighted on page 114.

The **"Red Death" had long devastated** the country. No pestilence had ever been so fatal, or so hideous. Blood was its Avatar and its seal—the redness and horror of blood. There were sharp pains, and sudden dizziness, and then profuse bleeding at the pores, with dissolution. The scarlet stains upon the body, and especially upon the face of the victim, were the pest ban which shut him out from the aid and from the sympathy of his fellow men. And the whole seizure, progress, and termination of the disease were the incidents of half an hour.

But the Prince Prospero was happy and <u>dauntless</u> and <u>sagacious</u>. When his dominions were half depopulated, he

WORDS TO KNOW

dauntless (dônt'lĭs) *adj.* fearless
sagacious (sə-gā'shəs) *adj.* wise

Use this guide for help with unfamiliar words and difficult passages.

✏️ MARK IT UP WORD POWER

Mark words that you'd like to add to your **Personal Word List**. After reading, you can record the words and their meanings beginning on page 344.

1 **devastated** (dĕv′ə-stā′tĭd): laid waste to.
2 **pestilence** (pĕs′tə-ləns): a very destructive infectious disease.
4 **Avatar** (ăv′ə-tär′): an appearance in physical form of an unseen force.

8 **dissolution:** death.

10 **pest ban:** a proclamation announcing that a person is sick with the plague.

✏️ JOT IT DOWN Reread Lines 8–12

Why do people show no pity for the victims of the Red Death? (Clarify) summoned to his presence a thousand hale and lighthearted friends from among the knights and dames of his court, and with these retired to the deep seclusion of one of his castellated abbeys. This was an extensive and magnificent structure, the creation of the prince's own eccentric yet august taste. A strong and lofty wall girded it in. This wall had gates of iron. The <u>courtiers</u>, having entered, brought furnaces and massy hammers and welded the bolts. They resolved to leave means neither of ingress or egress to the sudden impulses of despair or of frenzy from within. The abbey was amply provisioned. With such precautions the courtiers might bid defiance to <u>contagion</u>. The external world could take care of itself. In the meantime it was folly to grieve, or to think. The prince had provided all the appliances of pleasure. There were buffoons, there were improvisatori, there were ballet-dancers, there were musicians, there was Beauty, there was wine. All these and security were within. Without was the "Red Death."

Pause & Reflect

FOCUS

Read to find out about the seven rooms in which Prince Prospero holds the masked ball. Pay close attention to what is different about the black room.

It was toward the close of the fifth or sixth month of his seclusion, and while the pestilence raged most furiously abroad, that the Prince Prospero entertained his thousand friends at a masked ball of the most unusual magnificence.

It was a voluptuous scene, that masquerade. But first let me tell of the rooms in which it was held. There were seven— an imperial suite. In many palaces, however, such suites form a long and straight vista, while the folding doors slide back nearly to the walls on either hand, so that the view of the whole extent is scarcely impeded. Here the case was very different; as might have been expected from the duke's love of the *bizarre*. The apartments were so irregularly disposed that the vision embraced but little more than one at a time. There was a sharp turn at every twenty or thirty yards, and at each turn a novel effect. To the right and left, in the middle of each

WORDS TO KNOW

courtier (kôr′tē-ər) *n.* a member of a royal court
contagion (kən-tā′jən) *n.* the spreading of disease

20 castellated abbey (kăs´tə-lā´tĭd ăb´ē)**:** a fortified building formerly used as, or built to resemble, a monastery.

25 ingress (ĭn´grĕs´) **or egress** (ē´grĕs´)**:** entry or exit.

26–33 Inside the abbey, Prospero tries to create a world filled with amusements.

27 provisioned: provided with supplies.

31 improvisatori (ĭm-prŏv´ĭ-zə-tôr´ē)**:** poets who recite verses that they make up as they go along.

41 voluptuous (və-lŭp´cho͞o-əs)**:** appealing to the senses; luxurious.

47 The duke and Prince Prospero are the same person.

51 novel: strikingly new, unusual, or different.

Pause **&** *Reflect*

1. What does Prince Prospero do to try to escape this disease? **(Infer)**

_____

_____

_____

_____

2. Review the details you circled as you read. Then underline the phrase below that describes life inside the abbey. **(Infer)**

devoted to prayer

dedicated to caring for the sick

filled with a variety of pleasures

wall, a tall and narrow Gothic window looked out upon a closed corridor which pursued the windings of the suite. These windows were of stained glass whose color varied in accordance with the prevailing hue of the decorations of the chamber into which it opened. That at the eastern extremity was hung, for example, in blue—and vividly blue were its windows. The second chamber was purple in its ornaments and tapestries, and here the panes were purple. The third was green throughout, and so were the casements. The fourth was furnished and lighted with orange—the fifth with white—the sixth with violet. The seventh apartment was closely shrouded in black velvet tapestries that hung all over the ceiling and down the walls, falling in heavy folds upon a carpet of the same material and hue. But in this chamber only, the color of the windows failed to correspond with the decorations. The panes here were scarlet—a deep blood color. Now in no one of the seven apartments were there any lamp or candelabrum amid the profusion of golden ornaments that lay scattered to and fro or depended from the roof. There was no light of any kind emanating from lamp or candle within the suite of chambers. But in the corridors that followed the suite, there stood, opposite to each window, a heavy tripod, bearing a brazier of fire that projected its rays through the tinted glass and so glaringly illumined the room. And thus were produced a multitude of gaudy and fantastic appearances. But in the western or black chamber the effect of the firelight that streamed upon the dark hangings through the blood-tinted panes, was ghastly in the extreme, and produced so wild a look upon the countenances of those who entered, that there were few of the company bold enough to set foot within its precincts at all.

It was in this apartment, also, that there stood against the western wall a gigantic clock of ebony. Its pendulum swung to and fro with a dull, heavy, monotonous clang; and when the minute hand made the circuit of the face, and the hour was to be stricken, there came from the brazen lungs of the clock a sound which was clear and loud and deep and exceedingly musical, but of so peculiar a note and emphasis that, at each lapse of an hour, the musicians of the orchestra were constrained to pause, momentarily, in their performance, to hearken to the sound; and thus the waltzers perforce ceased their evolutions; and there was a brief

JOT IT DOWN **Reread Lines 56–65**

Fill in the chart below by listing the missing colors. One is shown. **(Clarify)**

Rooms in the abbey

| 1st blue | 2nd | 3rd | 4th | 5th | 6th | 7th |

eastern   western

READ ALOUD **Lines 62–67**

What makes the black room different from the six other rooms? **(Compare and Contrast)**

_____

_____

_____

59 **tapestries:** woven cloths hung on walls.
60 **casements:** windows.

74 **brazier** (brā′zhər): metal pan for holding a fire.

80 **countenances** (koun′tə-nən-səz): faces.

84 **ebony** (ĕb′ə-nē): a hard, very dark wood.

87 **brazen:** brass.

93 **evolutions:** intricate patterns of movement.

disconcert of the whole gay company; and, while the chimes of the clock yet rang, it was observed that the giddiest turned pale, and the more aged and sedate passed their hands over their brows as if in confused reverie or meditation. But when the echoes had fully ceased, a light laughter at once <u>pervaded</u> the assembly; the musicians looked at each other and smiled as if at their own nervousness and folly, and made whispering vows, each to the other, that the next chiming of the clock should produce in them no similar emotion; and then, after the lapse of sixty minutes (which embrace three thousand and six hundred seconds of the Time that flies), there came yet another chiming of the clock, and then were the same disconcert and tremulousness and meditation as before.

Pause & Reflect

FOCUS
Read to find out about the guests' costumes and behavior at the masked ball.

But in spite of these things, it was a gay and magnificent revel. The tastes of the duke were peculiar. He had a fine eye for colors and effects. He disregarded the *decora* of mere fashion. His plans were bold and fiery, and his conceptions glowed with barbaric luster. There are some who would have thought him mad. His followers felt that he was not. It was necessary to hear and see and touch him to be *sure* that he was not.

He had directed, in great part, the movable embellishments of the seven chambers, upon occasion of this great *fête;* and it was his own guiding taste which had given character to the masqueraders. Be sure they were <u>grotesque</u>. There were much glare and glitter and piquancy and phantasm—much of what has been seen since in *Hernani*. There were arabesque figures with unsuited limbs and appointments. There were delirious fancies such as the madman fashions. There was much of the beautiful, much of the wanton, much of the *bizarre,* something of the terrible, and not a little of that which might have excited disgust. To and fro in the seven chambers there

WORDS
TO
KNOW

pervade (pər-vād′) *v.* to spread throughout
grotesque (grō-těsk′) *adj.* having a bizarre, fantastic
    appearance

118

94 disconcert: confusion.

97 reverie: daydreaming.

108 revel: a celebration.

111 _decora:_ fine things.

114 mad: insane.

116–138 Notice the comparison of the masqueraders to dreams, phantasms, and a madman's fancies.
116 movable embellishments: furnishings and decorations.
120 phantasm (făn'tăz'əm): a shifting appearance.
121 _Hernani_ (ĕr'nä-nē): a play by Victor Hugo, first staged in 1830, known for its use of color and spectacle; **arabesque** (ăr'ə-bĕsk'): characterized by complicated decorations.

Pause & Reflect

✎ **MARK IT UP** **1.** What happens whenever the ebony clock chimes? Write the answer below. Then circle details on pages 116 and 118 that led you to your answer. **(Cause and Effect)**

_____

_____

_____

_____

2. What do you think might occur in the black room? **(Predict)**

_____

_____

_____

_____

📖 **READ ALOUD** **Lines 119–126**

The boxed sentences describe the guests' costumes at the masked ball. Check the two words below that apply to these costumes. **(Evaluate)**

ordinary   amusing

strange   disturbing

---

stalked, in fact, a multitude of dreams. And these—the
dreams—writhed in and about, taking hue from the rooms,
and causing the wild music of the orchestra to seem as the
echo of their steps. And, anon, there strikes the ebony clock
which stands in the hall of velvet. And then, for a moment, all
is still, and all is silent save the voice of the clock. The dreams
are stiff-frozen as they stand. But the echoes of the chime die
away—they have endured but an instant—and a light, half-
subdued laughter floats after them as they depart. And now
again the music swells, and the dreams live, and writhe to and
fro more merrily than ever, taking hue from the many-tinted
windows through which stream the rays of the tripods. But to
the chamber which lies most westwardly of the seven, there
are now none of the maskers who venture; for the night is
waning away; and there flows a ruddier light through the
blood-colored panes; and the blackness of the sable drapery
appalls; and to him whose foot falls upon the sable carpet,
there comes from the near clock of ebony a muffled peal more
solemnly emphatic than any which reaches *their* ears who
indulge in the more remote gaieties of the other apartments.

Pause **&** *Reflect*

FOCUS

At midnight a masked
figure suddenly
appears at the ball.
Read to find out about
this figure and
Prospero's reaction
to it.

MARK IT UP As you
read, circle any details
that help you picture
this figure.

But these other apartments were densely
crowded, and in them beat feverishly
the heart of life. And the revel went
whirlingly on, until at length there
commenced the sounding of midnight
upon the clock. And then the music
ceased, as I have told; and the
evolutions of the waltzes were quieted;
and there was an uneasy cessation of
all things as before. But now there were
twelve strokes to be sounded by the bell of the clock; and
thus it happened, perhaps, that more of thought crept, with
more of time, into the meditations of the thoughtful among
those who reveled. And thus, too, it happened, perhaps, that
before the last echoes of the last chime had utterly sunk into
silence, there were many individuals in the crowd who had
found leisure to become aware of the presence of a masked
figure which had arrested the attention of no single individual

127 The **dreams** are not literal dreams. The guests wear costumes so fantastic that they look as though they have stepped out of a dream.

128 writhed (rīthd)**:** made twisting or turning movements.

138-146 The dancers avoid the black room because the combination of red and black in the room and the loud chiming of the clock frightens them; **appalls:** fills with dread.

1. Prospero's followers believe that he *is / is not* insane. **(Clarify)**

2. Would you like to be a guest at Prospero's masked ball? *Yes / No,* because_____

_____

_____

_____.

(Connect)

before. And the rumor of this new presence having spread itself whisperingly around, there arose at length from the whole company a buzz, or murmur, expressive of disapprobation and surprise—then, finally of terror, of horror, and of disgust.

In an assembly of phantasms such as I have painted, it may well be supposed that no ordinary appearance could have excited such sensation. In truth the masquerade <u>license</u> of the night was nearly unlimited; but the figure in question had out-Heroded Herod, and gone beyond the bounds of even the prince's indefinite decorum. There are chords in the hearts of the most reckless which cannot be touched without emotion. Even with the utterly lost, to whom life and death are equally jests, there are matters of which no jest can be made. The whole company, indeed, seemed now deeply to feel that in the costume and bearing of the stranger neither wit nor propriety existed. The figure was tall and gaunt, and shrouded from head to foot in the habiliments of the grave. The mask which concealed the visage was made so nearly to resemble the countenance of a stiffened corpse that the closest scrutiny must have difficulty in detecting the cheat. And yet all this might have been endured, if not approved, by the mad revellers around. But the mummer had gone so far as to assume the type of the Red Death. His vesture was dabbed in *blood*—and his broad brow, with all the features of the face, was besprinkled with the scarlet horror.

When the eyes of Prince Prospero fell upon this spectral image (which with a slow and solemn movement, as if more fully to sustain its *role*, stalked to and fro among the waltzers), he was seen to be convulsed, in the first moment with a strong shudder either of terror or distaste; but, in the next, his brow reddened with rage.

"Who dares?" he demanded hoarsely of the courtiers who stood near him—"who dares insult us with this blasphemous mockery? Seize him and unmask him—that we may know whom we have to hang at sunrise, from the battlements!"

Pause & *Reflect*

WORDS
TO
KNOW
license (lī′səns) *n.* a lack of restrictions on behavior; freedom

174 out-Heroded Herod: been more extreme than the biblical king Herod, who ordered the deaths of all male babies up to two years old in an effort to kill the infant Jesus. This expression is used in Shakespeare's *Hamlet*.

182 habiliments (hə-bĭl'ə-mənts)**:** clothing.
183 visage (vĭz'ĭj)**:** face.

187 mummer: a person dressed for a masquerade.

198 blasphemous (blăs'fə-məs)**:** mocking something holy.

Pause **&** *Reflect*

1. Review the details you circled as you read. What makes the masked figure so horrible? **(Infer)**

_____
_____
_____
_____

MARK IT UP **2.** How does Prospero react to the masked figure? Cross out the word below that does *not* describe his reaction. Then underline any details on page 122 that led you to the answer. **(Clarify)**

frightened

angry

sympathetic

disgusted

It was in the eastern or blue chamber in which stood the Prince Prospero as he uttered these words. They rang throughout the seven rooms loudly and clearly—for the prince was a bold and robust man, and the music had become hushed at the waving of his hand.

It was in the blue room where stood the prince, with a group of pale courtiers by his side. At first, as he spoke, there was a slight rushing movement of this group in the direction of the intruder, who at the moment was also near at hand, and now, with deliberate and stately step, made closer approach to the speaker. But from a certain nameless awe with which the mad assumptions of the mummer had inspired the whole party, there were found none who put forth a hand to seize him; so that, unimpeded, he passed within a yard of the prince's person; and, while the vast assembly, as if with one impulse, shrank from the centers of the rooms to the walls, he made his way uninterruptedly, but with the same solemn and measured step which had distinguished him from the first, through the blue chamber to the purple—through the purple to the green—through the green to the orange—through this again to the white—and even thence to the violet, ere a decided movement had been made to arrest him. It was then, however, that the Prince Prospero, maddening with rage and the shame of his own momentary cowardice, rushed hurriedly through the six chambers while none followed him on account of a deadly terror that had seized upon all. He bore aloft a drawn dagger, and had approached, in rapid <u>impetuosity</u>, to within three or four feet of the retreating figure, when the latter, having attained the extremity of the velvet apartment, turned suddenly and confronted his pursuer. There was a sharp cry— and the dagger dropped gleaming upon the sable carpet, upon which, instantly afterwards, fell prostrate in death the Prince Prospero. Then, summoning the wild courage of despair, a throng of the revellers at once threw themselves into the

WORDS
TO
KNOW

impetuosity (ĭm-pĕch′ oo-ŏs′ ĭ-tē) *n.* unthinking action

206 robust (rō-bŭst′)**:** full of health and strength.

212–225 The masked figure walks through the rooms with great dignity and no haste.

◤ **JOT IT DOWN** **Reread Lines 213-225**

Why do you think the masked figure is allowed to walk the length of the rooms uninterrupted? **(Infer)**

_____

_____

_____

_____

◤ **MARK IT UP** **WORD POWER**

Remember to mark words that you'd like to add to your **Personal Word List.** Later, you can record the words and their meanings beginning on page 344.

236–242 When a group of revellers rip off the figure's costume, there is nothing underneath.

black apartment, and seizing the mummer, whose tall figure stood erect and motionless within the shadow of the ebony clock, gasped in unutterable horror at finding the grave-cerements and corpselike mask, which they handled with so violent a rudeness, <u>untenanted</u> by any <u>tangible</u> form.

And now was acknowledged the presence of the Red Death. He had come like a thief in the night. And one by one dropped the revellers in the blood-bedewed halls of their revel, and died each in the despairing posture of his fall. And the life of the ebony clock went out with that of the last of the gay. And the flames of the tripods expired. And Darkness and Decay and the Red Death held illimitable dominion over all.

Pause & *Reflect*

WORDS
TO
KNOW

untenanted (ŭn-tĕn′ən-tĭd) *adj.* not occupied
tangible (tăn′jə-bəl) *adj.* able to be touched or felt

241 cerements (sĕr′ə-mənts)**:** cloth wrappings for the dead.

249 illimitable dominion (ĭ-lĭm′ĭ-tə-bəl də-mĭn′yən)**:** unlimited power.

Pause **&** Reflect

1. Describe Prospero's death. **(Clarify)**

_____

_____

_____

_____

MARK IT UP **2.** What happens to Prospero's guests? Circle the sentence on page 126 that tells the answer. **(Clarify)**

READ ALOUD **3.** Read aloud the boxed sentence on page 126. Then restate its idea in your own words. **(Paraphrase)**

_____

_____

_____

_____

....

....

....

....

....

....

CHALLENGE

Irony is the contrast between what is expected and what actually exists or happens. For example, Prospero, who tries to escape the Red Death, actually rushes toward it at his own party. Highlight other examples of irony in this story. What view of the world does Poe suggest with these ironies? **(Analyze)**

Wrapping Up

If you are using The *Language of Literature,* you can now move to the questions and activities on pages 462–463 of that book.

Active Reading SkillBuilder

Clarifying Meaning

In "The Masque of the Red Death," Poe uses unusual, old-fashioned vocabulary to help reinforce the story's setting in the past. The following strategies can help **clarify** the meanings of particular words and passages: use the Guide for Reading notes; reread difficult passages carefully, then **paraphrase** them (state them in your own words); **summarize** difficult passages; use **context clues** (clues found in the surrounding phrases) to figure out the meanings of unfamiliar words. Use these strategies while reading the story. Record on the chart below any difficult words and passages, questions about them, and possible meanings for each word or passage. An example is given.

Difficult Words and Passages	Questions	Possible Meanings
The courtiers might bid defiance to contagion.	What does "bid defiance" mean?	The courtiers thought they were safe from the disease.

Literary Analysis SkillBuilder

Allegory

"The Masque of the Red Death" can be read as an **allegory,** a literary work in which the characters, objects, and events represent abstract qualities, such as kindness or greed. An allegory has a second level of meaning in addition to its literal meaning. Some allegories are intended to teach moral lessons. Use the chart below to analyze allegorical elements in Poe's story. Give a possible meaning for the listed elements and explain how Poe uses each one to convey a moral lesson.

Person, Object, Event	Possible Meaning	Possible Moral of Story
The prince	*selfishness*	*Selfish people in the end destroy themselves.*
The abbey		
The series of seven rooms		
The clock		
The stranger		

Follow Up: Compare your chart with that of a partner; defend your interpretations of allegorical elements in Poe's story.

Words to Know SkillBuilder

Words to Know

contagion	dauntless	impetuosity	pervade	tangible
courtier	grotesque	license	sagacious	untenanted

A. Fill in each set of blanks with the correct word from the word list. The boxed letters will spell out what the Red Death turned out to be.

1. Children sometimes act as if this has been granted to them when their teacher is replaced by a substitute.

   _ □ _ _ _ _ _

2. This is what you are if a visit to the dentist, noises in the night, and an algebra exam fail to bother you.

   _ _ _ □ _ _ _ _ _

3. This is one who spends time bowing, attending royal banquets, and saying "Your Highness."

   _ _ _ _ _ _ □ _

4. This describes some high-fashion items and many things possessed by people with truly horrible taste.

   _ _ _ _ _ □ _ _ _

5. This describes someone who knows that a stitch in time saves nine and too many cooks spoil the broth.

   _ _ _ _ □ _ _ _ _

6. This is what vaccines prevent and what we try to limit by covering our mouths when we cough.

   _ _ _ _ □ _ _ _ _

7. This could cause you to jump into a lake to save a drowning child or to dye your hair green on a dare.

   _ _ □ _ _ _ _ _ _ _ _

8. This could describe an abandoned house, a dead body, or a hive after the bees have vacated it.

   _ _ _ _ _ _ □ _ _ _ _

9. This describes a wedding ring but not the words "I do," or a piece of apple pie but not the taste.

   _ _ _ _ _ _ □ □ _

10. Solids cannot do this to the spaces they occupy, but sounds, moods, and gases can.

    _ □ _ _ _ _ _

B. Write the invitation that Prince Prospero sent out to a thousand of his subjects when he got his clever idea. Use at least **four** of the Words to Know.

Before You Read

If you are using *The Language of Literature* . . .

- Use the information on page 500 of that book to prepare for reading.

- Look at the art on pages 501, 505, and 511. What two contrasting **moods** do you see?

Reading Tips

Because this short story was written more than 150 years ago, some of the words and phrases may seem formal and old-fashioned. It may take a while to get used to the **style**.

- If you are having trouble following a long sentence, try to break it down into smaller chunks. Look for each subject and verb.

- Use **context clues** to figure out the meaning of unfamiliar words.

- Use the notes in the Guide for Reading to help you understand difficult words and passages.

MARK IT UP KEEP TRACK

As you read, you can use these marks to keep track of your understanding.

✔ ..... I understand.

? ..... I don't understand this.

! ..... Interesting or surprising idea

Dr. Heidegger's Experiment

NATHANIEL HAWTHORNE

PREVIEW In this story, written in the early 1800s, an elderly doctor wants to carry out a mysterious experiment with four of his elderly friends. He offers them water that he says has the power to make them young again. They don't believe him, but they try the water anyway. The effects produce some surprising consequences. Whether the experiment is successful is a matter of opinion—the doctor's, the friends', and the reader's.

FOCUS

The first part of the story introduces Dr. Heidegger and his four friends. It also describes the doctor's study.

MARK IT UP As you read, underline details that describe what each of the four friends has wasted or lost. An example is highlighted.

10

That very singular man, old Dr. Heidegger, once invited four <u>venerable</u> friends to meet him in his study. There were three white-bearded gentlemen, Mr. Medbourne, Colonel Killigrew, and Mr. Gascoigne, and a withered gentlewoman, whose name was the Widow Wycherly. They were all melancholy old creatures, who had been unfortunate in life, and whose greatest misfortune it was, that they were not long ago in their graves. Mr. Medbourne, in the vigor of his age, had been a prosperous merchant, but had lost his all by a frantic speculation, and was now little better than a mendicant. Colonel Killigrew had wasted his best years, and his health and substance, in the pursuit of sinful pleasures, which had

---

WORDS
TO
KNOW

venerable (vĕn'ər-ə-bəl) *adj.* worthy of respect because of age, dignity, or character

Use this guide for help with unfamiliar words and difficult passages.

6 Gascoigne: (găs-coin´).

10–11 whose . . . graves: The most unfortunate aspect of their lives was that they were not already dead.

14 speculation: risky business deals; **mendicant** (měn´dǐ-kənt): beggar.

✎ **MARK IT UP** WORD POWER

Mark words that you'd like to add to your **Personal Word List.** After reading, you can record the words and their meanings beginning on page 344.

given birth to a brood of pains, such as the gout, and divers other torments of soul and body. Mr. Gascoigne was a ruined politician, a man of evil fame, or at least had been so, till time had buried him from the knowledge of the present generation, and made him obscure instead of infamous. As for the Widow Wycherly, tradition tells us that she was a great beauty in her day; but, for a long while past, she had lived in deep seclusion, on account of certain scandalous stories, which had prejudiced the gentry of the town against her. It is a circumstance worth mentioning, that each of these three old gentlemen, Mr. Medbourne, Colonel Killigrew, and Mr. Gascoigne, were early lovers of the Widow Wycherly, and had once been on the point of cutting each other's throats for her sake. And, before proceeding farther, I will merely hint, that Dr. Heidegger and all his four guests were sometimes thought to be a little beside themselves; as is not unfrequently the case with old people, when worried either by present troubles or woeful recollections.

"My dear old friends," said Dr. Heidegger, motioning them to be seated, "I am desirous of your assistance in one of those little experiments with which I amuse myself here in my study."

If all stories were true, Dr. Heidegger's study must have been a very curious place. It was a dim, old-fashioned chamber, festooned with cobwebs, and besprinkled with antique dust. Around the walls stood several oaken book-cases, the lower shelves of which were filled with rows of gigantic folios, and black-letter quartos, and the upper with little parchment covered duodecimos. Over the central book-case was a bronze bust of Hippocrates, with which, according to some authorities, Dr. Heidegger was accustomed to hold consultations, in all difficult cases of his practice. In the obscurest corner of the room stood a tall and narrow oaken closet, with its door ajar, within which doubtfully appeared a skeleton. Between two of the book-cases hung a looking-glass, presenting its high and dusty plate within a tarnished gilt frame. Among many wonderful stories related of this mirror, it was fabled that the spirits of all the doctor's deceased patients dwelt within its verge, and would stare him in the face whenever he looked thitherward. The opposite side of the chamber was ornamented with the full length portrait of a young lady, arrayed in the faded magnificence of silk, satin, and brocade, and with a visage as faded as her

17 gout (gout): a painful disease of the joints, once thought to be caused by eating too much rich food.

21 obscure instead of infamous (ĭn'fə-məs): little known rather than well-known for wickedness.

25 gentry: respectable or socially high-ranking people.

JOT IT DOWN Reread Lines 26–30

What relationship did the four guests have in their youth? **(Clarify)**

32 beside themselves: upset; not rational.

40 festooned: decorated in draping curves.

43–44 folios . . . quartos . . . duodecimos: books of different sizes.
45 Hippocrates (hĭ-pŏk'rə-tēz'): a Greek physician, considered to be the father of medicine.

50–55 This is no ordinary mirror. People say that Dr. Heidegger can see in the glass the ghosts of patients who have died.

54 verge: border.
55 thitherward: in that direction.

58 visage (vĭz'ĭj): face.

dress. Above half a century ago, Dr. Heidegger had been on the point of marriage with this young lady; but, being affected with some slight disorder, she had swallowed one of her lover's prescriptions, and died on the bridal evening.

The greatest curiosity of the study remains to be mentioned: it was a ponderous folio volume, bound in black leather, with massive silver clasps. There were no letters on the back, and nobody could tell the title of the book. But it was well known to be a book of magic; and once, when a chambermaid had lifted it, merely to brush away the dust, the skeleton had rattled in its closet, the picture of the young lady had stepped one foot upon the floor, and several ghastly faces had peeped forth from the mirror; while the brazen head of Hippocrates frowned, and said—"Forbear!"

Such was Dr. Heidegger's study. On the summer afternoon of our tale, a small round table, as black as ebony, stood in the center of the room, sustaining a cut-glass vase, of beautiful form and elaborate workmanship. The sunshine came through the window, between the heavy festoons of two faded damask curtains, and fell directly across this vase; so that a mild splendor was reflected from it on the ashen visages of the five old people who sat around. Four champagne glasses were also on the table.

Pause **&** *Reflect*

FOCUS

Dr. Heidegger demonstrates the experiment he wants to carry out with his friends. He will try to make an old dried-up rose bloom again. As you read, look for magical elements in the demonstration.

"My dear old friends," repeated Dr. Heidegger, "may I reckon on your aid in performing an exceedingly curious experiment?"

Now Dr. Heidegger was a very strange old gentleman, whose eccentricity had become the nucleus for a thousand fantastic stories. Some of these fables, to my shame be it spoken, might possibly be traced back to mine own veracious self; and if any passages of the present tale

64 ponderous folio volume: a large book. The magical effects of this book are described later in this paragraph.

72 forbear: stop; cease.

78 damask (dăm'əsk): A patterned cloth.

89–94 The narrator admits to having told fables, or untrue stories, about Dr. Heidegger in the past.

92 veracious (və-rā'shəs): truthful.

Pause & Reflect

1. Review the details that you underlined as you read. For each of the four guests, write one word or phrase that describes what that character has lost or wasted. **(Clarify)**

Mr. Medbourne: _____

Colonel Killigrew: _____

Mr. Gascoigne: _____

Widow Wycherly: _____

2. Why has Dr. Heidegger invited his friends to his study? **(Clarify)**

_____

_____

_____

_____

MARK IT UP 3. Review lines 39–81. Circle words and phrases that help you to **visualize** Dr. Heidegger's study and its mysterious contents.

should startle the reader's faith, I must be content to bear the <u>stigma</u> of a fiction-monger.

When the doctor's four guests heard him talk of his proposed experiment, they anticipated nothing more wonderful than the murder of a mouse in an air-pump, or the examination of a cobweb by the microscope, or some similar nonsense, with which he was constantly in the habit of pestering his intimates. But without waiting for a reply, Dr. Heidegger hobbled across the chamber, and returned with the same ponderous folio, bound in black leather, which common report affirmed to be a book of magic. Undoing the silver clasps, he opened the volume, and took from among its black-letter pages a rose, or what was once a rose, though now the green leaves and crimson petals had assumed one brownish hue, and the ancient flower seemed ready to crumble to dust in the doctor's hands.

"This rose," said Dr. Heidegger, with a sigh, "this same withered and crumbling flower, blossomed five-and-fifty years ago. It was given me by Sylvia Ward, whose portrait hangs yonder; and I meant to wear it in my bosom at our wedding. Five-and-fifty years it has been treasured between the leaves of this old volume. Now, would you deem it possible that this rose of half a century could ever bloom again?"

"Nonsense!" said the Widow Wycherly, with a peevish toss of her head. "You might as well ask whether an old woman's wrinkled face could ever bloom again."

"See!" answered Dr. Heidegger.

He uncovered the vase, and threw the faded rose into the water which it contained. At first, it lay lightly on the surface of the fluid, appearing to imbibe none of its moisture. Soon, however, a singular change began to be visible. The crushed and dried petals stirred, and assumed a deepening tinge of crimson, as if the flower were reviving from a death-like slumber; the slender stalk and twigs of foliage became green; and there was the rose of half a century, looking as fresh as when Sylvia Ward had first given it to her lover. It was scarcely full-blown; for some of its delicate red leaves curled modestly around its moist bosom, within which two or three dewdrops were sparkling.

WORDS
TO
KNOW

stigma (stĭg′mə) *n.* a mark of disgrace

94 fiction-monger: liar.

95–100 The guests are used to being called in to watch Dr. Heidegger's experiments. They expect nothing unusual.

> ✎ **MARK IT UP** **Reread Lines 109–114**
>
> Who gave Dr. Heidegger the rose and how old is it? Circle words in the boxed passage that tell the answers. **(Clarify)**

116 peevish: irritable.

122 imbibe: absorb.

> ✎ **JOT IT DOWN** **Reread Lines 122–131**
>
> What happens to the rose? **(Summarize)**
>
> _____
>
> _____
>
> _____

129 full-blown: completely open.

"That is certainly a very pretty deception," said the doctor's friends; carelessly, however, for they had witnessed greater miracles at a conjurer's show: "pray how was it effected?"

"Did you never hear of the 'Fountain of Youth,'" asked Dr. Heidegger, "which Ponce De Leon, the Spanish adventurer, went in search of, two or three centuries ago?"

"But did Ponce De Leon ever find it?" said the Widow Wycherly.

"No," answered Dr. Heidegger, "for he never sought it in the right place. The famous Fountain of Youth, if I am rightly informed, is situated in the southern part of the Floridian peninsula, not far from Lake Macaco. Its source is overshadowed by several gigantic magnolias, which, though numberless centuries old, have been kept as fresh as violets, by the virtues of this wonderful water. An acquaintance of mine, knowing my curiosity in such matters, has sent me what you see in the vase."

"Ahem!" said Colonel Killigrew, who believed not a word of the doctor's story: "and what may be the effect of this fluid on the human frame?"

"You shall judge for yourself, my dear colonel," replied Dr. Heidegger; "and all of you, my respected friends, are welcome to so much of this admirable fluid, as may restore to you the bloom of youth. For my own part, having had much trouble in growing old, I am in no hurry to grow young again. With your permission, therefore, I will merely watch the progress of the experiment."

While he spoke, Dr. Heidegger had been filling the four champagne glasses with the water of the Fountain of Youth. It was apparently impregnated with an effervescent gas, for little bubbles were continually ascending from the depths of the glasses, and bursting in silvery spray at the surface. As the liquor diffused a pleasant perfume, the old people doubted not that it possessed cordial and comfortable properties; and, though utter skeptics as to its rejuvenescent power, they were inclined to swallow it at once. But Dr. Heidegger besought them to stay a moment.

"Before you drink, my respectable old friends," said he, "it would be well that, with the experience of a life-time to direct you, you should draw up a few general rules for your guidance, in passing a second time through the perils of

134 conjurer's: magician's.

137 Ponce De Leon (pŏns′ də lē-ōn′)**:** Spanish explorer who went to Florida in 1513.

✎ **JOT IT DOWN**   **Reread Lines 142–149**

Where did the water for Dr. Heidegger's experiment come from? **(Clarify)**

✎ **JOT IT DOWN**   **Reread Lines 156–158**

Why doesn't Dr. Heidegger want to drink the water himself? **(Infer)**

---

162 was apparently . . . gas: seemed to have a bubbling gas dissolved in it.

166 cordial (kôr′jəl)**:** stimulating.
167 rejuvenescent (rĭ-jōō′və-nĕs′ənt)**:** producing renewed youth.
168–169 besought them to stay: begged them to wait.
170–176 Dr. Heidegger warns his friends against making the same mistakes they made in their youth. He fully expects them to regain their youth.

youth. Think what a sin and shame it would be, if, with your peculiar advantages, you should not become patterns of virtue and wisdom to all the young people of the age!"

The doctor's four venerable friends made him no answer, except by a feeble and <u>tremulous</u> laugh; so very ridiculous was the idea, that, knowing how closely repentance treads behind the steps of error, they should ever go astray again.

"Drink, then," said the doctor, bowing: "I rejoice that I have so well selected the subjects of my experiment."

Pause & Reflect

FOCUS

The four guests are about to drink the magical water. Read on to see if your prediction on page 143 was correct.

MARK IT UP Underline details that show how each guest acts after drinking the water.

With palsied hands, they raised the glasses to their lips. The liquor, if it really possessed such virtues as Dr. Heidegger imputed to it, could not have been bestowed on four human beings who needed it more woefully. They looked as if they had never known what youth or pleasure was, but had been the offspring of Nature's dotage, and always the gray, <u>decrepit</u>, sapless, miserable creatures, who now sat stooping round the doctor's table, without life enough in their souls or bodies to be animated even by the prospect of growing young again. They drank off the water, and replaced their glasses on the table.

Assuredly there was an almost immediate improvement in the aspect of the party, not unlike what might have been produced by a glass of generous wine, together with a sudden glow of cheerful sunshine, brightening over all their visages at once. There was a healthful suffusion on their cheeks, instead of the ashen hue that had made them look so corpselike. They gazed at one another, and fancied that some magic power had really begun to smooth away the deep and sad inscriptions which Father Time had been so long engraving on their brows. The Widow Wycherly adjusted her cap, for she felt almost like a woman again.

WORDS
TO
KNOW

tremulous (trĕm′yə-ləs) *adj.* marked by trembling, quivering, or shaking
decrepit (dĭ-krĕp′ĭt) *adj.* weakened, worn out, or broken down by old age or hard use

177–180 At this point, the four friends are certain that they would never repeat the errors of their past.

183 palsied: trembling.

186 imputed: attributed; credited.

191 dotage (dō'tĭj)**:** feebleness due to old age.

198 aspect: appearance.

201 healthful suffusion: rosy glow of health.

203–206 fancied . . . power: The narrator does not tell you whether the changes are really happening or are just in the characters' minds.

Pause **&** *Reflect*

1. Briefly describe the magical event that Dr. Heidegger shows to his friends. **(Summarize)**

_____

_____

_____

▲ MARK IT UP **2.** When Dr. Heidegger first tells his friends that he has found the secret of youth, do they believe him? Underline words and phrases on pages 138 and 140 that support your answer. **(Infer)**

_____

_____

_____

3. The guests seem willing to go along with the experiment. What do you think will happen when they drink the water? **(Predict)**

_____

_____

_____

_____

4. If you were one of the guests, would you join in the experiment? Give your reasons. **(Connect)**

_____

_____

_____

....

....

....

....

....

....

....

....

"Give us more of this wondrous water!" cried they, eagerly. "We are younger—but we are still too old! Quick!—give us more!"

"Patience, patience!" quoth Dr. Heidegger, who sat watching the experiment, with philosophic coolness. "You have been a long time growing old. Surely, you might be content to grow young in half an hour! But the water is at your service."

Again he filled their glasses with the liquor of youth, enough of which still remained in the vase to turn half the old people in the city to the age of their own grand-children. While the bubbles were yet sparkling on the brim, the doctor's four guests snatched their glasses from the table, and swallowed the contents at a single gulp. Was it delusion? Even while the draught was passing down their throats, it seemed to have wrought a change on their whole systems. Their eyes grew clear and bright; a dark shade deepened among their silvery locks; they sat around the table, three gentlemen of middle age, and a woman, hardly beyond her buxom prime.

"My dear widow, you are charming!" cried Colonel Killigrew, whose eyes had been fixed upon her face, while the shadows of age were flitting from it like darkness from the crimson day-break.

The fair widow knew, of old, that Colonel Killigrew's compliments were not always measured by sober truth; so she started up and ran to the mirror, still dreading that the ugly visage of an old woman would meet her gaze. Meanwhile, the three gentlemen behaved in such a manner, as proved that the water of the Fountain of Youth possessed some intoxicating qualities; unless, indeed, their <u>exhilaration</u> of spirits were merely a lightsome dizziness, caused by the sudden removal of the weight of years. Mr. Gascoigne's mind seemed to run on political topics, but whether relating to the past, present, or future, could not easily be determined, since the same ideas and phrases have been in vogue these fifty years. Now he rattled forth full-throated sentences about patriotism, national glory, and the people's right; now he muttered some

WORDS
TO
KNOW

exhilaration (ĭg-zĭl′ə-rā′shən) *n.* a lively delight

READ ALOUD | Reread Lines 208–221

As you read this passage aloud, try to express the excitement and impatience of the guests.

221 delusion: trick; deception.
222 draught (drăft): the amount taken in a single act of drinking.

MARK IT UP | KEEP TRACK

Remember to use these marks to keep track of your understanding.

✔ ..... I understand.

? ..... I don't understand this.

! ..... Interesting or surprising idea

perilous stuff or other, in a sly and doubtful whisper, so cautiously that even his own conscience could scarcely catch the secret; and now, again, he spoke in measured accents, and a deeply <u>deferential</u> tone, as if a royal ear were listening to his well-turned periods. Colonel Killigrew all this time had been trolling forth a jolly bottle-song, and ringing his glass in symphony with the chorus, while his eyes wandered towards the buxom figure of the Widow Wycherly. On the other side of the table, Mr. Medbourne was involved in a calculation of dollars and cents, with which was strangely intermingled a project for supplying the East Indies with ice, by harnessing a team of whales to the polar icebergs.

As for the Widow Wycherly, she stood before the mirror, curtseying and simpering to her own image, and greeting it as the friend whom she loved better than all the world beside. She thrust her face close to the glass, to see whether some long-remembered wrinkle or crow's-foot had indeed vanished. She examined whether the snow had so entirely melted from her hair, that the venerable cap could be safely thrown aside. At last, turning briskly away, she came with a sort of dancing step to the table.

"My dear old doctor," cried she, "pray favor me with another glass!"

"Certainly, my dear madam, certainly!" replied the complaisant doctor; "See! I have already filled the glasses."

There, in fact, stood the four glasses, brim full of this wonderful water, the delicate spray of which, as it effervesced from the surface, resembled the tremulous glitter of diamonds. It was now so nearly sunset, that the chamber had grown duskier than ever; but a mild and moon-like splendor gleamed from within the vase, and rested alike on the four guests, and on the doctor's venerable figure. He sat in a high-backed, elaborately-carved, oaken arm-chair, with a gray dignity of aspect that might have well befitted that very Father Time, whose power had never been <u>disputed</u>, save by this fortunate company. Even while quaffing the third draught of the Fountain of Youth, they were almost awed by the expression of his mysterious visage.

WORDS
TO
KNOW

deferential (dĕf′ə-rĕn′shəl) *adj.* extremely respectful
dispute (dĭ-spyōōt′) *v.* to question or doubt

246 perilous stuff: dangerous information; Mr. Gascoigne's mind is moving so fast that he talks about all kinds of political subjects, including some secret ones.

259 simpering: smiling in a silly, self-conscious way.

270 complaisant (kəm-plā′sənt): willing to please.

277–283 Dr. Heidegger remains calm, though his guests are quite excited.

281 quaffing (kwŏf′ĭng): drinking heartily.

READ ALOUD Lines 271–277

Listen for the repetition of *s, m,* and *n* sounds. Try to picture the scene that is described.

But, the next moment, the exhilarating gush of young life shot through their veins. They were now in the happy prime of youth. Age, with its miserable train of cares, and sorrows, and diseases, was remembered only as the trouble of a dream, from which they had joyously awoke. The fresh gloss of the soul, so early lost, and without which the world's successive scenes had been but a gallery of faded pictures, again threw its enchantment over all their prospects. They felt like new-created beings, in a new-created universe.

"We are young! We are young!" they cried, <u>exultingly</u>.

Youth, like the extremity of age, had <u>effaced</u> the strongly marked characteristics of middle life, and mutually assimilated them all. They were a group of merry youngsters, almost maddened with the exuberant frolicksomeness of their years. The most singular effect of their gayety was an impulse to mock the infirmity and decrepitude of which they had so lately been the victims. They laughed loudly at their old-fashioned attire, the wide-skirted coats and flapped waistcoats of the young men, and the ancient cap and gown of the blooming girl. One limped across the floor, like a gouty grandfather; one set a pair of spectacles astride of his nose, and pretended to pore over the black-letter pages of the book of magic; a third seated himself in an arm-chair, and strove to imitate the venerable dignity of Dr. Heidegger. Then all shouted mirthfully, and leaped about the room. The Widow Wycherly—if so fresh a damsel could be called a widow—tripped up to the doctor's chair, with a mischievous merriment in her rosy face.

> "Doctor, you dear old soul," cried she, "get up and dance with me!" And then the four young people laughed louder than ever, to think what a queer figure the poor old doctor would cut.
>
> "Pray excuse me," answered the doctor, quietly. "I am old and rheumatic, and my dancing days were over long ago. But either of these gay young gentlemen will be glad of so pretty a partner."

Pause **Reflect**

WORDS
TO
KNOW

exultingly (ĭg-zŭl'tĭng-lē) *adv.* in a joyful and triumphant way
efface (ĭ-fās') *v.* to rub or wipe out; erase

296 assimilated: absorbed.

297 exuberant (ĭg–zoo'bər-ənt)
frolicksomeness: joyous playfulness.

298–315 The four guests begin to make fun of old people, even mocking Dr. Heidegger.

308 mirthfully: joyfully.

317 rheumatic (roo-măt'ĭk)**:** made stiff by a condition such as arthritis.

Pause & Reflect

1. Look back at the details that you marked as you read. How do the four guests act after drinking the water? **(Summarize)**

_____

_____

_____

_____

2. In an **allegory,** people and objects represent certain qualities. Write the name of the character who might stand for each of the following qualities:

living for pleasure _____

political corruption _____

pride about appearance _____

love of money _____
(Interpret Allegory)

3. Reread the boxed passage, lines 312–319. Compare the behavior of the four guests with the behavior of Dr. Heidegger.
(Compare and Contrast)

_____

_____

_____

_____

320

FOCUS
Read to discover the final results of Dr. Heidegger's experiment.

"Dance with me, Clara!" cried Colonel Killigrew.

"No, no, I will be her partner!" shouted Mr. Gascoigne.

"She promised me her hand, fifty years ago!" exclaimed Mr. Medbourne.

They all gathered round her. One caught both her hands in his passionate grasp—another threw his arm about her waist—the third buried his hand among the glossy curls that clustered beneath the widow's cap. Blushing, panting, struggling, chiding, laughing, her warm breath fanning each of their faces by turns, she strove to disengage herself, yet still remained in their triple embrace. Never was there a livelier picture of youthful rivalship, with bewitching beauty for the prize. Yet, by a strange deception, owing to the duskiness of the chamber, and the antique dresses which they still wore, the tall mirror is said to have reflected the figures of the three old, gray, withered grand-sires, ridiculously contending for the skinny ugliness of a shrivelled grand-dam.

But they were young: their burning passions proved them so. Inflamed to madness by the coquetry of the girl-widow, who neither granted nor quite withheld her favors, the three rivals began to interchange threatening glances. Still keeping hold of the fair prize, they grappled fiercely at one another's throats. As they struggled to and fro, the table was overturned, and the vase dashed into a thousand fragments. The precious Water of Youth flowed in a bright stream across the floor, moistening the wings of a butterfly, which, grown old in the decline of summer, had alighted there to die. The insect fluttered lightly through the chamber, and settled on the snowy head of Dr. Heidegger.

"Come, come, gentlemen!—come, Madam Wycherly," exclaimed the doctor, "I really must protest against this riot."

They stood still, and shivered; for it seemed as if gray Time were calling them back from their sunny youth, far down into the chill and darksome vale of years. They looked at old Dr. Heidegger, who sat in his carved arm-chair, holding the rose of half a century, which he had rescued from among the fragments of the shattered vase. At the motion of his hand, the four rioters resumed their seats; the more readily, because their violent exertions had wearied them, youthful though they were.

331 strove to disengage herself:
struggled to free herself.

337–338 grand-sires . . . grand-dam: old
men . . . old woman.

340 coquetry (kō′kĭ-trē)**:** flirtatious
behavior.

355 vale: valley.

JOT IT DOWN **Reread Lines 334–338**

The narrator is unclear about whether the
reflection is real or not. What does the image
in the mirror reveal? **(Clarify)**

_____

_____

_____

_____

MARK IT UP WORD POWER

Remember to mark words that you'd like to
add to your **Personal Word List**. Later, you
can record the words and their meanings
beginning on page 344.

"My poor Sylvia's rose!" ejaculated Dr. Heidegger, holding it in the light of the sunset clouds: "it appears to be fading again."

And so it was. Even while the party were looking at it, the flower continued to shrivel up, till it became as dry and fragile as when the doctor had first thrown it into the vase. He shook off the few drops of moisture which clung to its petals.

"I love it as well thus, as in its dewy freshness," observed he, pressing the withered rose to his withered lips. While he spoke, the butterfly fluttered down from the doctor's snowy head, and fell upon the floor.

His guests shivered again. A strange chillness, whether of the body or spirit they could not tell, was creeping gradually over them all. They gazed at one another, and fancied that each fleeting moment snatched away a charm, and left a deepening furrow where none had been before. Was it an illusion? Had the changes of a life-time been crowded into so brief a space, and were they now four aged people, sitting with their old friend, Dr. Heidegger?

"Are we grown old again, so soon!" cried they, dolefully.

In truth, they had. The Water of Youth possessed merely a virtue more <u>transient</u> than that of wine. The delirium which it created had effervesced away. Yes! they were old again. With a shuddering impulse, that showed her a woman still, the widow clasped her skinny hands before her face, and wished that the coffin-lid were over it, since it could be no longer beautiful.

"Yes, friends, ye are old again," said Dr. Heidegger; "and lo! the Water of Youth is all lavished on the ground. Well—I bemoan it not; for if the fountain gushed at my very doorstep, I would not stoop to bathe my lips in it—no, though its delirium were for years instead of moments. Such is the lesson ye have taught me!"

But the doctor's four friends had taught no such lesson to themselves. They resolved forthwith to make a pilgrimage to Florida, and quaff at morning, noon, and night, from the Fountain of Youth.

Pause & Reflect

| WORDS TO KNOW | **transient** (trăn′shənt) *adj.* lasting or existing for only a short time |

362 ejaculated: exclaimed.

369–370 Note that Dr. Heidegger still loves the rose, even though it is now old again.

383 delirium (dĭ-lîr′ē-əm)**:** a state of uncontrolled excitement or emotion.

389 lavished: wasted

Pause **&** **Reflect**

▲ **MARK IT UP** **1.** In the middle of the struggle over Widow Wycherly, the vase is broken and the water spills. Underline the sentences on pages 150 and 152 that reveal what happens to the butterfly, the rose, and the guests. **(Clarify)**

2. What do the four guests decide to do at the end of the story? **(Clarify)**

_____

_____

_____

_____

3. What lesson has Dr. Heidegger learned? **(Infer)**

_____

_____

_____

_____

▲ **CHALLENGE**

Several times the author seems to create uncertainty about whether the four guests really become young again. Do you think the changes are real or imaginary? Mark evidence from the story to support your opinion. Why do you think the author introduces the element of uncertainty? **(Draw Conclusions)**

Wrapping Up

If you are using *The Language of Literature,* you can now move on to the questions and activities on pages 514–515 of that book.

Active Reading SkillBuilder

Interpreting Allegory

An **allegory** is a work of literature in which people, objects, and events represent general qualities, such as good and evil. Allegories are written not only to entertain but also to teach lessons. As you read "Dr. Heidegger's Experiment," complete the following chart by identifying a quality or idea that each guest in the story might represent. An example is given.

Character	What he or she loses or wastes	What happens when he or she is given a second youth	What he or she might represent
Mr. Medbourne	wealth	schemes to make money again	greed
Col. Killigrew			
Mr. Gascoigne			
Widow Wycherly			

Literary Analysis SkillBuilder

Foreshadowing

Foreshadowing is a writer's use of hints or clues to indicate events that will occur later in a story. It is a technique that builds suspense and arouses the reader's curiosity. For example, the eerie effects that occur when the chambermaid lifts the book of magic foreshadow the strange effects of drinking the water. Use the following diagram to record two other effective examples of foreshadowing that Hawthorne uses in "Dr. Heidegger's Experiment."

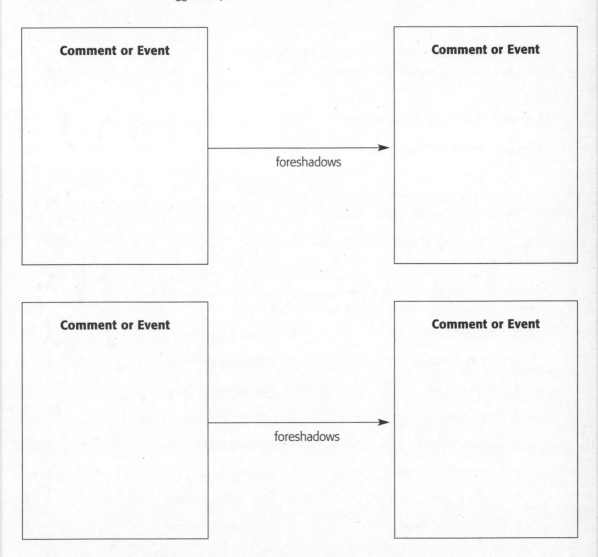

Follow Up: Explain whether foreshadowing added to or took away from your enjoyment of this story.

Words to Know SkillBuilder

Words to Know

decrepit	dispute	exhilaration	stigma	tremulous
deferential	efface	exultingly	transient	venerable

A. On each blank line, write the word from the word list that the rhyme describes.

1. If you have to speak in public and it makes you quite uneasy,
Your knees are this, your mouth is dry, your stomach's
rather queasy.

   TREMULOUS
   _____
   (1)

2. The tides do this to footprints that are pressed into the sand.
Rustlers try to do it to the legal owner's brand.

   _____
   (2)

3. This causes dishonor, it makes you feel shame,
Like a bad reputation, a blot on your name.

   _____
   (3)

4. The reason that it's hard to get much thinner
Is that this describes one's fullness after dinner.

   _____
   (4)

5. Proud and haughty, stuffy people may become unglued
If they are not treated with this kind of attitude.

   _____
   (5)

6. The opposite of misery, of sadness and despair,
This is the feeling of walking on air.

   _____
   (6)

B. For each phrase in the first column, find the phrase in the second column that is closest in meaning. Write the letter of that phrase in the blank.

1. a transient terror	A. suspect the statistics
2. a decrepit dwelling	B. a distinguished doctor
3. dispute the data	C. great gaiety
4. deeply deferential	D. a rickety residence
5. exultingly express	E. a passing panic
6. a venerable veterinarian	F. triumphantly talk
7. a tremulous tester	G. really, really respectful
8. exceptional exhilaration	H. a quivering questioner

C. Write a commercial for Dr. Heidegger's Fountain of Youth Elixir. Use at least **four** of the Words to Know.

A ROSE for EMILY

William Faulkner

PREVIEW This story is set in a town in Mississippi. The narrator, who speaks for the entire town, tells about Miss Emily Grierson. She was from an upper-class family. Proud and strong-willed, she cut herself off from the community. Years passed, and the town changed. Few people ever saw Miss Emily, and no one set foot inside her house. There was something mysterious about her and her house—especially about one of the rooms upstairs.

I

FOCUS

The narrator tells about Miss Emily's funeral and describes her house and street. The narrator also tells how a former mayor helped her.

MARK IT UP As you read, circle details that help you picture how her house and street have changed over the years. An example is highlighted.

When Miss Emily Grierson died, our whole town went to her funeral: the men through a sort of respectful affection for a fallen monument, the women mostly out of curiosity to see the inside of her house, which no one save an old manservant—a combined gardener and cook—had seen in at least ten years.

It was a big, squarish frame house that had once been white, decorated with cupolas and spires and scrolled balconies in the heavily lightsome style of the seventies,[1] set on what had once been our most select street. But garages and cotton gins[2] had

---

1. **the seventies:** the 1870s.
2. **cotton gins:** machines that separate the seeds and other small objects from the fibers of cotton.

Before You Read

If you are using *The Language of Literature* . . .

- Use the information on page 516 of that book to prepare for reading.
- Look at the art on pages 520–521 to help you **visualize** Miss Emily's house.

Reading Tips

William Faulkner once stated, "There is no such thing as *was*—only *is*." This view of the past led him to tell stories in new ways, shuffling the order of events. In this story, for example, the **narrator** recalls events from Miss Emily's life, not in **sequence** but as memory might link them.

- Some sentences in this story are long. When you come upon them, look for the main clause and pick out the subject and the verb. That will take you to the heart of the sentence.
- You will also come upon poetic passages, rich with **figurative language.** Read them at your usual pace and mark them. After reading the story, reread these passages and examine the language.

MARK IT UP KEEP TRACK

As you read, you can use these marks to keep track of your understanding.

✔ ..... I understand.

? ..... I don't understand this.

! ..... Interesting or surprising idea

encroached and <u>obliterated</u> even the august names of that neighborhood; only Miss Emily's house was left, lifting its stubborn and <u>coquettish</u> decay above the cotton wagons and the gasoline pumps—an eyesore among eyesores. And now Miss Emily had gone to join the representatives of those
- 20 august names where they lay in the cedar-bemused[3] cemetery among the ranked and anonymous graves of Union and Confederate soldiers who fell at the battle of Jefferson.

Alive, Miss Emily had been a tradition, a duty, and a care; a sort of hereditary obligation upon the town, dating from that day in 1894 when Colonel Sartoris, the mayor—he who fathered the <u>edict</u> that no Negro woman should appear on the streets without an apron—remitted her taxes, the dispensation dating from the death of her father on into perpetuity.[4] Not that Miss Emily would have accepted charity.
- 30 Colonel Sartoris invented an involved tale to the effect that Miss Emily's father had loaned money to the town, which the town, as a matter of business, preferred this way of repaying. Only a man of Colonel Sartoris' generation and thought could have invented it, and only a woman could have believed it.

Pause & **Reflect**

FOCUS

A committee of aldermen visits Miss Emily to force her to pay her taxes. Read to find out how she reacts to them.

- 40

When the next generation, with its more modern ideas, became mayors and aldermen, this arrangement created some little dissatisfaction. On the first of the year they mailed her a tax notice. February came, and there was no reply. They wrote her a formal letter, asking her to call at the sheriff's office at her convenience. A week

---

3. **cedar-bemused:** almost lost in cedar trees (literally, confused by cedars).

4. **remitted . . . perpetuity:** released her from paying taxes forever after the time of her father's death.

WORDS TO KNOW	**encroach** (ĕn-krōch') *v.* to advance beyond original limits; intrude **obliterate** (ə-blĭt'ə-rāt') *v.* to wipe out, leaving no trace **coquettish** (kō-kĕt'ĭsh) *adj.* flirtatious **edict** (ē'dĭkt') *n.* an order put out by a person in authority

later the mayor wrote her himself, offering to call or to send his car for her, and received in reply a note on paper of an archaic shape, in a thin, flowing calligraphy[5] in faded ink, to the effect that she no longer went out at all. The tax notice was also enclosed, without comment.

They called a special meeting of the Board of Aldermen. A deputation[6] waited upon her, knocked at the door through which no visitor had passed since she ceased giving china-painting lessons eight or ten years earlier. They were admitted by the old Negro into a dim hall from which a stairway mounted into still more shadow. It smelled of dust and disuse—a close, <u>dank</u> smell. The Negro led them into the parlor. It was furnished in heavy, leather-covered furniture. When the Negro opened the blinds of one window, they could see that the leather was cracked; and when they sat down, a faint dust rose sluggishly about their thighs, spinning with slow motes[7] in the single sun-ray. On a tarnished gilt easel before the fireplace stood a crayon portrait of Miss Emily's father.

They rose when she entered—a small, fat woman in black, with a thin gold chain descending to her waist and vanishing into her belt, leaning on an ebony cane with a tarnished gold head. Her skeleton was small and spare; perhaps that was why what would have been merely plumpness in another was obesity in her. She looked bloated, like a body long submerged in motionless water, and of that <u>pallid</u> hue. Her eyes, lost in the fatty ridges of her face, looked like two small pieces of coal pressed into a lump of dough as they moved from one face to another while the visitors stated their errand.

She did not ask them to sit. She just stood in the door and listened quietly until the spokesman came to a stumbling halt. Then they could hear the invisible watch ticking at the end of the gold chain.

Her voice was dry and cold. "I have no taxes in Jefferson. Colonel Sartoris explained it to me. Perhaps one of you can gain access to the city records and satisfy yourselves."

"But we have. We are the city authorities, Miss Emily. Didn't you get a notice from the sheriff, signed by him?"

---

5. **calligraphy:** beautiful handwriting.

6. **deputation:** a small group representing a larger one.

7. **motes:** specks.

WORDS
TO
KNOW

dank (dăngk) *adj.* unpleasantly damp; moist and chilly
pallid (păl′ĭd) *adj.* abnormally pale

MARK IT UP WORD POWER

Mark words that you'd like to add to your **Personal Word List.** After reading, you can record the words and their meanings beginning on page 344.

READ ALOUD **Lines 62–71**

Read aloud the boxed passage. Then circle the two phrases below that are true of Miss Emily. **(Infer)**

is overweight

looks healthy

wears a bright dress

keeps her watch hidden

Pause **&** **Reflect**

<u>MARK IT UP</u> **1.** The aldermen are shown into a dim hall and then into the parlor. Circle details on page 159 that help you visualize these rooms. **(Visualize)**

2. What is strange about Miss Emily's order to "see Colonel Sartoris"? **(Evaluate)**

_____

_____

_____

_____

"I received a paper, yes," Miss Emily said. "Perhaps he considers himself the sheriff . . . I have no taxes in Jefferson."

"But there is nothing on the books to show that, you see. We must go by the—"

"See Colonel Sartoris. I have no taxes in Jefferson."

"But, Miss Emily—"

"See Colonel Sartoris." (Colonel Sartoris had been dead almost ten years.) "I have no taxes in Jefferson. Tobe!" The Negro appeared. "Show these gentlemen out."

Pause **&** **Reflect**

II

90

FOCUS
Read to find out about the smell coming from Miss Emily's house.

So she vanquished them, horse and foot, just as she had vanquished their fathers thirty years before about the smell. That was two years after her father's death and a short time after her sweetheart— the one we believed would marry her—had deserted her. After her father's death she went out very little; after her sweetheart went away, people hardly saw her at all. A few of the ladies had the <u>temerity</u> to call, but were not received, and the only sign of life about the place was the Negro man—a young man

100 then—going in and out with a market basket.

"Just as if a man—any man— could keep a kitchen properly," the ladies said; so they were not surprised when the smell developed. It was another link between the gross, teeming world and the high and mighty Griersons.

A neighbor, a woman, complained to the mayor, Judge Stevens, eighty years old.

"But what will you have me do about it, madam?" he said.

"Why, send her word to stop it," the woman said. "Isn't there a law?"

110 "I'm sure that won't be necessary," Judge Stevens said. "It's probably just a snake or a rat that nigger[8] of hers killed in the yard. I'll speak to him about it."

---

8. This character uses an offensive term. Faulkner helps create the setting of this story by using language typical of certain people living in the South at that time.

WORDS
TO
KNOW

temerity (tə-mĕr′ĭ-tē) *n.* foolish boldness

The next day he received two more complaints, one from a man who came in <u>diffident</u> deprecation.[9] "We really must do something about it, Judge. I'd be the last one in the world to bother Miss Emily, but we've got to do something." That night the Board of Aldermen met—three graybeards and one younger man, a member of the rising generation.

"It's simple enough," he said. "Send her word to have her place cleaned up. Give her a certain time to do it in, and if she don't . . ."

"Dammit, sir," Judge Stevens said, "will you accuse a lady to her face of smelling bad?"

So the next night, after midnight, four men crossed Miss Emily's lawn and slunk about the house like burglars, sniffing along the base of the brickwork and at the cellar openings while one of them performed a regular sowing motion with his hand out of a sack slung from his shoulder. They broke open the cellar door and sprinkled lime there, and in all the outbuildings. As they recrossed the lawn, a window that had been dark was lighted and Miss Emily sat in it, the light behind her, and her upright torso motionless as that of an idol. They crept quietly across the lawn and into the shadow of the locusts that lined the street. After a week or two the smell went away.

Pause & Reflect

FOCUS

Read to find out about Miss Emily's relationship with her father and her reaction to his death.
MARK IT UP As you read, underline any details that help you understand this relationship.

That was when people had begun to feel really sorry for her. People in our town, remembering how old lady Wyatt, her great-aunt, had gone completely crazy at last, believed that the Griersons held themselves a little too high for what they really were. None of the young men were quite good enough for Miss Emily and such. We had long thought of them as a tableau,[10] Miss Emily a slender figure in white in the

---

9. **deprecation:** disapproval.
10. **tableau** (tăb′lō′): dramatic scene or picture.

diffident (dĭf′ĭ-dənt) *adj.* shy and timid; lacking self-confidence

Pause & Reflect

MARK IT UP **1.** Circle the sentence on page 160 that tells when the smell develops. (Clarify)

2. What steps do the aldermen take to deal with this problem? (Summarize)

_____

_____

_____

_____

1. Review the details you underlined as you read. The narrator pictures Miss Emily's father standing with his back to her and holding a horsewhip. Circle the phrase below that tells whom Miss Emily's father is driving from his house. **(Infer)**

a tax collector

a committee of aldermen

one of Emily's suitors, or boyfriends

2. Reread the boxed sentence on this page. How would you restate this idea in your own words? **(Paraphrase)**

_____

_____

_____

_____

MARK IT UP 3. What does Miss Emily tell the doctors and ministers who come for her father's body? Circle the sentence on this page that tells the answer. **(Clarify)**

....

....

....

....

....

....

....

....

....

background, her father a spraddled silhouette in the foreground, his back to her and clutching a horsewhip, the two of them framed by the back-flung front door. So when she got to be thirty and was still single, we were not pleased exactly, but vindicated; even with insanity in the family she wouldn't have turned down all of her chances if they had really materialized.

When her father died, it got about that the house was all that was left to her; and in a way, people were glad. At last they could pity Miss Emily. Being left alone, and a pauper, she had become humanized. Now she too would know the old thrill and the old despair of a penny more or less.

The day after his death all the ladies prepared to call at the house and offer condolence and aid, as is our custom. Miss Emily met them at the door, dressed as usual and with no trace of grief on her face. She told them that her father was not dead. She did that for three days, with the ministers calling on her, and the doctors, trying to persuade her to let them dispose of the body. Just as they were about to resort to law and force, she broke down, and they buried her father quickly.

We did not say she was crazy then. We believed she had to do that. We remembered all the young men her father had driven away, and we knew that with nothing left, she would have to cling to that which had robbed her, as people will.

Pause & Reflect

III

FOCUS

After her father's death, Emily meets Homer Barron. Read to find out about their relationship.

MARK IT UP As you read, circle any details that help you form impressions of Homer Barron.

She was sick for a long time. When we saw her again, her hair was cut short, making her look like a girl, with a vague resemblance to those angels in colored church windows—sort of tragic and serene.

The town had just let the contracts for paving the sidewalks, and in the summer after her father's death they began the work. The construction company came with niggers and mules and machinery, and a foreman named Homer Barron, a Yankee—a big, dark, ready man, with a big voice and eyes lighter than his face. The little boys would follow in groups to hear him cuss the niggers, and the niggers singing in time to the rise and fall of picks. Pretty soon he knew everybody in town. Whenever you heard a lot of laughing anywhere about the square, Homer Barron would be in the center of the group. Presently we began to see him and Miss Emily on Sunday afternoons driving in the yellow-wheeled buggy and the matched team of bays from the livery stable.

190   At first we were glad that Miss Emily would have an interest, because the ladies all said, "Of course a Grierson would not think seriously of a Northerner, a day laborer." But there were still others, older people, who said that even grief could not cause a real lady to forget *noblesse oblige*[11]— without calling it *noblesse oblige.* They just said, "Poor Emily. Her kinsfolk should come to her." She had some kin in Alabama; but years ago her father had fallen out with them over the estate of old lady Wyatt, the crazy woman, and there was no communication between the two families. They had

200 not even been represented at the funeral.

And as soon as the old people said, "Poor Emily," the whispering began. "Do you suppose it's really so?" they said to one another. "Of course it is. What else could . . ." This behind their hands; rustling of craned[12] silk and satin behind jalousies[13] closed upon the sun of Sunday afternoon as the thin, swift clop-clop-clop of the matched team passed: "Poor Emily."

She carried her head high enough—even when we believed that she was fallen. It was as if she demanded more than ever

210 the recognition of her dignity as the last Grierson; as if it had wanted that touch of earthiness to reaffirm her imperviousness. Like when she bought the rat poison, the arsenic. That was over a year after they had begun to say "Poor Emily," and while the two female cousins were visiting her.

Pause **&** *Reflect*

---

11. *noblesse oblige* (nō-blěs′ ō-blēzh′): the responsibility of people of high social position to behave in a noble fashion.

12. **craned:** stretched.

13. **jalousies** (jăl′ə-sēz): doors or windows containing overlapping slats that can be opened or closed.

A Rose for Emily 163

Pause **&** *Reflect*

1. Review the details you circled as you read. Then cross out the phrase below that is *not* true of Homer Barron. **(Infer)**

takes Miss Emily for carriage rides

comes from a well-to-do Southern family

works as the foreman of a construction crew

is popular in town

2. Why do you think Emily began seeing Homer? **(Infer)**

_____

_____

_____

_____

READ ALOUD **3.** Read aloud the boxed sentences on this page. What do the older people think of Miss Emily's new boyfriend? **(Draw Conclusions)**

_____

_____

_____

_____

FOCUS
Read to find out what Miss Emily buys from the druggist.

"I want some poison," she said to the druggist. She was over thirty then, still a slight woman, though thinner than usual, with cold, haughty black eyes in a face the flesh of which was strained across the temples and about the eye-sockets as you imagine a lighthouse-keeper's face ought to look. "I want some poison," she said.

"Yes, Miss Emily. What kind? For rats and such? I'd recom—"

"I want the best you have. I don't care what kind."

The druggist named several. "They'll kill anything up to an elephant. But what you want is—"

"Arsenic," Miss Emily said. "Is that a good one?"

"Is . . . arsenic? Yes, ma'am. But what you want—"

"I want arsenic."

The druggist looked down at her. She looked back at him, erect, her face like a strained flag. "Why, of course," the druggist said. "If that's what you want. But the law requires you to tell what you are going to use it for."

Miss Emily just stared at him, her head tilted back in order to look him eye for eye, until he looked away and went and got the arsenic and wrapped it up. The Negro delivery boy brought her the package; the druggist didn't come back. When she opened the package at home there was written on the box, under the skull and bones: "For rats."

Pause & Reflect

IV

FOCUS
Read to find out more about Miss Emily and Homer Barron and the town's opinion of them.

So the next day we all said, "She will kill herself"; and we said it would be the best thing. When she had first begun to be seen with Homer Barron, we had said, "She will marry him." Then we said, "She will persuade him yet," because Homer himself had remarked—he liked men, and it was known that he drank with the younger men in the Elks' Club—that he was not a marrying man. Later we said, "Poor Emily" behind the jalousies as they passed on Sunday afternoon in the glittering buggy, Miss Emily with her head high and Homer Barron

Pause & Reflect

📖 **READ ALOUD** 1. Read aloud the boxed passage on this page. Miss Emily refuses to tell the druggist why she wants to buy arsenic. Why does he sell it to her anyway? **(Infer)**

_____
_____
_____
_____

2. What do you think Miss Emily will do with the arsenic? **(Predict)**

_____
_____
_____
_____

with his hat cocked and a cigar in his teeth, reins and whip in a yellow glove.

Then some of the ladies began to say that it was a disgrace to the town and a bad example to the young people. The men did not want to interfere, but at last the ladies forced the Baptist minister—Miss Emily's people were Episcopal—to call upon her. He would never <u>divulge</u> what happened during that interview, but he refused to go back again. The next Sunday they again drove about the streets, and the following day the minister's wife wrote to Miss Emily's relations in Alabama.

So she had blood-kin under her roof again and we sat back to watch developments. At first nothing happened. Then we were sure that they were to be married. We learned that Miss Emily had been to the jeweler's and ordered a man's toilet set in silver, with the letters H. B. on each piece. Two days later we learned that she had bought a complete outfit of men's clothing, including a nightshirt, and we said, "They are married." We were really glad. We were glad because the two female cousins were even more Grierson than Miss Emily had ever been.

So we were not surprised when Homer Barron—the streets had been finished some time since—was gone. We were a little disappointed that there was not a public blowing-off,[14] but we believed that he had gone on to prepare for Miss Emily's coming, or to give her a chance to get rid of the cousins. (By that time it was a cabal,[15] and we were all Miss Emily's allies to help <u>circumvent</u> the cousins.) Sure enough, after another week they departed. And, as we had expected all along, within three days Homer Barron was back in town. A neighbor saw the Negro man admit him at the kitchen door at dusk one evening.

And that was the last we saw of Homer Barron. And of Miss Emily for some time. The Negro man went in and out with the market basket, but the front door remained closed. Now and then we would see her at a window for a moment, as the men did that night when they sprinkled the lime, but for almost six months she did not appear on the streets. Then we knew that this was to be expected too; as if that quality of

---

14. **blowing-off:** celebration.

15. **cabal** (kə-băl′): a group united in a secret plot.

WORDS
TO
KNOW

divulge (dĭ-vŭlj′) v. to make known something private
circumvent (sûr′kəm-věnt′) v. to avoid or get around by clever maneuvering

NOTES

MARK IT UP **KEEP TRACK**

Remember to use these marks to keep track of your understanding.

✔ ..... I understand.

? ..... I don't understand this.

! ..... Interesting or surprising idea

1. Some of the ladies in the town get the minister's wife to write to Emily's relations in Alabama. These ladies regard Emily's relationship with Homer Barron as a (circle one) *blessing / disgrace.* **(Infer)**

MARK IT UP **2.** After a time, the townspeople assume that Miss Emily and Homer Barron are married. Circle the two sentences on page 165 that tell why they think so. **(Cause and Effect)**

3. The last time Homer Barron is seen is when_____

_____

_____.

(Clarify)

her father which had <u>thwarted</u> her woman's life so many times had been too <u>virulent</u> and too furious to die.

FOCUS
Read to find out about Miss Emily's later years. **MARK IT UP** As you read, circle details that describe her appearance and actions.

When we next saw Miss Emily, she had grown fat and her hair was turning gray. During the next few years it grew grayer and grayer until it attained an even pepper-and-salt iron-gray, when it ceased turning. Up to the day of her death at seventy-four it was still that vigorous iron-gray, like the hair of an active man.

From that time on her front door remained closed, save for a period of six or seven years, when she was about forty, during which she gave lessons in china-painting. She fitted up a studio in one of the downstairs rooms, where the daughters and granddaughters of Colonel Sartoris' contemporaries were sent to her with the same regularity and in the same spirit that they were sent to church on Sundays with a twenty-five-cent piece for the collection plate. Meanwhile her taxes had been remitted.

Then the newer generation became the backbone and the spirit of the town, and the painting pupils grew up and fell away and did not send their children to her with boxes of color and <u>tedious</u> brushes and pictures cut from the ladies' magazines. The front door closed upon the last one and remained closed for good. When the town got free postal delivery, Miss Emily alone refused to let them fasten the metal numbers above her door and attach a mailbox to it. She would not listen to them.

Daily, monthly, yearly we watched the Negro grow grayer and more stooped, going in and out with the market basket. Each December we sent her a tax notice, which would be returned by the post office a week later, unclaimed. Now and then we would see her in one of the downstairs windows—she had evidently shut up the top floor of the house—like the carven torso of an idol in a niche,[16] looking or not looking at

---

16. **niche** (nĭch): an indented space in a wall.

WORDS TO KNOW	**thwart** (thwôrt) *v.* to block or hinder; prevent the fulfillment of **virulent** (vĭr′yə-lənt) *adj.* extremely poisonous or harmful **tedious** (tē′dē-əs) *adj.* boring because of dullness

us, we could never tell which. Thus she passed from generation to generation—dear, inescapable, impervious, tranquil, and perverse.

And so she died. Fell ill in the house filled with dust and shadows, with only a doddering Negro man to wait on her. We did not even know she was sick; we had long since given up trying to get any information from the Negro. He talked to no one, probably not even to her, for his voice had grown harsh and rusty, as if from disuse.

She died in one of the downstairs rooms, in a heavy walnut bed with a curtain, her gray head propped on a pillow yellow and moldy with age and lack of sunlight.

Pause & Reflect

V

FOCUS

Read to find out about Miss Emily's funeral and what the townspeople find in the locked room.

MARK IT UP As you read, circle any details that help you picture what is in this room.

The Negro met the first of the ladies at the front door and let them in, with their hushed, sibilant[17] voices and their quick, curious glances, and then he disappeared. He walked right through the house and out the back and was not seen again.

The two female cousins came at once. They held the funeral on the second day, with the town coming to look at Miss Emily beneath a mass of bought flowers, with the crayon face of her father musing <u>profoundly</u> above the bier[18] and the ladies sibilant and macabre; and the very old men—some in their brushed Confederate uniforms—on the porch and the lawn, talking of Miss Emily as if she had been a contemporary of theirs, believing that they had danced with her and courted her perhaps, confusing time with its mathematical progression, as the old do, to whom all the past is not a diminishing road but, instead, a huge meadow which no winter ever quite touches, divided from them now by the narrow bottle-neck of the most recent decade of years.

---

17. **sibilant** (sĭb′ə-lənt): making a hissing sound.

18. **bier** (bîr) a platform for a coffin.

WORDS
TO
KNOW
profoundly (prə-found′lē) *adv.* deeply; intensely

Pause & Reflect

1. Review the details you circled as you read. Then list two of Miss Emily's physical changes after Homer Barron disappears. **(Clarify)**

_____

_____

_____

_____

2. Which phrase below is true of Miss Emily in her later years? Circle or check it. **(Infer)**

allows a mailbox to be attached to her door

often visits the top floor of her house

frequently writes to Homer Barron

does not pay her taxes

READ ALOUD Lines 346–354

This passage, which is part of a long sentence, is beautifully written and rich in figurative language. It suggests a view of the past that Miss Emily may have shared. Notice the rhythm Faulkner creates by using present participles—*talking, believing, and confusing.*

1. What does Miss Emily's servant do after letting the ladies into the house? Underline the sentence on page 167 that tells the answer. **(Clarify)**

2. Review the details you circled as you read. Among the items in the room are "toilet things backed with . . . silver so tarnished that the monogram [the initials of a name] was obscured." Write the initials that are covered over. **(Infer)**

_____

_____

3. On the second pillow, a strand of hair is found. Whose hair is it? **(Infer)**

_____

_____

The whole town attends Miss Emily's funeral. The relationship, therefore, between Emily and the **narrator**, who represents the townspeople, is important. Mark passages that help you understand this relationship. What do you learn about the narrator and his or her attitude toward Miss Emily? How much does the narrator know? How does the narrator influence the reader's understanding of events?

Wrapping Up

If you are using **The Language of Literature,** you can now turn to the questions and activities on pages 525–526 of that book.

Already we knew that there was one room in that region above stairs which no one had seen in forty years, and which would have to be forced. They waited until Miss Emily was decently in the ground before they opened it.

The violence of breaking down the door seemed to fill this
360 room with pervading dust. A thin, acrid pall[19] as of the tomb seemed to lie everywhere upon this room decked and furnished as for a bridal:[20] upon the valance curtains of faded rose color, upon the rose-shaded lights, upon the dressing table, upon the delicate array of crystal and the man's toilet things backed with tarnished silver, silver so tarnished that the monogram was obscured. Among them lay a collar and tie, as if they had just been removed, which, lifted, left upon the surface a pale crescent in the dust. Upon a chair hung the suit, carefully folded; beneath it the two mute shoes and the
370 discarded socks.

The man himself lay in the bed.

For a long while we just stood there, looking down at the profound and fleshless grin. The body had apparently once lain in the attitude of an embrace, but now the long sleep that outlasts love, that conquers even the grimace of love, had cuckolded him.[21] What was left of him, rotted beneath what was left of the nightshirt, had become inextricable from the bed in which he lay; and upon him and upon the pillow beside him lay that even coating of the patient and
380 biding dust.

Then we noticed that in the second pillow was the indentation of a head. One of us lifted something from it, and leaning forward, that faint and invisible dust dry and acrid in the nostrils, we saw a long strand of iron-gray hair.

Pause & Reflect

_____

19. **acrid pall** (ăk′rĭd pôl′): bitter-smelling covering.

20. **bridal:** wedding.

21. **cuckolded him:** made his wife or lover unfaithful to him.

Active Reading SkillBuilder

Sequencing Events

Faulkner often shuffled the order of events in his stories by using flashbacks—scenes that interrupt the present action to describe events that took place at an earlier time. Sentences beginning with the words *when, after,* and *during* can help the reader follow Faulkner's unusual approach to **sequencing events.** After reading each part of the story, record on the lines below important events in Miss Emily's life. Write them in chronological order—the order in which they occurred in time. After reading the entire story, use the information you have recorded to complete the time line that has been started below. Examples are shown.

Part I *taxes remitted* *receives tax notice* *confronts aldermen* *Emily's funeral*

Part II _____ _____ _____ _____

Part III _____ _____ _____ _____

Part IV _____ _____ _____ _____

Part V _____ _____ _____ _____

Miss Emily's Life

taxes remitted

funeral

Literary Analysis SkillBuilder

Characterization

Characterization refers to the techniques writers use to develop characters. A writer may reveal a character through physical description; the character's actions, words, and feelings; the actions, words, and feelings of other characters; or the narrator's direct comments about a character. Fill in the following diagram with at least three specific examples of characterization in the story that help you learn more about Miss Emily. An example is shown.

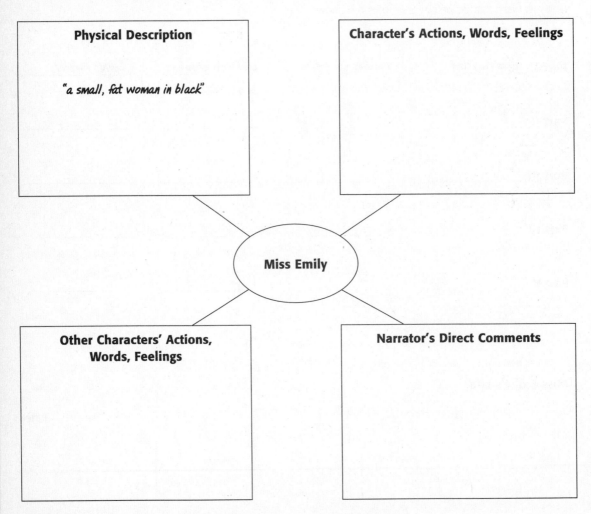

Physical Description

"a small, fat woman in black"

Character's Actions, Words, Feelings

Miss Emily

Other Characters' Actions, Words, Feelings

Narrator's Direct Comments

Follow Up: Compare your examples of characterization with those of your classmates. Then discuss which techniques Faulkner uses most effectively to reveal the character of Miss Emily.

Words to Know SkillBuilder

Words to Know

circumvent	diffident	encroach	pallid	temerity
coquettish	divulge	obliterate	profoundly	thwart
dank	edict	obscure	tedious	virulent

A. Decide which word from the word list belongs in each numbered blank. Then write the word on the blank line on the right. Use each word only once.

Resting at the edge of the forest, he heard the distant sounds of his pursuers. Their steady, lumbering progress showed their mindless determination to (1) his escape. He was afraid of the forest, (2) afraid, but the need to flee was deeper than that fear.

What had he done that was so terrible? Different as he was, he had liked these oddly shaped beings with their (3) skin the color of moonbeams and their small, glittering eyes. He had pitied them for the harshness of their rulers. Listening, unseen, to meetings of their high council, he had heard the secrets of their ruthless plans and then, foolishly, had the (4) to (5) those secrets.

He had done this only to help these creatures, and they had turned on him. Their unthinking obedience and their viciousness astounded him. Would he have been so brave if he had known how (6) the council's counterattack would be? It had issued an (7) that he was to be shot on sight. Now, hounded and persecuted, he had to get to the ship and the others.

The sun sent flirting glances, like those of a (8) maiden, through the hideous trees. Then the clouds and the horrible, flesh-colored leaves moved to (9) the light. Still, he waited in the dark, humid forest, its (10) air clinging to his face.

He didn't know whose land he was about to (11) upon, but trespassing did not concern him. It would take cleverness to (12) his pursuers. Had he managed to (13) his tracks, or did some small trace of them remain? If only he could find the ship!

Suddenly, there was a shuffling in the tall, stinging grass, and he whirled, weapon ready, only to see a tiny animal peeking out at him in a (14) way. Its bashfulness overcame its curiosity, and it hopped away. Relief left him almost faint. At just that moment, a hand grasped his shoulder—a glistening green hand, covered with scales. Three deep black eyes stared into his own.

"Here you are, Zanoz," said a voice like a saw. "At long last. It was beginning to get (15) waiting for you, and I do dislike being bored. Let's get out of here before the humans catch up with you."

(1) _____

(2) _____

(3) _____

(4) _____

(5) _____

(6) _____

(7) _____

(8) _____

(9) _____

(10) _____

(11) _____

(12) _____

(13) _____

(14) _____

(15) _____

B. Write a brief summary of "A Rose for Emily," using at least **six** of the Words to Know.

Before You Read

If you are using *The Language of Literature* . . .

- Use the information on page 580 of that book to prepare for reading.
- Look at the art on page 587 to help you **visualize** the **setting**.

Reading Tips

The author of this **short story** served in the Civil War and later worked as a journalist. As you might expect, some paragraphs read like those in a news story.

There are some long sentences and complicated paragraphs. When you come upon them, ask yourself one or more of the five "reporter's questions":

- *Who* is being described?
- *What* is happening?
- *Where* are the people positioned?
- *When* does the event occur?
- *Why* does it happen?

MARK IT UP KEEP TRACK

As you read, you can use these marks to keep track of your understanding.

✔..... I understand.

?..... I don't understand this.

!..... Interesting or surprising idea

AN OCCURRENCE AT OWL CREEK BRIDGE

Ambrose Bierce

PREVIEW This short story is set in Alabama during the Civil War (1861–1865). As the story begins, a Southern gentleman is about to be hanged by Federal, or Union, soldiers. With the rope around his neck and his final seconds ticking away, he suddenly thinks of a way to escape. Will he succeed?

I

FOCUS
The first three paragraphs of this story describe a scene in almost photographic detail. Read to find out about the soldiers and their prisoner.

MARK IT UP As you read, circle the details that suggest why the soldiers and the prisoner are on the bridge. An example is highlighted.

A man stood upon a railroad bridge in northern Alabama, looking down into the swift water twenty feet below. The man's hands were behind his back, the wrists bound with a cord. A rope closely encircled his neck. It was attached to a stout cross-timber above his head and the slack fell to the level of his knees. Some loose boards laid upon the sleepers[1] supporting the metals of the railway supplied a footing for him and his executioners—two private soldiers of the Federal army, directed by a sergeant who in civil life may have been a deputy sheriff. At a short remove upon the same temporary platform was an officer in the uniform of his rank, armed. He was a captain. A sentinel at each end of the bridge stood with his rifle in the position known as "support," that is to say, vertical in front of the left shoulder, the hammer resting on the forearm thrown straight across the chest—a formal and unnatural position, enforcing an erect carriage of the body. It did not appear to be the duty of these two men to know what was occurring at the center of

---

1. **sleepers:** railroad ties.

the bridge; they merely blockaded the two ends of the foot planking that traversed it.

Beyond one of the sentinels nobody was in sight; the railroad ran straight away into a forest for a hundred yards, then, curving, was lost to view. Doubtless there was an outpost farther along. The other bank of the stream was open ground—a gentle acclivity[2] topped with a stockade of vertical tree trunks, loopholed for rifles, with a single embrasure[3] through which protruded the muzzle of a brass cannon commanding the bridge. Midway of the slope between bridge and fort were the spectators—a single company of infantry in line, at "parade rest," the butts of the rifles on the ground, the barrels inclining slightly backward against the right shoulder, the hands crossed upon the stock. A lieutenant stood at the right of the line, the point of his sword upon the ground, his left hand resting upon his right. Excepting the group of four at the center of the bridge, not a man moved. The company faced the bridge, staring stonily, motionless. The sentinels, facing the banks of the stream, might have been statues to adorn the bridge. The captain stood with folded arms, silent, observing the work of his <u>subordinates</u>, but making no sign. Death is a dignitary who when he comes announced is to be received with formal manifestations of respect, even by those most familiar with him. In the code of military etiquette silence and fixity are forms of deference.[4]

The man who was engaged in being hanged was apparently about thirty-five years of age. He was a civilian, if one might judge from his habit, which was that of a planter.[5] His features were good—a straight nose, firm mouth, broad forehead, from which his long, dark hair was combed straight back, falling behind his ears to the collar of his well-fitting frock-coat. He wore a mustache and pointed beard, but no whiskers; his eyes were large and dark gray, and had a kindly expression which one would hardly have expected in one whose neck was in the hemp. Evidently this was no vulgar assassin.

---

2. **acclivity** (ə-klĭv′ĭ-tē): an upward slope of ground.

3. **embrasure** (ĕm-brā′zhər): an opening with the sides slanting outward to increase the angle of fire of a gun.

4. **deference** (dĕf′ər-əns): courteous respect.

5. **planter**: the owner of a plantation.

WORDS TO KNOW

subordinate (sə-bôr′dn-ĭt) *n.* one who is lower in rank

MARK IT UP WORD POWER

Mark words that you'd like to add to your **Personal Word List**. After reading, you can record the words and their meanings beginning on page 344.

MARK IT UP Lines 49–57

What details create a positive image of the prisoner? Underline these details. **(Evaluate)**

1. Review the details you circled as you read. Why are the soldiers and the prisoner on the bridge? **(Infer)**

_____

_____

_____

_____

2. Circle the word below that applies to the soldiers. **(Clarify)**

amused   noisy

motionless   bored

The liberal military code makes provision for hanging many kinds of persons, and gentlemen are not excluded.

Pause & Reflect

60 **FOCUS**
The prisoner is standing on the bridge with a noose around his neck. Read to find out about his thoughts and sensations.

The preparations being complete, the two private soldiers stepped aside and each drew away the plank upon which he had been standing. The sergeant turned to the captain, saluted and placed himself immediately behind that officer, who in turn moved apart one pace. These movements left the condemned man and the sergeant standing on the two ends of the same plank, which spanned three of the cross-ties of the bridge. The end upon which the **70** civilian stood almost, but not quite, reached a fourth. This plank had been held in place by the weight of the captain; it was now held by that of the sergeant. At a signal from the former the latter would step aside, the plank would tilt and the condemned man go down between two ties. The arrangement commended itself to his judgment as simple and effective. His face had not been covered nor his eyes bandaged. He looked a moment at his "unsteadfast footing," then let his gaze wander to the swirling water of the stream racing madly beneath his feet. A piece of dancing driftwood **80** caught his attention and his eyes followed it down the current. How slowly it appeared to move! What a sluggish stream!

He closed his eyes in order to fix his last thoughts upon his wife and children. The water, touched to gold by the early sun, the brooding mists under the banks at some distance down the stream, the fort, the soldiers, the piece of drift—all had distracted him. And now he became conscious of a new disturbance. Striking through the thought of his dear ones was a sound which he could neither ignore nor understand, a sharp, distinct, metallic percussion like the stroke of a **90** blacksmith's hammer upon the anvil; it had the same ringing quality. He wondered what it was, and whether immeasurably distant or near by—it seemed both. Its recurrence was regular, but as slow as the tolling of a death knell.[6] He awaited each

---

6. **tolling of a death knell:** the slow, steady ringing of a bell at a funeral.

stroke with impatience and—he knew not why—apprehension. The intervals of silence grew progressively longer; the delays became maddening. With their greater infrequency the sounds increased in strength and sharpness. They hurt his ear like the thrust of a knife; he feared he would shriek. What he heard was the ticking of his watch.

100   He unclosed his eyes and saw again the water below him. "If I could free my hands," he thought, "I might throw off the noose and spring into the stream. By diving I could <u>evade</u> the bullets and, swimming vigorously, reach the bank, take to the woods and get away home. My home, thank God, is as yet outside their lines; my wife and little ones are still beyond the invader's farthest advance."

    As these thoughts, which have here to be set down in words, were flashed into the doomed man's brain rather than evolved from it the captain nodded to the sergeant. The 110 sergeant stepped aside.

Pause & Reflect

II

FOCUS
This section—a **flashback**—interrupts the action of the story to describe earlier events. Read to find out about the prisoner, Peyton Farquhar, before his capture.

MARK IT UP As you read, circle details that help you learn about his character.

120

Peyton Farquhar was a well-to-do planter, of an old and highly respected Alabama family. Being a slave owner and like other slave owners a politician he was naturally an original secessionist[7] and ardently devoted to the Southern cause. Circumstances of an imperious nature, which it is unnecessary to relate here, had prevented him from taking service with the gallant army that had fought the disastrous campaigns ending with the fall of Corinth,[8] and he chafed under the inglorious

---

7. **secessionist** (sǐ-sěsh'ə-nǐst): one who supported the withdrawal of Southern states from the Union.

8. **Corinth**: a town in Mississippi that was the site of a Civil War battle in 1862.

WORDS
TO
KNOW
    evade (ǐ-vād') v. to escape or avoid

Pause & Reflect

1. Circle the phrase below that tells what the prisoner tries to fix his thoughts on. **(Clarify)**

  boyhood friends

  his parents

  his wife and children

  the Confederate flag

MARK IT UP **2.** What sound tortures the prisoner as he closes his eyes? Underline the phrase at the top of this page that answers the question. **(Clarify)**

3. Why does the captain nod to the sergeant? **(Infer)**

_____

_____

_____

_____

restraint, longing for the release of his energies, the larger life of the soldier, the opportunity for distinction. That opportunity, he felt, would come, as it comes to all in war time. Meanwhile he did what he could. No service was too humble for him to perform in aid of the South, no adventure too perilous for him to undertake if consistent with the character of a civilian who was at heart a soldier, and who in good faith and without too
130 much qualification assented to at least a part of the frankly villainous dictum that all is fair in love and war.

One evening while Farquhar and his wife were sitting on a rustic bench near the entrance to his grounds, a gray-clad soldier rode up to the gate and asked for a drink of water. Mrs. Farquhar was only too happy to serve him with her own white hands. While she was fetching the water her husband approached the dusty horseman and inquired eagerly for news from the front.

"The Yanks are repairing the railroads," said the man,
140 "and are getting ready for another advance. They have reached the Owl Creek bridge, put it in order and built a stockade on the north bank. The commandant has issued an order, which is posted everywhere, declaring that any civilian caught interfering with the railroad, its bridges, tunnels or trains will be <u>summarily</u> hanged. I saw the order."

"How far is it to the Owl Creek bridge?" Farquhar asked.

"About thirty miles."

"Is there no force on this side the creek?"

"Only a picket post[9] half a mile out, on the railroad, and a
150 single sentinel at this end of the bridge."

"Suppose a man—a civilian and student of hanging—should elude the picket post and perhaps get the better of the sentinel," said Farquhar, smiling, "what could he accomplish?"

The soldier reflected. "I was there a month ago," he replied. "I observed that the flood of last winter had lodged a great quantity of driftwood against the wooden pier at this end of the bridge. It is now dry and would burn like tow."[10]

---

9. **picket post:** the camp of soldiers who are assigned to guard against a surprise attack.

10. **tow:** coarse, dry fiber.

WORDS
TO
KNOW

summarily (sə-mĕr′ə-lē) *adv.* in a way that is quick and bypasses usual procedures

The lady had now brought the water, which the soldier
160 drank. He thanked her ceremoniously, bowed to her husband
and rode away. An hour later, after nightfall, he repassed the
plantation, going northward in the direction from which he
had come. He was a Federal scout.

Pause & Reflect

III

FOCUS
Read to find out what
happens to Farquhar
shortly after he falls
through the bridge.
MARK IT UP As you
read, underline details
that describe his
sensations.

As Peyton Farquhar fell straight
downward through the bridge he
lost consciousness and was as one
already dead. From this state he was
awakened—ages later, it seemed to
him—by the pain of a sharp pressure
upon his throat, followed by a sense of
suffocation. Keen, poignant[11] agonies
seemed to shoot from his neck downward through every fiber
of his body and limbs. These pains appeared to flash along
well-defined lines of ramification[12] and to beat with an
inconceivably rapid periodicity.[13] They seemed like streams of
pulsating fire heating him to an intolerable temperature. As to
his head, he was conscious of nothing but a feeling of
fullness—of congestion. These sensations were unaccompanied
by thought. The intellectual part of his nature was already
180 effaced; he had power only to feel, and feeling was torment.
He was conscious of motion. Encompassed in a luminous
cloud, of which he was now merely the fiery heart, without
material substance, he swung through unthinkable arcs of
oscillation, like a vast pendulum. Then all at once, with
terrible suddenness, the light about him shot upward with the
noise of a loud plash; a frightful roaring was in his ears, and
all was cold and dark. The power of thought was restored; he
knew that the rope had broken and he had fallen into the
stream. There was no additional strangulation; the noose
190 about his neck was already suffocating him and kept the
water from his lungs. To die of hanging at the bottom of a

---

11. **poignant** (poin′yənt): physically painful.
12. **flash . . . ramification:** spread out rapidly along branches from a
    central point.
13. **periodicity** (pĭr′ē-ə-dĭs′ĭ-tē): recurring at regular intervals.

Owl Creek Bridge **177**

Pause & **Reflect**

1. Review the details that you
circled as you read. Why does
Farquhar want to be a soldier?
(Infer)

_____

_____

_____

_____

2. Reread the boxed sentences on
page 176. What do you think
Farquhar did that led to his
arrest? **(Draw Conclusions)**

_____

_____

_____

_____

3. Why is it important that the man
who stops for a drink is a
Federal scout, not a Confederate
soldier? **(Cause and Effect)**

_____

_____

_____

_____

river!—the idea seemed to him <u>ludicrous</u>. He opened his eyes in the darkness and saw above him a gleam of light, but how distant, how <u>inaccessible</u>! He was still sinking, for the light became fainter and fainter until it was a mere glimmer. Then it began to grow and brighten, and he knew that he was rising toward the surface—knew it with reluctance, for he was now very comfortable. "To be hanged and drowned," he thought, "that is not so bad; but I do not wish to be shot. No; I will

200 not be shot; that is not fair."

He was not conscious of an effort, but a sharp pain in his wrist <u>apprised</u> him that he was trying to free his hands. He gave the struggle his attention, as an idler might observe the feat of a juggler, without interest in the outcome. What splendid effort!—what magnificent, what superhuman strength! Ah, that was a fine endeavor! Bravo! The cord fell away; his arms parted and floated upward, the hands dimly seen on each side in the growing light. He watched them with a new interest as first one and then the other pounced upon

210 the noose at his neck. They tore it away and thrust it fiercely aside, its undulations resembling those of a water-snake. "Put it back, put it back!" He thought he shouted these words to his hands, for the undoing of the noose had been succeeded by the direst pang that he had yet experienced. His neck ached horribly; his brain was on fire; his heart, which had been fluttering faintly, gave a great leap, trying to force itself out at his mouth. His whole body was racked and wrenched with an insupportable anguish![14] But his disobedient hands gave no heed to the command. They beat the water vigorously with

220 quick, downward strokes, forcing him to the surface. He felt his head emerge; his eyes were blinded by the sunlight; his chest expanded convulsively, and with a supreme and crowning agony his lungs engulfed a great draught of air, which instantly he expelled in a shriek!

He was now in full possession of his physical senses. They were, indeed, <u>preternaturally</u> keen and alert. Something in the awful disturbance of his organic system had so exalted and

---

14. **racked . . . anguish:** stretched and twisted with unendurable physical pain.

MARK IT UP **KEEP TRACK**

Remember to use these marks to keep track of your understanding.

✔ ..... I understand.

? ..... I don't understand this.

! ..... Interesting or surprising idea

WORDS TO KNOW	**ludicrous** (lōō'dĭ-krəs) *adj.* laughably absurd; ridiculous
	inaccessible (ĭn'ăk-sĕs'ə-bəl) *adj.* not obtained easily, if at all; unreachable
	apprise (ə-prīz') *v.* to give notice to; inform
	preternaturally (prē'tər-năch'ər-əl-ē) *adv.* more than naturally; extraordinarily

refined them that they made record of things never before perceived. He felt the ripples upon his face and heard their
230 separate sounds as they struck. He looked at the forest on the bank of the stream, saw the individual trees, the leaves and the veining of each leaf—saw the very insects upon them: the locusts, the brilliant-bodied flies, the gray spiders stretching their webs from twig to twig. He noted the prismatic colors[15] in all the dewdrops upon a million blades of grass. The humming of the gnats that danced above the eddies of the stream, the beating of the dragon-flies' wings, the strokes of the water-spiders' legs, like oars which had lifted their boat—all these made audible music. A fish slid along beneath his
240 eyes and he heard the rush of its body parting the water.

Pause & Reflect

FOCUS

Farquhar reaches the surface of the water. Read to find out what happens as the soldiers try to gun him down.

MARK IT UP As you read, list key events in the margins.

He had come to the surface facing down the stream; in a moment the visible world seemed to wheel slowly round, himself the pivotal point, and he saw the bridge, the fort, the soldiers upon the bridge, the captain, the sergeant, the two privates, his executioners. They were in silhouette against the blue sky. They shouted and gesticulated,[16]
250 pointing at him. The captain had drawn his pistol, but did not fire; the others were unarmed. Their movements were grotesque and horrible, their forms gigantic.

Suddenly he heard a sharp report and something struck the water smartly within a few inches of his head, spattering his face with spray. He heard a second report, and saw one of the sentinels with his rifle at his shoulder, a light cloud of blue smoke rising from the muzzle. The man in the water saw the eye of the man on the bridge gazing into his own through the sights of the rifle. He observed that it was a gray eye and
260 remembered having read that gray eyes were keenest, and that all famous marksmen had them. Nevertheless, this one had missed.

---

15. **prismatic colors** (prĭz-mătˈĭk): basic colors produced by passing light through a prism.
16. **gesticulated** (jĕ-stĭkˈyə-lātˈĭd): gestured with the hands.

Pause & Reflect

 MARK IT UP **1.** Review the details you underlined as you read. Then tell what happens to Farquhar after he falls through the bridge. **(Summarize)**

_____

_____

_____

_____

2. What happens to the rope around Farquhar's neck? **(Clarify)**

_____

_____

_____

_____

 MARK IT UP **3.** Reread the boxed sentences on this page. They suggest that Farquhar's senses are amazingly sharp. Underline details that show his heightened sense of hearing. **(Supporting Details)**

A counter-swirl had caught Farquhar and turned him half round; he was again looking into the forest on the bank opposite the fort. The sound of a clear, high voice in a monotonous singsong now rang out behind him and came across the water with a distinctness that pierced and subdued all other sounds, even the beating of the ripples in his ears. Although no soldier, he had frequented camps enough to

270   know the dread significance of that deliberate, drawling, aspirated chant; the lieutenant on shore was taking a part in the morning's work. How coldly and pitilessly—with what an even, calm intonation, presaging,[17] and enforcing tranquillity in the men—with what accurately measured intervals fell those cruel words:

"Attention, company! . . . Shoulder arms! . . . Ready! . . . Aim! . . . Fire!"

Farquhar dived—dived as deeply as he could. The water roared in his ears like the voice of Niagara, yet he heard the

280   dulled thunder of the volley and, rising again toward the surface, met shining bits of metal, singularly flattened, oscillating slowly downward. Some of them touched him on the face and hands, then fell away, continuing their descent. One lodged between his collar and neck; it was uncomfortably warm and he snatched it out.

As he rose to the surface, gasping for breath, he saw that he had been a long time under water; he was <u>perceptibly</u> farther down stream—nearer to safety. The soldiers had almost finished reloading; the metal ramrods flashed all at once in the

290   sunshine as they were drawn from the barrels, turned in the air, and thrust into their sockets. The two sentinels fired again, independently and ineffectually.

The hunted man saw all this over his shoulder; he was now swimming vigorously with the current. His brain was as energetic as his arms and legs; he thought with the rapidity of lightning.

"The officer," he reasoned, "will not make that martinet's[18] error a second time. It is as easy to dodge a volley as a single

---

17. **presaging** (prĕs′ĭj-ĭng): predicting.

18. **martinet** (mär′tn-ĕt′): strict disciplinarian; one who demands that regulations be followed exactly.

MARK IT UP **WORD POWER**

Remember to mark words that you'd like to add to your **Personal Word List**. Later, you can record the words and their meanings beginning on page 344.

WORDS
TO
KNOW

perceptibly (pər-sĕp′tə-blē) *adv.* in a way that can be perceived by the senses or the mind; noticeably

shot. He has probably already given the command to fire at
⬤300 will. God help me, I cannot dodge them all!"

An appalling plash within two yards of him was followed
by a loud, rushing sound, *diminuendo*,[19] which seemed to
travel back through the air to the fort and died in an
explosion which stirred the very river to its deeps! A rising
sheet of water curved over him, fell down upon him, blinded
him, strangled him! The cannon had taken a hand in the
game. As he shook his head free from the commotion of the
smitten water he heard the deflected shot humming through
the air ahead, and in an instant it was cracking and smashing
⬤310 the branches in the forest beyond.

"They will not do that again," he thought; "the next time
they will use a charge of grape.[20] I must keep my eye upon the
gun; the smoke will apprise me—the report arrives too late; it
lags behind the missile. That is a good gun."

Suddenly he felt himself whirled round and round—
spinning like a top. The water, the banks, the forests, the now
distant bridge, fort and men—all were commingled and
blurred. Objects were represented by their colors only;
circular horizontal streaks of color—that was all he saw. He
⬤320 had been caught in a vortex[21] and was being whirled on with
a velocity of advance and gyration that made him giddy and
sick. In a few moments he was flung upon the gravel at the
foot of the left bank of the stream—the southern bank—and
behind a projecting point which concealed him from his
enemies. The sudden arrest of his motion, the abrasion of one
of his hands on the gravel, restored him, and he wept with
delight. He dug his fingers into the sand, threw it over himself
in handfuls and audibly blessed it. It looked like diamonds,
rubies, emeralds; he could think of nothing beautiful which it
⬤330 did not resemble. The trees upon the bank were giant garden
plants; he noted a definite order in their arrangement, inhaled
the fragrance of their blooms. A strange, roseate light shone
through the spaces among their trunks and the wind made in
their branches the music of æolian harps.[22] He had no wish
to perfect his escape—was content to remain in that

READ ALOUD **Lines 315–325**

Read aloud the boxed passage
on this page. Then circle the
word or phrase below that
completes the following
sentence correctly:

Farquhar finally escapes the
soldiers mainly because of his

cleverness

swimming skills

luck

(Draw Conclusions)

---

19. *diminuendo* (dǐ-mǐn′yōō-ĕn′dō) *Italian:* gradually decreasing in loudness.

20. **grape:** short for *grapeshot*, a cluster of several small iron balls fired in one
    shot from a cannon.

21. **vortex:** a whirlpool or spinning water.

22. **music of æolian** (ē-ō′lē-ən) **harps:** heavenly music.

1. Review the list of key events that
you wrote in the margin. Why
are the soldiers unsuccessful in
their attempts to shoot
Farquhar? **(Cause and Effect)**

_____

_____

_____

_____

2. Do you think Farquhar will get
back home safely? *Yes / No,*
because_____

_____

_____ .

(Predict)

enchanting spot until retaken.

A whiz and rattle of grapeshot among the branches high
above his head roused him from his dream. The baffled
cannoneer had fired him a random farewell. He sprang to his
340 feet, rushed up the sloping bank, and plunged into the forest.

Pause **&** **Reflect**

> **FOCUS**
> Read to find out what
> finally happens to
> Farquhar.

All that day he traveled, laying his course
by the rounding sun. The forest seemed
<u>interminable</u>; nowhere did he discover a
break in it, not even a woodman's road.
He had not known that he lived in so
wild a region. There was something uncanny in the revelation.

By night fall he was fatigued, footsore, famishing. The
thought of his wife and children urged him on. At last he
found a road which led him in what he knew to be the right
350 direction. It was as wide and straight as a city street, yet it
seemed untraveled. No fields bordered it, no dwelling
anywhere. Not so much as the barking of a dog suggested
human habitation. The black bodies of the trees formed a
straight wall on both sides, terminating on the horizon in a
point, like a diagram in a lesson in perspective. Overhead, as
he looked up through this rift in the wood, shone great golden
stars looking unfamiliar and grouped in strange constellations.
He was sure they were arranged in some order which had a
secret and malign[23] significance. The wood on either side was
360 full of singular noises, among which—once, twice, and again,
he distinctly heard whispers in an unknown tongue.

His neck was in pain and lifting his hand to it he found it
horribly swollen. He knew that it had a circle of black where
the rope had bruised it. His eyes felt congested; he could no
longer close them. His tongue was swollen with thirst;
he relieved its fever by thrusting it forward from between his
teeth into the cold air. How softly the turf had carpeted the
untraveled avenue—he could no longer feel the roadway
beneath his feet!

---

23. **malign** (mə-līn′): evil; harmful; threatening harm or evil.

WORDS
TO
KNOW   **interminable** (ĭn-tûr′mə-nə-bəl) *adj.* endless

370   Doubtless, despite his suffering, he had fallen asleep while walking, for now he sees another scene—perhaps he has merely recovered from a delirium.[24] He stands at the gate of his own home. All is as he left it, and all bright and beautiful in the morning sunshine. He must have traveled the entire night. As he pushes open the gate and passes up the wide white walk, he sees a flutter of female garments; his wife, looking fresh and cool and sweet, steps down from the veranda to meet him. At the bottom of the steps she stands waiting, with a smile of <u>ineffable</u> joy, an attitude of matchless

380 grace and dignity. Ah, how beautiful she is! He springs forward with extended arms. As he is about to clasp her he feels a stunning blow upon the back of the neck; a blinding white light blazes all about him with a sound like the shock of a cannon—then all is darkness and silence!

     Peyton Farquhar was dead; his body, with a broken neck, swung gently from side to side beneath the timbers of the Owl Creek bridge.

Pause Reflect

Pause & Reflect

MARK IT UP   **1.** Reread the boxed sentences on page 182. What details make the surroundings look unreal? Circle these details. **(Analyze)**

2. What kills Farquhar? **(Infer)**

_____

_____

_____

_____

3. Did you like the ending of this story? _Yes / No,_ because _____

_____

_____

_____

_____ .

(Connect)

CHALLENGE

Irony is a contrast between what is expected and what actually occurs. Bierce's finest stories show the ironies of war. One irony in this story is that the prisoner is not a "vulgar assassin," but a well-bred gentleman. Mark other examples of irony in this story. What **theme,** or message, about war do these ironies suggest? **(Analyze)**

Wrapping Up

If you are using **The Language of Literature,** you can now move to the questions and activities on pages 591–592.

---

24. **delirium** (dĭ-lîr′ē-əm): a temporary state of extreme mental confusion, marked by hallucinations.

WORDS
TO
KNOW   **ineffable** (ĭn-ĕf′ə-bəl) *adj.* unable to be expressed in words

Active Reading SkillBuilder

Analyzing Structure

The **structure** of a work of literature is the arrangement of its parts. This story, for example, is arranged in three numbered sections. Each section signals a change in time. To help keep track of the sequence of events in the story and to clarify what happens, use the chart below to record your responses to the reading strategy questions. An example is shown.

Reading Strategy Questions	Answers
Section I Whose thoughts and feelings does the narrator relate?	*the thoughts and feelings of the condemned man*
What does the captain's nod mean?	
Section II When do these events occur and what do they explain?	
Section III Would these be the thoughts of a man on the brink of death?	
Can you account for the changes in the surroundings?	
What kills Farquhar?	

Literary Analysis SkillBuilder

Point of View

Point of view is the perspective from which events in a story are narrated. The first three paragraphs of this story are told from a **third-person omniscient,** or all-knowing, point of view. In the fourth paragraph, the perspective shifts to focus on Farquhar's personal thoughts and sensations. This focus on one person's inner life is called **third-person limited** point of view. Identify the point of view in sections II and III of the story. Indicate where the point of view shifts. An example is shown.

Section II

Point of View: *third person limited*

Where It Shifts:
Line:
Page

New Point of View:

Section III

Point of View:

Where It Shifts:
Line:
Page:

New Point of View:

Follow Up: Why do you think Bierce did not use a consistent point of view to tell this story?

Words to Know SkillBuilder

Words to Know

apprise	inaccessible	interminable	perceptibly	subordinate
evade	ineffable	ludicrous	preternaturally	summarily

A. Fill in each set of blanks with the correct word from the word list. The boxed letters will spell out a word that describes the forces Peyton Farquhar supports.

1. This describes Chicken Little's belief that the sky was falling or the idea of a cow jumping over the moon.

   _ _ _ _ □ _ □ _ _

2. This describes your emotion when you are speechless with dismay, happiness, or fear.

   _ □ _ _ □ _ _ _ _

3. This is what the pyramid builders hoped would describe the treasures hidden in the pharaohs' tombs.

   _ _ _ _ _ _ □ _ _ _ _

4. This is a private to a sergeant, a sergeant to a captain, and a captain to a colonel.

   _ _ _ _ _ _ □ _ _ _ _ □

5. This is how shocked you are when you gasp and how sleepy you are when you yawn.

   _ _ □ _ _ _ _ _ _ _ _

6. This is how people wed when they elope and how people execute prisoners when they lynch them.

   _ _ _ _ □ _ _ _ _

7. This describes the motion of the waves, the spinning of the Earth, and what a boring lecture seems to be.

   _ _ □ _ _ _ _ _ _ _ _ □

Write the word the boxed letters spell out. _____

B. Fill in each blank with the correct word from the word list.

1. Sleeping Beauty snoozed for a _____ long time.

2. People tend to give up if their goals seem _____.

3. Warning signs _____ the public of danger.

4. A gazelle's speed helps it _____ a pursuing lion.

5. A giggling person is _____ amused.

C. Write the report the captain might have submitted to his superior officer regarding the occurrence at Owl Creek Bridge. Use at least **four** of the Words to Know.

from LIFE ON THE
Mississippi

M A R K   T W A I N

PREVIEW In this excerpt, Mark Twain recalls his on-the-job training as a riverboat pilot on the *Paul Jones*. The **setting** is the Mississippi River in 1856, when Twain was 21. He tells how a famous riverboat pilot, Mr. Bixby, taught him the art of steering a riverboat, even at night. He describes how his view of the river changed as he learned to look at it with a trained eye.

MEMOIR

Before You Read

If you are using *The Language of Literature* . . .

- Use the information on page 669 of that book to prepare for reading.

- Look at the picture on page 671 to get an idea of what riverboats looked like in the 1850s.

Reading Tips

A **memoir** is a form of **autobiographical writing** in which a person recalls actual events in his or her life.

- The first two sections are like brief stories. Read them as you would any other **narratives.** Pay close attention to what happens and when. Keep track of the **sequence** of events.

- The third section relies more on **description.** You may find it difficult because of its long sentences and many details. As you read, slow down your pace. Picture in your mind what the author describes.

FOCUS

Twain tells how he came to be a pilot in training on a riverboat. Read to find out how young Twain does his first day on the job.

MARK IT UP As you read, circle details that show his difficulty in steering the riverboat. An example is highlighted on page 188.

A Cub-Pilot's Experience

What with lying on the rocks four days at Louisville, and some other delays, the poor old *Paul Jones* fooled away about two weeks in making the voyage from Cincinnati to New Orleans. This gave me a chance to get acquainted with one of the pilots, and he taught me how to steer the boat, and thus made the fascination

10 of river life more potent than ever for me. . . .

I soon discovered two things. One was that a vessel would not be likely to sail for the mouth of the Amazon under ten or twelve years; and the other was that the nine or ten dollars still left in my pocket would not suffice for so impossible an exploration as I had planned, even if I could afford to wait for a ship. Therefore it followed that I must contrive a new career. The *Paul Jones* was now bound for St. Louis. I planned a siege against my pilot, and at the end of three hard days he surrendered. He agreed to teach me the Mississippi River from

20 New Orleans to St. Louis for five hundred dollars, payable out of the first wages I should receive after graduating. I entered upon the small enterprise of "learning" twelve or

---

MARK IT UP **KEEP TRACK**

As you read, you can use these marks to keep track of your understanding.

✔ ..... I understand.

? ..... I don't understand this.

! ..... Interesting or surprising idea

thirteen hundred miles of the great Mississippi River with the easy confidence of my time of life. If I had really known what I was about to require of my faculties,[1] I should not have had the courage to begin. I supposed that all a pilot had to do was to keep his boat in the river, and I did not consider that that could be much of a trick, since it was so wide.

The boat backed out from New Orleans at four in the afternoon, and it was "our watch" until eight. Mr. Bixby, my chief, "straightened her up," plowed her along past the sterns of the other boats that lay at the Levee,[2] and then said, "Here, take her; shave those steamships as close as you'd peel an apple." I took the wheel, and my heartbeat fluttered up into the hundreds; for it seemed to me that we were about to scrape the side off every ship in the line, we were so close. I held my breath and began to claw the boat away from the danger; and I had my own opinion of the pilot who had known no better than to get us into such peril, but I was too wise to express it. In half a minute I had a wide margin of safety intervening between the *Paul Jones* and the ships; and within ten seconds more I was set aside in disgrace, and Mr. Bixby was going into danger again and flaying me alive with abuse of my cowardice. I was stung, but I was obliged to admire the easy confidence with which my chief loafed from side to side of his wheel, and trimmed the ships so closely that disaster seemed ceaselessly imminent.[3] When he had cooled a little he told me that the easy water was close ashore and the current outside, and therefore we must hug the bank, upstream, to get the benefit of the former, and stay well out, downstream, to take advantage of the latter. In my own mind I resolved to be a downstream pilot and leave the upstreaming to people dead to prudence.[4]

Now and then Mr. Bixby called my attention to certain things. Said he, "This is Six-Mile Point." I assented. It was pleasant enough information, but I could not see the bearing of it. I was not conscious that it was a matter of any interest to me. Another time he said, "This is Nine-Mile Point." Later he said, "This is Twelve-Mile Point." They were all about level with the water's edge; they all looked about alike to me;

✎ **MARK IT UP** WORD POWER

Mark words that you'd like to add to your **Personal Word List**. After reading, you can record the words and their meanings beginning on page 344.

---

1. **faculties:** abilities.
2. **Levee** (lĕv′ē): a landing place for boats on a river.
3. **imminent** (ĭm′ə-nənt): about to happen.
4. **dead to prudence:** lacking good judgment.

they were monotonously unpicturesque. I hoped Mr. Bixby would change the subject. But no; he would crowd up around a point, hugging the shore with affection, and then say: "The slack water ends here, abreast this bunch of China trees; now we cross over." So he crossed over. He gave me the wheel once or twice, but I had no luck. I either came near chipping off the edge of a sugar plantation, or I yawed⁵ too far from shore, and so dropped back into disgrace again and got abused.

70 The watch was ended at last, and we took supper and went to bed. At midnight the glare of a lantern shone in my eyes, and the night watchman said, "Come, turn out!" And then he left. I could not understand this extraordinary procedure; so I presently gave up trying to, and dozed off to sleep. Pretty soon the watchman was back again, and this time he was gruff. I was annoyed. I said,

"What do you want to come bothering around here in the middle of the night for? Now, as like as not, I'll not get to sleep again to-night."

80 The watchman said, "Well, if this ain't good, I'm blessed."

The "offwatch" was just turning in, and I heard some brutal laughter from them, and such remarks as "Hello, watchman! ain't the new cub turned out yet? He's delicate, likely. Give him some sugar in a rag, and send for the chambermaid to sing 'Rock-a-by Baby' to him."

About this time Mr. Bixby appeared on the scene. Something like a minute later I was climbing the pilothouse steps with some of my clothes on and the rest in my arms. Mr. Bixby was close behind, commenting. Here was something

90 fresh⁶—this thing of getting up in the middle of the night to go to work. It was a detail in piloting that had never occurred to me at all. I knew that boats ran all night, but somehow I had never happened to reflect that somebody had to get up out of a warm bed to run them. I began to fear that piloting was not quite so romantic as I had imagined it was; there was something very real and worklike about this new phase of it. . . .

Pause & Reflect

Pause & Reflect

1. Review the details you circled as you read. What mistakes did Twain make in steering the riverboat? **(Draw Conclusions)**

_____

_____

_____

_____

2. What does Mr. Bixby call young Twain's attention to as they go up the river? **(Clarify)**

_____

_____

_____

_____

READ ALOUD 3. Read aloud the boxed passage on this page. Then circle the phrase below that tells how the other crew members view young Twain. **(Infer)**

with affection

with mockery

with respect

---

5. **yawed:** swerved.

6. **fresh:** new.

FOCUS

Mr. Bixby steers the riverboat through the dark night. Read to find out why Mr. Bixby gets angry at young Twain and what happens as a result.

100

Mr. Bixby made for the shore and soon was scraping it, just the same as if it had been daylight. And not only that, but singing:

Father in heaven, the day is declining, etc.

It seemed to me that I had put my life in the keeping of a peculiarly reckless outcast. Presently he turned on me and said, "What's the name of the first point above New Orleans?"

I was gratified to be able to answer promptly, and I did. I said I didn't know.

"Don't *know?*"

110 This manner jolted me. I was down at the foot[7] again, in a moment. But I had to say just what I had said before.

"Well, you're a smart one!" said Mr. Bixby. "What's the name of the *next* point?"

Once more I didn't know.

"Well, this beats anything. Tell me the name of *any* point or place I told you."

I studied awhile and decided that I couldn't.

"Look here! What do you start out from, above Twelve-Mile Point, to cross over?"

120 "I—I—don't know."

"You—you—don't know?" mimicking my drawling manner of speech. "What *do* you know?"

"I—I—nothing, for certain."

"By the great Caesar's ghost, I believe you! You're the stupidest dunderhead I ever saw or ever heard of, so help me Moses! The idea of *you* being a pilot—you! Why, you don't know enough to pilot a cow down a lane."

Oh, but his wrath was up! He was a nervous man, and he shuffled from one side of his wheel to the other as if the floor 130 was hot. He would boil awhile to himself, and then overflow and scald me again.

"Look here! What do you suppose I told you the names of those points for?"

I tremblingly considered a moment, and then the devil of temptation provoked me to say, "Well to—to—be entertaining, I thought."

7. **down at the foot:** at the bottom of the class.

This was a red rag to the bull. He raged and stormed so (he was crossing the river at the time) that I judged it made him blind, because he ran over the steering oar of a trading scow.[8] Of course the traders sent up a volley of red-hot profanity. Never was a man so grateful as Mr. Bixby was, because he was brimful, and here were subjects who could *talk back*. He threw open a window, thrust his head out, and such an irruption followed as I never had heard before. The fainter and farther away the scowmen's curses drifted, the higher Mr. Bixby lifted his voice and the weightier his adjectives grew. When he closed the window he was empty. You could have drawn a seine[9] through his system and not caught curses enough to disturb your mother with. Presently he said to me in the gentlest way, "My boy, you must get a little memorandum book; and every time I tell you a thing, put it down right away. There's only one way to be a pilot, and that is to get this entire river by heart. You have to know it just like A B C."

That was a dismal revelation to me, for my memory was never loaded with anything but blank cartridges. However, I did not feel discouraged long. I judged that it was best to make some allowances, for doubtless Mr. Bixby was "stretching."[10] . . .

By the time we had gone seven or eight hundred miles up the river, I had learned to be a tolerably plucky upstream steersman, in daylight; and before we reached St. Louis I had made a trifle of progress in night work, but only a trifle. I had a notebook that fairly bristled with the names of towns, "points," bars, islands, bends, reaches, etc.; but the information was to be found only in the notebook—none of it was in my head. It made my heart ache to think I had only got half of the river set down; for as our watch was four hours off and four hours on, day and night, there was a long four-hour gap in my book for every time I had slept since the voyage began. . . .

Pause & *Reflect*

Pause & Reflect

1. Mr. Bixby gets angry at young Twain because _____ _____ _____.

Filled with anger, Mr. Bixby makes the mistake of _____ _____ _____.

(Cause and Effect)

2. What does young Twain jot down in his notebook? **(Clarify)**

_____ _____ _____ _____

3. What grade should young Twain get as a student pilot? Jot down the grade you would give him and the reason why. **(Evaluate)**

_____ _____ _____

---

8. **scow:** a flat-bottomed boat used chiefly to transport freight.

9. **seine** (sān): large fishing net.

10. **"stretching":** exaggerating.

READ ALOUD Lines 178–188

Twain says that the Mississippi River is more fascinating than a book. In this passage, Twain creates a rolling rhythm by repeating the word *never* and by using parallel word groups.

MARK IT UP KEEP TRACK

Remember to use these marks to keep track of your understanding.

✔ ..... I understand.

? ..... I don't understand this.

! ..... Interesting or surprising idea

FOCUS

Twain compares the Mississippi River to a book. He then tells what he has gained and what he has lost by learning his trade.

MARK IT UP As you read, underline any details that help you understand what he has gained and what he has lost.

... **The face of the water,** in time, became a wonderful book—a book that was a dead language to the uneducated passenger, but which told its mind to me without reserve, delivering its most cherished secrets as clearly as if it uttered them with a voice. And it was not a book to be read once and thrown aside, for it had a new story to tell every day. Throughout the long twelve hundred miles there was never a page that was void of interest, never one that you could leave unread without loss, never one that you would want to skip, thinking you could find higher enjoyment in some other thing. There never was so wonderful a book written by man; never one whose interest was so absorbing, so unflagging, so sparklingly renewed with every reperusal.[11] The passenger who could not read it was charmed with a peculiar sort of faint dimple on its surface (on the rare occasions when he did not overlook it altogether); but to the pilot that was an *italicized* passage; indeed, it was more than that, it was a legend of the largest capitals,[12] with a string of shouting exclamation points at the end of it, for it meant that a wreck or a rock was buried there that could tear the life out of the strongest vessel that ever floated. It is the faintest and simplest expression the water ever makes, and the most hideous to a pilot's eye. In truth, the passenger who could not read this book saw nothing but all manner of pretty pictures in it, painted by the sun and shaded by the clouds, whereas to the trained eye these were not pictures at all, but the grimmest and most dead earnest of reading matter.

Now when I had mastered the language of this water, and had come to know every trifling feature that bordered the great river as familiarly as I knew the letters of the alphabet, I had made a valuable acquisition. But I had lost something, too. I had lost something which could never be restored to me while I lived. All the grace, the beauty, the poetry, had gone out of the majestic river! I still kept in mind a certain wonderful sunset which I witnessed when steamboating was new to me. A broad expanse of the river was turned to blood;

---

11. **reperusal** (rē′pə-rōō′zəl): rereading.

12. **a legend of the largest capitals:** an inscription in large capital letters.

in the middle distance the red hue brightened into gold, through which a solitary log came floating, black and conspicuous; in one place a long, slanting mark lay sparkling upon the water; in another the surface was broken by boiling, tumbling rings, that were as many-tinted as an opal; where the ruddy flush was faintest, was a smooth spot that was covered with graceful circles and radiating lines, ever so delicately traced; the shore on our left was densely wooded,

220 and the somber shadow that fell from this forest was broken in one place by a long, ruffled trail that shone like silver; and high above the forest wall a clean-stemmed dead tree waved a single leafy bough that glowed like a flame in the unobstructed splendor that was flowing from the sun. There were graceful curves, reflected images, woody heights, soft distances; and over the whole scene, far and near, the dissolving lights drifted steadily, enriching it every passing moment with new marvels of coloring.

I stood like one bewitched. I drank it in, in a speechless
230 rapture. The world was new to me, and I had never seen anything like this at home. But as I have said, a day came when I began to cease from noting the glories and the charms which the moon and the sun and the twilight wrought upon the river's face; another day came when I ceased altogether to note them. Then, if that sunset scene had been repeated, I should have looked upon it without rapture, and should have commented upon it, inwardly, after this fashion: "This sun means that we are going to have wind tomorrow; that floating log means that the river is rising, small thanks to it; that
240 slanting mark on the water refers to a bluff reef[13] which is going to kill somebody's steamboat one of these nights, if it keeps on stretching out like that; those tumbling 'boils' show a dissolving bar and a changing channel there; the lines and circles in the slick water over yonder are a warning that that troublesome place is shoaling up[14] dangerously; that silver streak in the shadow of the forest is the 'break' from a new snag, and he has located himself in the very best place he could have found to fish for steamboats; that tall dead tree, with a single living branch, is not going to last long, and then
250 how is a body ever going to get through this blind place at night without the friendly old landmark?"

---

13. **bluff reef:** an underwater ridge of rock.

14. **shoaling up:** becoming too shallow for safe navigation, because of a buildup of sand or silt in the riverbed.

MARK IT UP WORD POWER

Remember to mark words that you'd like to add to your **Personal Word List**. Later, you can record the words and their meanings beginning on page 344.

1. Review the details you underlined as you read. Then **summarize** what Twain feels he has lost by learning to pilot a steamboat.

_____

_____

_____

2. List one piece of useful information Twain learns from "reading" the river's appearance. **(Clarify)**

_____

_____

_____

READ ALOUD 3. Read aloud the boxed sentences on this page. Then restate Twain's **main idea** in your own words. **(Paraphrase)**

_____

_____

_____

CHALLENGE

Twain compares Mr. Bixby's temper to boiling water: "He would boil awhile to himself, and then overflow and scald me again." Circle other examples of **figurative language** that refer to Mr. Bixby. What does each example convey about his **character? (Analyze)**

Wrapping Up

If you are using **The Language of Literature,** you can now move to the questions and activities on pages 676–677 of that book.

No, the romance and beauty were all gone from the river. All the value any feature of it had for me now was the amount of usefulness it could furnish toward compassing the safe piloting of a steamboat. Since those days, I have pitied doctors from my heart. What does the lovely flush in a beauty's cheek mean to a doctor but a "break" that ripples above some deadly disease? Are not all her visible charms sown thick with what are to him the signs and symbols of hidden decay? Does he ever see her beauty at all, or doesn't he simply view her professionally, and comment upon her unwholesome condition all to himself? And doesn't he sometimes wonder whether he has gained most or lost most by learning his trade?

Pause & Reflect

Active Reading SkillBuilder

Visualizing

When writers skillfully describe a scene or character, they help readers **visualize,** or form mental pictures of, whatever is being described. Readers can visualize what the Mississippi River looks like from Twain's precise details. When reading the selection, use the chart below to record three vivid details and comparisons that Twain uses to help you visualize the Mississippi. Examples are given.

Mississippi Descriptions	
Details	**Comparison**
Sunset turns river to blood. A single log floats in the middle distance.	Leafy bough glows like a flame.

Literary Analysis SkillBuilder

Description

Description is a process by which a writer creates a picture in words of a scene, an event, or a character. One descriptive device is **imagery**—descriptive words and phrases that re-create sensory experiences to help readers see, hear, smell, taste, or feel what is being described. Another descriptive device is the use of **analogies,** which show similarities between two dissimilar things. On the chart below, list two descriptive details from the selection. Identify each detail as an example of imagery or analogy, then record how it affects you as a reader. An example is shown.

Twain's Descriptions		
Detail	**Descriptive Device**	**Effect**
I ... began to claw the boat away from the danger.	imagery	It shows how slowly and painfully Twain steered his boat away from the others.

Follow Up: Which scene, event, or character do you picture most vividly as a result of Twain's description? Explain why.

A Wagner Matinee

Willa Cather

Before You Read

If you are using *The Language of Literature . . .*

- Use the information on page 688 of that book to prepare for reading.

- Look at the art on pages 691, 693, and 696. What impressions do the pictures give of the **main character** and the **settings** in the story?

Reading Tips

In "A Wagner Matinee," the author includes scenes from the past as well as from the present time of the story. Watch for shifts between the present and the past **settings** as you read.

- Put a *T* in the margin every time the story shifts from the present to the past or from the past to the present.

- Circle the word, phrase, or sentence that indicates a time shift has occurred.

PREVIEW "A Wagner Matinee" is set in Boston in the 1890s. Wagner (väg′ nər) was a famous German composer. His music plays a key role in this story. The main character, the narrator's Aunt Georgiana, has lived most of her adult life on a poor farm on the Nebraska frontier. When she visits her nephew in Boston after being gone for 30 years, he makes plans to take her to an afternoon concert. The matinee is an ordinary event to most of the audience. It stirs complicated feelings in the quiet, care-worn woman, however.

FOCUS

In this section, you will be introduced to Aunt Georgiana and learn something about her.

MARK IT UP As you read, circle details that give you some first impressions of Aunt Georgiana. An example is highlighted on page 198.

I received one morning a letter, written in pale ink on glassy, blue-lined note-paper, and bearing the postmark of a little Nebraska village. This communication, worn and rubbed, looking as though it had been carried for some days in a coat pocket that was none too clean, was from my Uncle Howard and informed me that his wife had been left a small legacy by a bachelor relative who had recently died, and that it would be necessary for her to go to Boston to attend to the settling of the estate. He requested me to meet her at the station and render her whatever services might be necessary. On examining the date indicated as that of her arrival, I found it no later than tomorrow. He had characteristically delayed writing until, had I been away from home for a day, I must have missed the good woman altogether.

MARK IT UP KEEP TRACK

As you read, you can use these marks to keep track of your understanding.

✔ ..... I understand.

? ..... I don't understand this.

! ..... Interesting or surprising idea

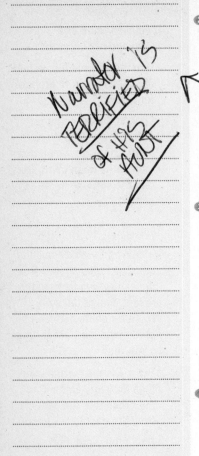

Narrator is TERRIFIED of his PAST

The name of my Aunt Georgiana called up not alone her own figure, at once <u>pathetic</u> and grotesque, but opened before my feet a gulf of recollection so wide and deep, that, as the letter dropped from my hand, I felt suddenly a stranger to all the present conditions of my existence, wholly ill at ease and out of place amid the familiar surroundings of my study. I became, in short, the gangling farmer-boy my aunt had known, scourged with chilblains[1] and bashfulness, my hands cracked and sore from the corn husking. I felt the knuckles of my thumb tentatively, as though they were raw again. I sat again before her parlor organ, fumbling the scales with my stiff, red hands, while she, beside me, made canvas mittens for the huskers.[2]

The next morning, after preparing my landlady somewhat, I set out for the station. When the train arrived I had some difficulty in finding my aunt. She was the last of the passengers to alight, and it was not until I got her into the carriage that she seemed really to recognize me. She had come all the way in a day coach; her linen duster had become black with soot and her black bonnet grey with dust during the journey. When we arrived at my boarding-house the landlady put her to bed at once and I did not see her again until the next morning.

Whatever shock Mrs. Springer experienced at my aunt's appearance, she considerately concealed. As for myself, I saw my aunt's misshapen figure with that feeling of awe and respect with which we behold explorers who have left their ears and fingers north of Franz-Josef-Land,[3] or their health somewhere along the Upper Congo.[4] My Aunt Georgiana had been a music teacher at the Boston Conservatory, somewhere back in the latter sixties. One summer, while visiting in the little village among the Green Mountains where her ancestors had dwelt for generations, she had kindled the <u>callow</u> fancy of

---

1. **chilblains:** painful swelling or sores on the feet or hands, caused by exposure to the cold.
2. **huskers:** farm workers who remove cornhusks by hand.
3. **Franz-Josef-Land:** a group of small, mostly ice-covered islands in the Arctic Ocean north of Russia.
4. **Upper Congo:** river in central Africa, now called the Zaire (zä-îr′) River.

WORDS TO KNOW	
	pathetic (pə-thĕt′ĭk) *adj.* arousing pity or compassion
	callow (kăl′ō) *adj.* lacking adult maturity or experience; immature

the most idle and shiftless of all the village lads, and had
conceived for this Howard Carpenter one of those
extravagant passions which a handsome country boy of
twenty-one sometimes inspires in an angular, spectacled
woman of thirty. When she returned to her duties in Boston,
Howard followed her, and the upshot of this <u>inexplicable</u>
infatuation was that she eloped with him, eluding the
<u>reproaches</u> of her family and the criticisms of her friends by
60 going with him to the Nebraska frontier. Carpenter, who, of
course, had no money, had taken a homestead in Red Willow
County, fifty miles from the railroad. There they had measured
off their quarter section themselves by driving across the
prairie in a wagon, to the wheel of which they had tied a red
cotton handkerchief, and counting off its revolutions. They
built a dugout in the red hillside, one of those cave dwellings
whose inmates so often reverted to primitive conditions. Their
water they got from the lagoons where the buffalo drank, and
their slender stock of provisions was always at the mercy of
70 bands of roving Indians. For thirty years my aunt had not been
further than fifty miles from the homestead.

But Mrs. Springer knew nothing of all this, and must have
been considerably shocked at what was left of my kinswoman.
Beneath the soiled linen duster which, on her arrival, was the
most conspicuous feature of her costume, she wore a black
stuff dress, whose ornamentation showed that she had
surrendered herself unquestioningly into the hands of a
country dressmaker. My poor aunt's figure, however, would
have presented astonishing difficulties to any dressmaker.
80 Originally stooped, her shoulders were now almost bent
together over her sunken chest. She wore no stays, and her
gown, which trailed unevenly behind, rose in a sort of peak
over her abdomen. She wore ill-fitting false teeth, and her skin
was as yellow as a Mongolian's from constant exposure to a
pitiless wind and to the alkaline water which hardens the
most transparent cuticle into a sort of flexible leather.

Pause & Reflect

Pause & Reflect

1. Look at the details that you
circled as you read. How would
you describe Aunt Georgiana at
this point? **(Visualize)**

_____

_____

_____

_____

2. Two consequences of Aunt
Georgiana's decision to marry
Howard Carpenter are_____

_____

and_____

_____.

3. Circle two phrases below that
describe how the narrator feels
toward his aunt. **(Infer)**

respects her

dislikes her

is annoyed by her

feels sympathy for her

WORDS
TO
KNOW

inexplicable (ĭn-ĕk′splĭ-kə-bəl) *adj.* difficult or impossible
   to explain
reproach (rĭ-prōch′) *n.* an expression of blame or
   disapproval

FOCUS

Read on to learn more about the narrator's life with his aunt in Nebraska. Find out what he is planning for her during her visit.

MARK IT UP Circle two passages that show how Aunt Georgiana treated the narrator when he was a boy.

I owed to this woman most of the good that ever came my way in my boyhood, and had a reverential affection for her. During the years when I was riding herd for my uncle, my aunt, after cooking the three meals—the first of which was ready at six o'clock in the morning—and putting the six children to bed, would often stand until midnight at her ironing-board with me at the kitchen table beside her, hearing me recite Latin declensions and conjugations,[5] gently shaking me when my drowsy head sank down over a page of irregular verbs. It was to her, at her ironing or mending, that I read my first Shakespeare, and her old text-book on mythology was the first that ever came into my empty hands. She taught me my scales and exercises, too—on the little parlor organ, which her husband had bought her after fifteen years, during which she had not so much as seen any instrument, but an accordion that belonged to one of the Norwegian farmhands. She would sit beside me by the hour, darning and counting while I struggled with the "Joyous Farmer," but she seldom talked to me about music, and I understood why. She was a <u>pious</u> woman; she had the consolations of religion and, to her at least, her martyrdom was not wholly <u>sordid</u>. Once when I had been doggedly beating out some easy passages from an old score of *Euryanthe*[6] I had found among her music books, she came up to me and, putting her hands over my eyes, gently drew my head back upon her shoulder, saying tremulously, "Don't love it so well, Clark, or it may be taken from you. Oh! dear boy, pray that whatever your sacrifice may be, it be not that."

When my aunt appeared on the morning after her arrival, she was still in a semi-somnambulant[7] state. She seemed not to realize that she was in the city where she had spent her youth, the place longed for hungrily half a lifetime. She had been so

---

5. **Latin declensions and conjugations** (kŏn'jə-gā'shəns): Latin word endings and verb forms.
6. *Euryanthe* (yōō'rē-ăn'thē): an opera by the German composer Carl Maria von Weber.
7. **Semi-somnambulant** (sŏm-năm'byə-lənt): half asleep or half-sleepwalking.

WORDS TO KNOW
pious (pī'əs) *adj.* having or showing reverence for God
sordid (sôr'dĭd) *adj.* wretched; dirty; morally degraded

wretchedly train-sick throughout the journey that she had no
recollection of anything but her discomfort, and, to all intents
and purposes, there were but a few hours of nightmare
between the farm in Red Willow County and my study on
Newbury Street. I had planned a little pleasure for her that
afternoon, to repay her for some of the glorious moments she
had given me when we used to milk together in the straw-
thatched cowshed and she, because I was more than usually
130 tired, or because her husband had spoken sharply to me,
would tell me of the splendid performance of the *Huguenots*[8]
she had seen in Paris, in her youth. At two o'clock the
Symphony Orchestra was to give a Wagner program, and I
intended to take my aunt; though, as I conversed with her, I
grew doubtful about her enjoyment of it. Indeed, for her own
sake, I could only wish her taste for such things quite dead,
and the long struggle mercifully ended at last. I suggested our
visiting the Conservatory and the Common[9] before lunch, but
she seemed altogether too timid to wish to venture out. She
140 questioned me absently about various changes in the city, but
she was chiefly concerned that she had forgotten to leave
instructions about feeding half-skimmed milk to a certain
weakling calf, "old Maggie's calf, you know, Clark," she
explained, evidently having forgotten how long I had been
away. She was further troubled because she had neglected to
tell her daughter about the freshly-opened kit of mackerel[10] in
the cellar, which would spoil if it were not used directly.

    I asked her whether she had ever heard any of the
Wagnerian operas,[11] and found that she had not, though she
150 was perfectly familiar with their respective situations, and had
once possessed the piano score of *The Flying Dutchman*. I
began to think it would have been best to get her back to Red
Willow County without waking her, and regretted having
suggested the concert.

Pause **&** *Reflect*

---

  8. *Huguenots* (hyōō′gə-nŏts′): an opera by the German composer
     Giacomo Meyerbeer.

  9. the Common: Boston Common, a public park.

10. mackerel: a fish commonly found in the Atlantic Ocean.

11. Wagnerian operas: The orchestra will play selections from several operas
    composed by Wagner, including *The Flying Dutchman, Tannhauser, Tristan
    and Isolde,* and a cycle of four operas called *The Ring of the Nibelung.*

Pause **&** *Reflect*

1. Look at the two passages that
you circled as you read. What do
they reveal about the kind of
person Aunt Georgiana is? **(Draw
Conclusions About Character)**

READ ALOUD 2. Read aloud
the boxed passage on page 200.
Aunt Georgiana is trying to tell
Clark

(Paraphrase)

3. How do you think it would feel to
give up your favorite activity or
your career for the rest of your
life? **(Connect)**

MARK IT UP 4. The
narrator begins to have doubts
about taking his aunt to the
concert. Underline two passages
on this page in which the
narrator expresses his doubts.
(Infer)

FOCUS

Clark and his aunt arrive at the concert hall, and the music begins.

✎ **MARK IT UP** Circle details that tell you something about how Aunt Georgiana reacts to the concert hall and to the music.

From the time we entered the concert hall, however, she was a trifle less passive and inert, and for the first time seemed to perceive her surroundings. I had felt some <u>trepidation</u> lest she might become aware of the absurdities of her attire, or might experience some painful embarrassment at stepping suddenly into the world to which she had been dead for a quarter of a century. But, again, I found how <u>superficially</u> I had judged her. She sat looking about her with eyes as impersonal, almost as stony, as those with which the granite Rameses[12] in a museum watches the froth and fret that ebbs and flows[13] about his pedestal—separated from it by the lonely stretch of centuries. I have seen this same aloofness in old miners who drift into the Brown hotel at Denver, their pockets full of bullion,[14] their linen soiled, their haggard faces unshaven; standing in the thronged corridors as solitary as though they were still in a frozen camp on the Yukon,[15] conscious that certain experiences have isolated them from their fellows by a gulf no haberdasher[16] could bridge.

We sat at the extreme left of the first balcony, facing the arc of our own and the balcony above us, veritable hanging gardens, brilliant as tulip beds. The matinée audience was made up chiefly of women. One lost the contour of faces and figures, indeed any effect of line whatever, and there was only the color of bodices past counting, the shimmer of fabrics soft and firm, silky and sheer; red, mauve, pink, blue, lilac, purple, ecru, rose, yellow, cream, and white, all the colors that an impressionist[17] finds in a sunlit landscape, with here and there the dead shadow of a frock coat. My Aunt Georgiana regarded them as though they had been so many daubs of tube-paint on a palette.

📖 **READ ALOUD** Lines 176–187

As you read these lines aloud, picture the scene described. What contrast is there between Aunt Georgiana and the other women at the matinee? **(Compare and Contrast)**

_____

_____

_____

_____

12. **Rameses** (răm′sēz′): one of the ancient kings of Egypt of that name.
13. **froth . . . flows:** happiness and sadness that comes and goes.
14. **bullion:** gold.
15. **Yukon** (yōō′kŏn′): a river in the Yukon Territory, in northwest Canada.
16. **haberdasher:** someone who sells men's clothing.
17. **impressionist:** member of a movement in French painting that emphasized the play of light and color.

WORDS
TO
KNOW

trepidation (trĕp′ĭ-dā′shən) *n.* fearful uncertainty or worry
superficially (sōō′pər-fĭsh′ə-lē) *adv.* in a shallow way; concerned with only what is obvious

When the musicians came out and took their places, she gave a little stir of anticipation and looked with quickening interest down over the rail at that invariable grouping, perhaps the first wholly familiar thing that had greeted her eye since she had left old Maggie and her weakling calf. I could feel how all those details sank into her soul, for I had not forgotten how they had sunk into mine when I came fresh from ploughing forever and forever between green aisles of corn, where, as in a treadmill, one might walk from daybreak to dusk without perceiving a shadow of change. The clean profiles of the musicians, the gloss of their linen, the dull black of their coats, the beloved shapes of the instruments, the patches of yellow light thrown by the green shaded lamps on the smooth, varnished bellies of the 'cellos and the bass viols in the rear, the restless, wind-tossed forest of fiddle necks and bows—I recalled how, in the first orchestra I had ever heard, those long bow strokes seemed to draw the heart out of me, as a conjurer's stick reels out yards of paper ribbon from a hat.

The first number was the *Tannhauser* overture. When the horns drew out the first strain of the Pilgrim's chorus, my Aunt Georgiana clutched my coat sleeve. Then it was I first realized that for her this broke a silence of thirty years; the inconceivable silence of the plains. With the battle between the two motives, with the frenzy of the Venusberg theme and its ripping of strings, there came to me an overwhelming sense of the waste and wear we are so powerless to combat; and I saw again the tall, naked house on the prairie, black and grim as a wooden fortress; the black pond where I had learned to swim, its margin pitted with sun-dried cattle tracks; the rain gullied clay banks about the naked house, the four dwarf ash seedlings where the dishcloths were always hung to dry before the kitchen door. The world there was the flat world of the ancients; to the east, a cornfield that stretched to daybreak; to the west, a corral that reached to sunset; between, the conquests of peace, dearer bought than those of war.

The overture closed, my aunt released my coat sleeve, but she said nothing. She sat staring at the orchestra through a dullness of thirty years, through the films made little by little by each of the three hundred and sixty-five days in every one of them. What, I wondered, did she get from it? She had been a good pianist in her day I knew, and her musical education had been broader than that of most music teachers of a

MARK IT UP KEEP TRACK

Remember to use these marks to keep track of your understanding.

✔ ..... I understand.

? ..... I don't understand this.

! ..... Interesting or surprising idea

1. Look back at the details that you
circled as you read. What do you
think Aunt Georgiana is feeling
when she arrives at the concert
hall? **(Draw Conclusions About
Character)**

_____

_____

_____

_____

2. How does Aunt Georgiana react
to hearing the first piece of
music? **(Clarify)**

_____

_____

_____

_____

230 quarter of a century ago. She had often told me of Mozart's operas and Meyerbeer's, and I could remember hearing her sing, years ago, certain melodies of Verdi's. When I had fallen ill with a fever in her house she used to sit by my cot in the evening—when the cool, night wind blew in through the faded mosquito netting tacked over the window and I lay watching a certain bright star that burned red above the cornfield—and sing "Home to our mountains, O, let us return!" in a way fit to break the heart of a Vermont boy near dead of home-sickness already.

Pause & Reflect

240 **FOCUS**
As the concert goes on, Clark watches his aunt closely.
MARK IT UP Underline passages that show Aunt Georgiana's changing responses to the music.

I watched her closely through the prelude to *Tristan and Isolde,* trying vainly to conjecture what that seething turmoil of strings and winds might mean to her, but she sat mutely staring at the violin bows that drove obliquely downward, like the pelting streaks of rain in a summer shower. Had this music any message for her? Had she enough left to at all comprehend this power which had kindled the world since she had left it? I

250 was in a fever of curiosity, but Aunt Georgiana sat silent upon her peak in Darien.[18] She preserved this utter immobility throughout the number from *The Flying Dutchman,* though her fingers worked mechanically upon her black dress, as though, of themselves, they were recalling the piano score they had once played. Poor old hands! They had been stretched and twisted into mere tentacles to hold and lift and knead with; the palms unduly swollen, the fingers bent and knotted—on one of them a thin, worn band that had once been a wedding ring. As I pressed and gently quieted one of

260 those groping hands, I remembered with quivering eyelids their services for me in other days.

---

18. **peak in Darien** (dâr′ē-ĕn′): an allusion to a poem by the English poet John Keats. In the poem Keats describes Spanish explorers on a mountain in Darien, a region that is now Panama. The Spaniards stand silent and amazed as they become the first Europeans to view the Pacific Ocean.

WORDS
TO
KNOW
conjecture (kən-jĕk′chər) v. to make a judgment on the basis of uncertain evidence; guess

Soon after the tenor began the "Prize Song," I heard a quick drawn breath and turned to my aunt. Her eyes were closed, but the tears were glistening on her cheeks, and I think, in a moment more, they were in my eyes as well. It never really died, then—the soul that can suffer so <u>excruciatingly</u> and so interminably; it withers to the outward eye only; like that strange moss which can lie on a dusty shelf half a century and yet, if placed in water, grows green again. She wept so
270 throughout the development and elaboration of the melody.

During the intermission before the second half of the concert, I questioned my aunt and found that the "Prize Song" was not new to her. Some years before there had drifted to the farm in Red Willow County a young German, a tramp cow puncher, who had sung the chorus at Bayreuth,[19] when he was a boy, along with the other peasant boys and girls. Of a Sunday morning he used to sit on his gingham-sheeted bed in the hands' bedroom which opened off the kitchen, cleaning the leather of his boots and saddle, singing
280 the "Prize Song," while my aunt went about her work in the kitchen. She had hovered about him until she had prevailed upon him to join the country church, though his sole fitness for this step, in so far as I could gather, lay in his boyish face and his possession of this divine melody. Shortly afterward he had gone to town on the Fourth of July, been drunk for several days, lost his money at a faro[20] table, ridden a saddled Texas steer on a bet, and disappeared with a fractured collar-bone. All this my aunt told me huskily, wanderingly, as though she were talking in the weak lapses of illness.
290 "Well, we have come to better things than the old *Trovatore*[21] at any rate, Aunt Georgie?" I queried, with a well meant effort at jocularity.

Her lip quivered and she hastily put her handkerchief up to her mouth. From behind it she murmured, "And you have been hearing this ever since you left me, Clark?" Her question was the gentlest and saddest of reproaches.

---

19. **Bayreuth** (bī-roit'): the Bayreuth Festival, an annual international music festival in Germany that presents Wagner's operas.
20. **faro:** a gambling game.
21. *Trovatore* (trô'vä-tô'rĕ): *Il Trovatore* is an opera by the Italian composer Giuseppe Verdi.

> **MARK IT UP** WORD POWER
>
> Remember to mark words that you'd like to add to your **Personal Word List**. Later, you can record the words and their meanings beginning on page 344.

WORDS TO KNOW

excruciatingly (ĭk-skrōō'shē-ā'tĭng-lə) *adv.* in a way that causes great pain or distress

A Wagner Matinee **205**

MARK IT UP **1.** Look at the passages that you underlined. Star three that show different reactions that Aunt Georgiana had. **(Clarify)**

2. During the intermission, Aunt Georgiana asks, "And you have been hearing this ever since you left me, Clark?" (lines 294–295). What does this tell you about what music meant to her? **(Draw Conclusions About Character)**

_____

_____

_____

_____

READ ALOUD **3.** Read aloud the boxed passage on this page. What are Aunt Georgiana's feelings at the end of the concert? **(Draw Conclusions About Character)**

_____

_____

_____

_____

CHALLENGE

In what ways do you think Aunt Georgiana has influenced the behavior and attitudes of the narrator? Review the story and mark passages that support your conclusions. **(Draw Conclusions)**

Wrapping Up

If you are using **_The Language of Literature,_** you can now move to the questions and activities on pages 697–699 of that book.

The second half of the program consisted of four numbers from the *Ring*, and closed with Siegfried's funeral march. My aunt wept quietly, but almost continuously, as a shallow vessel overflows in a rainstorm. From time to time her dim eyes looked up at the lights which studded the ceiling, burning softly under their dull glass globes; doubtless they were stars in truth to her. I was still perplexed as to what measure of musical comprehension was left to her, she who had heard nothing but the singing of Gospel Hymns at Methodist services in the square frame school-house on Section Thirteen for so many years. I was wholly unable to gauge how much of it had been dissolved in soapsuds, or worked into bread, or milked into the bottom of a pail.

The deluge of sound poured on and on; I never knew what she found in the shining current of it; I never knew how far it bore her, or past what happy islands. From the trembling of her face I could well believe that before the last numbers she had been carried out where the myriad graves are, into the grey, nameless burying grounds of the sea; or into some world of death vaster yet, where, from the beginning of the world, hope has lain down with hope and dream with dream and, renouncing,[22] slept.

The concert was over; the people filed out of the hall chattering and laughing, glad to relax and find the living level again, but my kinswoman made no effort to rise. The harpist slipped its green felt cover over his instrument; the flute-players shook the water from their mouthpieces; the men of the orchestra went out one by one, leaving the stage to the chairs and music stands, empty as a winter cornfield.

I spoke to my aunt. She burst into tears and sobbed pleadingly. "I don't want to go, Clark, I don't want to go!"

I understood. For her, just outside the door of the concert hall, lay the black pond with the cattle-tracked bluffs; the tall, unpainted house, with weather-curled boards; naked as a tower, the crook-backed ash seedlings where the dish-cloths hung to dry; the gaunt, molting turkeys picking up refuse about the kitchen door.

---

22. renouncing: giving up.

Active Reading SkillBuilder

Drawing Conclusions About Character

Readers **draw conclusions,** or make logical decisions, about what a character is like
by combining all the information that they learn about the character while reading
the story. When reading this story, pay close attention to details that reveal Aunt
Georgiana's personality, including what she says and does and how Cather
describes her. Fill in the chart below, explaining what these details reveal about the
kind of person Aunt Georgiana is. Later, you will use this evidence to draw
conclusions about her. Examples are given.

Observations	What They Reveal
Physical appearance *clothes covered with soot and dust*	*She is not interested in how she looks.*
Major decisions	
Actions and reactions *helped Clark with his Latin homework and taught him music*	*She is well-educated and continues to care about learning and music.*

Literary Analysis SkillBuilder

Setting

Setting is the time and place of the action of a literary work. The action may occur in a real or an imaginary place in the past, present, or future. In this story, Cather portrays two very different places—a Nebraska farm and the Boston concert hall—that have important effects on Aunt Georgiana. Review the story and use the "houses" below to record details that describe these two contrasting settings. Examples are given.

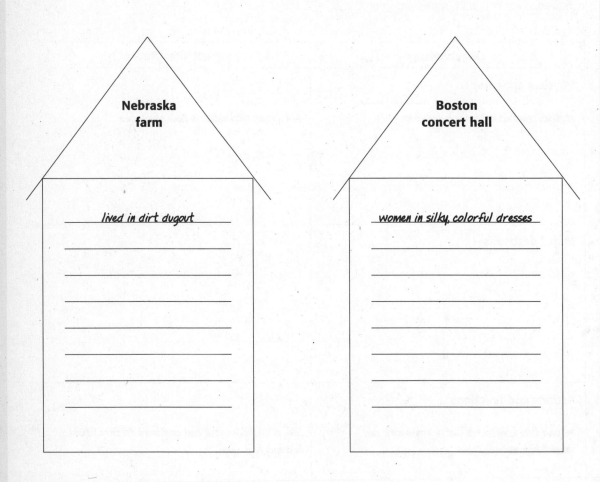

Nebraska farm

lived in dirt dugout

Boston concert hall

women in silky, colorful dresses

Follow Up: Using the details that you listed, sketch each of the settings. Then compare your drawings with those of your classmates.

Words to Know SkillBuilder

Words to Know

callow	excruciatingly	pathetic	reproach	superficially
conjecture	inexplicable	pious	sordid	trepidation

A. Each of the following sentences suggests a word in the word list. The word itself is hidden in the sentence. Underline the hidden word and then write it on the line. An example, using another word from the story, has been done for you.

Example: Between the verses is the familiar section I most like to <u>teach, or used</u> to, back when I had music students.

_____ *chorus*

1. Is the condition of this house the result of laziness, or did you think the filth and trash would disappear by magic?

_____ (1)

2. Your childish treatment of the topic keeps your report from being properly scientific. Allow me to add my mature wisdom.

_____ (2)

3. Pa, the ticks are so bad that poor Spot is covered with them. He's miserable, and I'm afraid he'll get sick!

_____ (3)

4. Appropriate music for church is rarely rock or rap, IOUs are not proper offerings, and swimwear offends the congregation.

_____ (4)

B. Decide which word from the word list belongs in each numbered blank. Then write the word on the blank line on the right.

The famine's cause was far from evident;
It was an (1) event.

_____ (1)

Your stern look makes me (2)
I'm about to get a lecture.

_____ (2)

When I messed up, the angry coach
Administered a sharp (3).
He couldn't help but blow a gasket.
I'd scored in the opponents' basket.

_____ (3)

A gnat or fly can drive you nuts, by acting irritatingly.
But either's better than a wasp, which stings (4).

_____ (4)

Before a test, I wouldn't call my mood anticipation.
It's quite a bit more accurate to call it (5).

_____ (5)

A lot of my confusion will remain
If you just (6) explain.

_____ (6)

C. Imagine that Aunt Georgiana decides to remain in Boston. Write a letter she might send to her husband explaining her decision. Use at least **five** of the Words to Know.

Before You Read

If you are using **The Language of Literature,** study the information on page 750 of that book to prepare for reading. Four of the eight poems presented there are in this lesson of **The InterActive Reader.**

Reading Tips

Many readers find Emily Dickinson's poems difficult. She often relies on suggestion, and she uses words in unusual ways. She is inventive in her capitalization and makes use of many dashes. To make sense of these poems, allow your imagination to run free.

- When you encounter an unusual phrase, try to guess what it might mean. Then see if your guess makes sense when applied to the poem.

- Don't worry if you can't understand every line. Focus on what you do understand—even if it's only one line or phrase— and try to build from that.

- Read each poem several times, and at least once aloud.

✐ **MARK IT UP** **KEEP TRACK**

As you read, you can use these marks to keep track of your understanding.

✔ ..... I understand.

? ..... I don't understand this.

! ..... Interesting or surprising idea

PREVIEW Emily Dickinson was a person of contrasts. She lived what appeared to be an extremely quiet and simple life in 19th-century New England. Yet she wrote many poems that are highly original in thought and style. They express strong feelings and ideas, and they often reveal insights in unexpected ways. Although only a few of her poems were published in her lifetime, Dickinson is now considered a major American poet.

"Hope" is the thing with feathers

Emily Dickinson

FOCUS

In this poem, Dickinson compares hope to a bird.

✐ **MARK IT UP** Underline words and phrases that describe a bird. An example is highlighted.

"Hope" is the thing with feathers—
That perches in the soul—
And sings the tune without the words—
And never stops—at all—

And sweetest—in the Gale[1]—is heard—
And sore[2] must be the storm—
That could abash[3] the little Bird
That kept so many warm—

I've heard it in the chillest land—
And on the strangest Sea—
Yet, never, in Extremity,[4]
It asked a crumb—of Me.

Pause **&** *Reflect*

Pause **&** **Reflect**

1. Look at the words and phrases that you underlined as you read. List the details about the bird that seem important to you. **(Evaluate)**

_____

_____

_____

_____

2. Circle the words below that describe both the bird and hope. **(Compare and Contrast)**

cheerful   demanding

fearful   strong

enduring   weak

READ ALOUD 3. Read aloud the two boxed lines. The bird doesn't ask for a crumb from the speaker, not even when it is in great need. What message about hope do you think the speaker may be expressing here? **(Reading Poetry)**

_____

_____

_____

_____

MARK IT UP **WORD POWER**

Mark words that you'd like to add to your **Personal Word List.** After reading, you can record the words and their meanings beginning on page 344.

1. **Gale:** extremely strong wind.
2. **sore:** severe.
3. **abash:** frustrate; baffle
4. **Extremity:** greatest need or peril.

My life closed twice *before* its close

Emily Dickinson

FOCUS

The speaker describes how it feels to lose someone you love. As you read, look for signs of how great the impact of loss can be.

My life closed twice before its close[1]—
It yet remains to see
If Immortality unveil
A third event to me[2]

5 So huge, so hopeless to conceive
As these that twice befell.[3]
Parting is all we know of heaven,[4]
And all we need of hell.

Pause & Reflect

Pause & Reflect

1. The speaker refers to two events that "closed" her life (line 1). What do you think she might be referring to? **(Infer)**

_____

_____

_____

_____

✎ **MARK IT UP** **2.** What feelings about loss are expressed in the poem? Write the answer below. Then underline the lines that help you answer that question. **(Analyze)**

_____

_____

_____

_____

3. Complete the following sentences:
Parting tells us "all we know of heaven" because _____

_____

_____.

Parting gives us "all we need of hell" because _____

_____

_____.

(Analyze)

---

1. **close:** end; the speaker's death.
2. **If . . . third event:** The speaker is referring to her own death. She wonders if she will experience an afterlife.
3. **befell** (bǐ-fěl′): happened.
4. **Parting . . . heaven:** When people die, it is often said that they have gone to heaven. Those left behind, of course, do not have any direct experience of heaven.

I heard a Fly buzz when I died

Emily Dickinson

I heard a Fly buzz—when I died—
The Stillness in the Room
Was like the Stillness in the Air—
Between the Heaves[1] of Storm—

5 The Eyes around—had wrung them dry—
And Breaths were gathering firm
For that last Onset—when the King[2]
Be witnessed—in the Room[3]—

I willed my Keepsakes—Signed away
10 What portion of me be
Assignable[4]—and then it was
There interposed[5] a Fly—

READ ALOUD **Lines 5–8**

Read aloud the boxed lines, paying attention to the capitalized words. In these lines the speaker describes the mourners. What does she observe about their "Eyes" and "Breaths"? (Clarify)

1. **Heaves:** risings and fallings.
2. **the King:** God.
3. **in the Room:** in the 19th century, people usually died at home in the presence of friends and family.
4. **I willed . . . Assignable:** The speaker seems to be referring to her physical possessions, such as those that might be included in a will. *Assignable* is a legal term referring to things that might be given away.
5. **interposed:** came between

1. To what does the speaker compare the "Stillness in the Room" (line 2)? **(Reading Poetry)**

_____

_____

_____

_____

2. Reread lines 9–11. What does the speaker take care of just before she dies? **(Clarify)**

_____

_____

_____

_____

3. Look back at the details you underlined as you read. Circle the pair of words below that you think best describes the speaker's attitude toward death. **(Analyze)**

terrified and uncertain

calm and objective

angry and resentful

With Blue—uncertain stumbling Buzz—
Between the light—and me—
 And then the Windows failed—and then
I could not see to see—

Pause **&** **Reflect**

Because I could not stop for Death

Emily Dickinson

FOCUS

In this poem, death is pictured as a carriage driver. The speaker imagines herself riding in death's carriage.

MARK IT UP Underline words and phrases that help you visualize death as a carriage driver.

Because I could not stop for Death—
He kindly stopped for me—
The Carriage held but just Ourselves—
And Immortality.

JOT IT DOWN Lines 1–4

Who is in the carriage with death and the speaker. **(Clarify)**
_____

5   We slowly drove—He knew no haste
And I had put away
My labor and my leisure too,
For His Civility[1]—

We passed the School, where Children strove
10   At Recess—in the Ring—
We passed the Fields of Gazing Grain[2]—
We passed the Setting Sun—

Or rather—He[3] passed Us—
The Dews drew quivering and chill[4]—
15   For only Gossamer,[5] my Gown—
My Tippet[6]—only Tulle[7]—

---

1. **Civility:** politeness.
2. **Gazing Grain:** grain leaning toward the sun.
3. **He:** the sun.
4. **The Dews . . . chill:** It is so cold that even the dew seems to shiver.
5. **Gossamer:** a thin, light cloth.
6. **Tippet:** shawl.
7. **Tulle** (tool): fine netting.

Pause & Reflect

1. Read through the words and phrases that you underlined as you read. How would you describe the character of the carriage driver? **(Reading Poetry)**

_____

_____

_____

_____

MARK IT UP **2.** Circle four things the speaker sees during the carriage ride (lines 9–12). **(Clarify)**

READ ALOUD **3.** Read lines 17–20 aloud. What do you think this house represents? **(Reading Poetry)**

_____

_____

CHALLENGE

Three of these poems are concerned with death. In two of them, the speaker is someone who has already died. What attitudes toward death does Dickinson reveal through these poems? Use evidence from the poems to support your opinion. **(Analyze)**

Wrapping Up

If you are using *The Language of Literature,* you can now move on to the questions and activities on pages 760–762 of that book. You may also want to review the questions on pages 752, 756, and 758.

216 The InterActive Reader

We paused before a House that seemed
A Swelling of the Ground—
The Roof was scarcely visible—
The Cornice[7]—in the Ground—

20

Since then—'tis Centuries—and yet
Feels shorter than the Day
I first surmised[8] the Horses' Heads
Were toward Eternity—

Pause & Reflect

---

7. **Cornice** (kôr′nĭs): the molding around the top of a building.
8. **surmised** (sər-mīzd): guessed.

Active Reading SkillBuilder

Strategies for Reading Poetry

The following suggestions can help readers increase their understanding and enjoyment of Dickinson's poetry. Read each poem once for overall impression and once for meaning; then read it aloud to appreciate Dickinson's unique **style, rhythm,** and **imagery;** note the **figurative language** and words that are capitalized for emphasis; pause when you encounter dashes, just as you do when you come to commas or periods in a poem.

Use the chart below to record your questions about any poetic element or device. One example is included.

Poems	Questions
"'Hope' is the thing with feathers—"	Why is "Gale" capitalized, but not "storm" (lines 5-6)?
"My life closed twice before its close—"	
"I heard a Fly buzz—when I died—"	
"Because I could not stop for Death—"	

Literary Analysis SkillBuilder

Figurative Language

Figurative language consists of groups of words that express ideas beyond the literal meaning of the words. Dickinson's poetry features such common figures of speech as **similes**—comparisons that use *like* or *as;* **metaphors**—direct comparisons between two unlike things; **extended metaphors**—comparisons of two things at length and in several ways; and **personification**—figurative language that gives human characteristics to an object, animal, or idea. Examples of personification and extended metaphor from Dickinson's poems are given below. In the four poems you have read, find one example of a simile and one example of a metaphor. Then fill in the remaining boxes.

Figures of Speech

Personification	Extended Metaphor
Death is personified as a kind gentleman in "Because I could not stop for Death."	"'Hope' is the thing with feathers" compares hope to a bird.
Simile	**Metaphor**

THE YELLOW WALLPAPER

CHARLOTTE PERKINS GILMAN

PREVIEW This story, set in the 1890s, is narrated by a young married woman whose husband is a doctor. He believes that his wife has a "nervous condition" and tells her to rest and do no work. The husband, John, has rented an old mansion for them for the summer. The narrator, who is never named, spends most of her time in a large top-floor room that has ugly yellow wallpaper. She pays more and more attention to the wallpaper and keeps a secret journal about what she sees and feels. Her journal—the story—lets us inside her mind as her thoughts and behavior become increasingly strange.

FOCUS

In this section, the narrator writes about her husband, the house where they are living, and her mental state.

MARK IT UP Underline words and phrases the narrator uses to describe the wallpaper in her room. Two examples have been highlighted on page 222.

It is very seldom that mere ordinary people like John and myself secure ancestral halls for the summer.

A colonial mansion, a hereditary estate, I would say a haunted house, and reach the height of romantic <u>felicity</u>—but that would be asking too much of fate!

Still I will proudly declare that there is something queer about it.

WORDS TO KNOW

felicity (fĭ-lĭs′ĭ-tē) *n.* happiness; bliss

Else, why should it be let[1] so cheaply? And why have stood so long untenanted?

John laughs at me, of course, but one expects that in marriage.

John is practical in the extreme. He has no patience with faith, an intense horror of superstition, and he scoffs openly at any talk of things not to be felt and seen and put down in figures.

John is a physician, and *perhaps*—(I would not say it to a living soul, of course, but this is dead paper and a great relief to my *mind*)—*perhaps* that is one reason I do not get well faster.

You see he does not believe I am sick!

And what can one do?

If a physician of high standing, and one's own husband, assures friends and relatives that there is really nothing the matter with one but temporary nervous depression—a slight hysterical[2] tendency—what is one to do?

My brother is also a physician, and also of high standing, and he says the same thing.

So I take phosphates or phosphites—whichever it is, and tonics, and journeys, and air, and exercise, and am absolutely forbidden to "work" until I am well again.

Personally, I disagree with their ideas.

Personally, I believe that congenial work, with excitement and change, would do me good.

But what is one to do?

I did write for a while in spite of them; but it *does* exhaust me a good deal—having to be so sly about it, or else meet with heavy opposition.

I sometimes fancy that in my condition if I had less opposition and more society and stimulus—but John says the very worst thing I can do is to think about my condition, and I confess it always makes me feel bad.

So I will let it alone and talk about the house.

The most beautiful place! It is quite alone, standing well back from the road, quite three miles from the village. It makes me think of English places that you read about, for there are hedges and walls and gates that lock, and lots of separate little houses for the gardeners and people.

---

1. **let**: rented.
2. **hysterical**: Hysteria is the presence of a physical ailment with no underlying physical cause.

50   There is a *delicious* garden! I never saw such a garden—
large and shady, full of box-bordered paths, and lined with
long grape-covered arbors with seats under them.

There were greenhouses, too, but they are all broken now.

There was some legal trouble, I believe, something about
the heirs and coheirs; anyhow, the place has been empty
for years.

That spoils my ghostliness, I am afraid, but I don't care—
there is something strange about the house—I can feel it.

I even said so to John one moonlight evening, but he said
60 what I felt was a draft, and shut the window.

I get unreasonably angry with John sometimes. I'm sure I
never used to be so sensitive. I think it is due to this nervous
condition.

But John says if I feel so, I shall neglect proper self-control;
so I take pains to control myself—before him, at least, and
that makes me very tired.

I don't like our room a bit. I wanted one downstairs that
opened on the piazza and had roses all over the window, and
such pretty old-fashioned chintz hangings! but John would
70 not hear of it.

He said there was only one window and not room for two
beds, and no near room for him if he took another.

He is very careful and loving, and hardly lets me stir
without special direction.

I have a schedule prescription for each hour in the day; he
takes all care from me, and so I feel <u>basely</u> ungrateful not to
value it more.

He said we came here solely on my account, that I was to
have perfect rest and all the air I could get. "Your exercise
80 depends on your strength, my dear," said he, "and your food
somewhat on your appetite; but air you can absorb all the
time." So we took the nursery at the top of the house.

It is a big, airy room, the whole floor nearly, with windows
that look all ways, and air and sunshine galore. It was nursery
first and then playroom and gymnasium, I should judge; for
the windows are barred for little children, and there are rings
and things in the walls.

MARK IT UP | WORD POWER

Mark words that you'd like to
add to your **Personal Word List**.
After reading, you can record
the words and their meanings
beginning on page 344.

WORDS
TO
KNOW

basely (bās′lē) *adv.* dishonorably; meanly

Pause & Reflect

1. Why is the narrator writing in secret? **(Cause and Effect)**

_____

_____

_____

_____

2. Describe the relationship between the narrator and her husband. **(Infer)**

_____

_____

_____

_____

3. Look at the words and phrases that you underlined as you read. What does the wallpaper look like? **(Visualize)**

_____

_____

_____

_____

The paint and paper look as if a boys' school had used it. It is stripped off—the paper—in great patches all around the head of my bed, about as far as I can reach, and in a great place on the other side of the room low down. I never saw a worse paper in my life.

One of those sprawling flamboyant patterns committing every artistic sin.

It is dull enough to confuse the eye in following, pronounced enough to constantly irritate and provoke study, and when you follow the lame uncertain curves for a little distance they suddenly commit suicide—plunge off at outrageous angles, destroy themselves in unheard of contradictions.

The color is repellent, almost revolting; a smouldering unclean yellow, strangely faded by the slow-turning sunlight.

It is a dull yet lurid orange in some places, a sickly sulphur tint in others.

No wonder the children hated it! I should hate it myself if I had to live in this room long.

There comes John, and I must put this away, —he hates to have me write a word.

Pause & Reflect

FOCUS

In this section, you will learn more about the narrator and how John treats her.

MARK IT UP As you read, underline details that tell about the narrator's state of mind.

We have been here two weeks, and I haven't felt like writing before, since that first day.

I am sitting by the window now, up in this <u>atrocious</u> nursery, and there is nothing to hinder my writing as much as I please, save lack of strength.

John is away all day, and even some nights when his cases are serious.

I am glad my case is not serious!

But these nervous troubles are dreadfully depressing.

John does not know how much I really suffer. He knows there is no *reason* to suffer, and that satisfies him.

WORDS
TO
KNOW

atrocious (ə-trō'shəs) *adj.* shockingly bad or lacking in taste; awful

Of course it is only nervousness. It does weigh on me so not to do my duty in any way!

I meant to be such a help to John, such a real rest and comfort, and here I am a comparative burden already!

Nobody would believe what an effort it is to do what little I am able,—to dress and entertain, and order things.

It is fortunate Mary is so good with the baby. Such a dear baby!

130 And yet I *cannot* be with him, it makes me so nervous.

I suppose John never was nervous in his life. He laughs at me so about this wallpaper!

At first he meant to repaper the room, but afterwards he said that I was letting it get the better of me, and that nothing was worse for a nervous patient than to give way to such fancies.

He said that after the wallpaper was changed it would be the heavy bedstead, and then the barred windows, and then that gate at the head of the stairs, and so on.

140 "You know the place is doing you good," he said, "and really, dear, I don't care to renovate the house just for a three months' rental."

"Then do let us go downstairs," I said, "there are such pretty rooms there."

Then he took me in his arms and called me a blessed little goose, and said he would go down to the cellar, if I wished, and have it whitewashed into the bargain.

But he is right enough about the beds and windows and things.

150 It is an airy and comfortable room as any one need wish, and, of course, I would not be so silly as to make him uncomfortable just for a whim.

I'm really getting quite fond of the big room, all but that horrid paper.

Out of one window I can see the garden, those mysterious deepshaded arbors, the riotous old-fashioned flowers, and bushes and gnarly trees.

Out of another I get a lovely view of the bay and a little private wharf belonging to the estate. There is a beautiful
160 shaded lane that runs down there from the house. I always fancy I see people walking in these numerous paths and arbors, but John has cautioned me not to give way to fancy in the least. He says that with my imaginative power and habit of story-making, a nervous weakness like mine is sure to lead

MARK IT UP Lines 140–152

Reread lines 140–152. Circle words or phrases that show John's attitude toward the narrator. (Analyze)

1. Review the details that you underlined as you read. Then circle the two phrases below that describe the narrator's state of mind. **(Infer)**

imagines she sees people walking outside

depressed by her nervous troubles

amused by the wallpaper

feels superior to her husband

2. The narrator mentions her writing several times in this section. Why do you think writing is important to her? **(Draw Conclusions)**

_____

_____

_____

_____

READ ALOUD Lines 189–197

How would you describe the narrator's imagination as a child? **(Infer)**

_____

_____

_____

_____

to all manner of excited fancies, and that I ought to use my will and good sense to check the tendency. So I try.

I think sometimes that if I were only well enough to write a little it would relieve the press of ideas and rest me.

But I find I get pretty tired when I try.

170 It is so discouraging not to have any advice and companionship about my work. When I get really well, John says we will ask Cousin Henry and Julia down for a long visit; but he says he would as soon put fireworks in my pillowcase as to let me have those stimulating people about now.

Pause & Reflect

FOCUS

Now the narrator gives more details about what she sees in the wallpaper. She also describes other parts of the room. As you
180 read, think about why the narrator reacts so strongly to the wallpaper.

I wish I could get well faster.

But I must not think about that. This paper looks to me as if it knew what a vicious influence it had!

There is a recurrent spot where the pattern lolls like a broken neck and two bulbous eyes stare at you upside down.

I get positively angry with the <u>impertinence</u> of it and the everlastingness.

Up and down and sideways they crawl, and those absurd, unblinking eyes are everywhere. There is one place where two breadths[3] didn't match, and the eyes go all up and down the line, one a little higher than the other.

I never saw so much expression in an <u>inanimate</u> thing before, and we all know how much expression they have! I
190 used to lie awake as a child and get more entertainment and terror out of blank walls and plain furniture than most children could find in a toystore.

I remember what a kindly wink the knobs of our big, old bureau used to have, and there was one chair that always seemed like a strong friend.

I used to feel that if any of the other things looked too fierce I could always hop into that chair and be safe.

---

3. **breadths:** strips of wallpaper of equal widths.

| WORDS TO KNOW | **impertinence** (ĭm-pûr′tn-əns) *n.* improper boldness; rudeness |
| | **inanimate** (ĭn-ăn′ə-mĭt) *adj.* not alive; lifeless |

The furniture in this room is no worse than inharmonious, however, for we had to bring it all from downstairs. I suppose
200 when this was used as a playroom they had to take the nursery things out, and no wonder! I never saw such ravages as the children have made here.

The wallpaper, as I said before, is torn off in spots, and it sticketh closer than a brother—they must have had <u>perseverance</u> as well as hatred.

Then the floor is scratched and gouged and splintered, the plaster itself is dug out here and there, and this great heavy bed which is all we found in the room, looks as if it had been through the wars.

210 But I don't mind it a bit—only the paper.

There comes John's sister. Such a dear girl as she is, and so careful of me! I must not let her find me writing.

She is a perfect and enthusiastic housekeeper, and hopes for no better profession. I verily believe she thinks it is the writing which made me sick!

But I can write when she is out, and see her a long way off from these windows.

There is one that commands the road, a lovely shaded winding road, and one that just looks off over the country.
220 A lovely country, too, full of great elms and velvet meadows.

This wallpaper has a kind of sub-pattern in a different shade, a particularly irritating one, for you can only see it in certain lights, and not clearly then.

But in the places where it isn't faded and where the sun is just so—I can see a strange, provoking, formless sort of figure, that seems to skulk about behind that silly and conspicuous front design.

There's sister on the stairs!

Pause **&** *Reflect*

Pause **&** *Reflect*

1. What does John's sister do in the house? **(Clarify)**

_____

_____

_____

2. Circle three words below that describe the narrator's reactions to the wallpaper. **(Infer)**

peaceful	happy
annoyed	angry
intrigued	uninterested

MARK IT UP **3.** The narrator sees something behind the wallpaper. Circle the passage in lines 225–228 that tells what she sees. **(Clarify)**

WORDS
TO
KNOW

perseverance (pûr′sə-vîr′əns) *n.* persistence in the face of difficulty; determination

FOCUS

The narrator is spending more time looking at the wallpaper.

MARK IT UP As you read, circle details that help you understand her worsening mental condition.

Well, the Fourth of July is over! The people are all gone and I am tired out. John thought it might do me good to see a little company, so we just had mother and Nellie and the children down for a week.

Of course I didn't do a thing. Jennie sees to everything now.

But it tired me all the same.

John says if I don't pick up faster he shall send me to Weir Mitchell[4] in the fall.

But I don't want to go there at all. I had a friend who was in his hands once, and she says he is just like John and my brother, only more so!

Besides, it is such an undertaking to go so far.

I don't feel as if it was worth while to turn my hand over for anything, and I'm getting dreadfully fretful and <u>querulous</u>.

I cry at nothing, and cry most of the time.

Of course I don't when John is here, or anybody else, but when I am alone.

And I am alone a good deal just now. John is kept in town very often by serious cases, and Jennie is good and lets me alone when I want her to.

So I walk a little in the garden or down that lovely lane, sit on the porch under the roses, and lie down up here a good deal.

I'm getting really fond of the room in spite of the wallpaper. Perhaps *because* of the wallpaper.

It dwells in my mind so!

I lie here on this great immovable bed—it is nailed down, I believe—and follow that pattern about by the hour. It is as good as gymnastics, I assure you. I start, we'll say, at the bottom, down in the corner over there where it has not been touched, and I determine for the thousandth time that I *will* follow that pointless pattern to some sort of a conclusion.

I know a little of the principle of design, and I know this thing was not arranged on any laws of radiation, or

---

4. **Weir Mitchell:** Dr. Silas Weir Mitchell, famous for his "rest cure" for nervous diseases, which is no longer considered effective.

WORDS TO KNOW

querulous (kwĕr′ə-ləs) *adj.* given to complaining

alternation, or repetition, or symmetry, or anything else that I ever heard of.

It is repeated, of course, by the breadths, but not otherwise.

270 Looked at in one way each breadth stands alone, the bloated curves and flourishes—a kind of "debased Romanesque"[5] with *delirium tremens*[6]—go waddling up and down in isolated columns of fatuity.[7]

But, on the other hand, they connect diagonally, and the sprawling outlines run off in great slanting waves of optic horror, like a lot of wallowing seaweeds in full chase.

The whole thing goes horizontally, too, at least it seems so, and I exhaust myself in trying to distinguish the order of its going in that direction.

280 They have used a horizontal breadth for a frieze[8], and that adds wonderfully to the confusion.

There is one end of the room where it is almost intact, and there, when the crosslights fade and the low sun shines directly upon it, I can almost fancy radiation after all,—the interminable grotesques seem to form around a common center and rush off in headlong plunges of equal distraction.

It makes me tired to follow it. I will take a nap I guess.

I don't know why I should write this.

I don't want to.

290 I don't feel able.

And I know John would think it absurd. But I *must* say what I feel and think in some way—it is such a relief!

But the effort is getting to be greater than the relief.

Half the time now I am awfully lazy, and lie down ever so much.

John says I mustn't lose my strength, and has me take cod liver oil and lots of tonics and things, to say nothing of ale and wine and rare meat.

Dear John! He loves me very dearly, and hates to have me 300 sick. I tried to have a real earnest reasonable talk with him the other day, and tell him how I wish he would let me go and make a visit to Cousin Henry and Julia.

But he said I wasn't able to go, nor able to stand it after I

---

5. **Romanesque**: an artistic style characterized by simple ornamentation.

6. *delirium tremens* (dĭ-lĭr´ē-əm trē´mənz): violent trembling and hallucinations caused by excessive drinking.

7. **fatuity** (fə-tōo´ĭ-tē): foolishness; smug stupidity.

8. **frieze** (frēz): a narrow band of wallpaper placed along the upper edge of a wall.

MARK IT UP KEEP TRACK

Remember to use these marks to keep track of your understanding.

✔ ..... I understand.

? ..... I don't understand this.

! ..... Interesting or surprising idea

Pause & Reflect

1. Look at the details that you circled as you read. Put an *X* next to the phrase below that does *not* apply to the narrator's mental condition. **(Clarify)**

___ cries all the time

___ has trouble thinking straight

___ screams at her husband

___ stares at the wallpaper

MARK IT UP **2.** The narrator says that she tries to "have a real earnest reasonable talk" with John (lines 300–302). Underline the lines that describe John's response. **(Cause and Effect)**

3. What kind of relationship does the narrator have with her baby? **(Evaluate)**

_____

_____

_____

_____

READ ALOUD **4.** Read aloud the boxed passage. What does the narrator now see "creeping behind" the wallpaper patterns? **(Visualize)**

_____

_____

_____

_____

got there; and I did not make out a very good case for myself, for I was crying before I had finished.

It is getting to be a great effort for me to think straight. Just this nervous weakness I suppose.

And dear John gathered me up in his arms, and just carried me upstairs and laid me on the bed, and sat by me and read 310 to me till it tired my head.

He said I was his darling and his comfort and all he had, and that I must take care of myself for his sake, and keep well.

He says no one but myself can help me out of it, that I must use my will and self-control and not let any silly fancies run away with me.

There's one comfort, the baby is well and happy, and does not have to occupy this nursery with the horrid wallpaper.

If we had not used it, that blessed child would have! What a fortunate escape! Why, I wouldn't have a child of mine, an 320 impressionable little thing, live in such a room for worlds.

I never thought of it before, but it is lucky that John kept me here after all, I can stand it so much easier than a baby, you see.

Of course I never mention it to them any more—I am too wise,—but I keep watch of it all the same.

There are things in that paper that nobody knows but me, or ever will.

> Behind that outside pattern the dim shapes get clearer every day.
> 330 It is always the same shape, only very numerous.
> And it is like a woman stooping down and creeping about behind that pattern. I don't like it a bit. I wonder—I begin to think—I wish John would take me away from here!

Pause & Reflect

FOCUS
In this section, the narrator tries again to talk to John.

MARK IT UP As you read, circle passages in which the narrator attempts to speak up 340 for herself.

It is so hard to talk with John about my case, because he is so wise, and because he loves me so.

But I tried it last night.

It was moonlight. The moon shines in all around just as the sun does.

I hate to see it sometimes, it creeps so

slowly, and always comes in by one window or another.

slowly, and always comes in by one window or another.

John was asleep and I hated to waken him, so I kept still and watched the moonlight on that <u>undulating</u> wallpaper till I felt creepy.

The faint figure behind seemed to shake the pattern, just as if she wanted to get out.

I got up softly and went to feel and see if the paper *did* move, and when I came back John was awake.

"What is it, little girl?" he said. "Don't go walking about 350 like that—you'll get cold."

I thought it was a good time to talk, so I told him that I really was not gaining here, and that I wished he would take me away.

"Why darling!" said he, "our lease will be up in three weeks, and I can't see how to leave before.

"The repairs are not done at home, and I cannot possibly leave town just now. Of course if you were in any danger, I could and would, but you really are better, dear, whether you can see it or not. I am a doctor, dear, and I know. You are 360 gaining flesh and color, your appetite is better, I feel really much easier about you."

"I don't weigh a bit more," said I, "nor as much; and my appetite may be better in the evening when you are here, but it is worse in the morning when you are away!"

"Bless her little heart!" said he with a big hug, "she shall be as sick as she pleases! But now let's improve the shining hours[9] by going to sleep, and talk about it in the morning!"

"And you won't go away?" I asked gloomily.

"Why, how can I, dear? It is only three weeks more and 370 then we will take a nice little trip of a few days while Jennie is getting the house ready. Really dear you are better!"

"Better in body perhaps—" I began, and stopped short, for he sat up straight and looked at me with such a stern, reproachful look that I could not say another word.

"My darling," said he, "I beg of you, for my sake and for our child's sake, as well as for your own, that you will never

---

9. **improve the shining hours:** make good use of time (an allusion to the poem "Against Idleness and Mischief" by Isaac Watts: "How doth the little busy bee / Improve each shining hour, / And gather honey all the day / From every opening flower!").

WORDS
TO
KNOW

undulating (ŭn′jə-lā′tĭng) *adj.* moving with a wavelike motion **undulate** *v.*

1. Review the passages that you
   circled as you read. The narrator

   asks John to _____

   _____.

   John's answer is _____

   because _____

   _____.

   (Clarify)

2. In line 349, John calls the
   narrator "little girl." Do you think
   he treats her like a little girl?
   Yes/No, because _____

   _____

   _____

   _____.

   (Draw Conclusions)

3. Do you feel sorry for the
   narrator? *Yes/No,* because

   _____

   _____

   _____

   _____.

   (Connect)

for one instant let that idea enter your mind! There is nothing so dangerous, so fascinating, to a temperament like yours. It is a false and foolish fancy. Can you not trust me as a physician 380 when I tell you so?"

So of course I said no more on that score, and we went to sleep before long. He thought I was asleep first, but I wasn't, and lay there for hours trying to decide whether that front pattern and the back pattern really did move together or separately.

Pause **&** Reflect

> **FOCUS**
> At this stage, the wall-paper controls the narrator's thoughts and daily activities.
>
> **MARK IT UP** As you
> 390 read, circle phrases
> that suggest the
> narrator's increasing
> mental unbalance.

On a pattern like this, by daylight, there is a lack of sequence, a defiance of law, that is a constant irritant to a normal mind.

The color is hideous enough, and unreliable enough, and infuriating enough, but the pattern is torturing.

You think you have mastered it, but just as you get well underway in following, it turns a back-somersault and there you are. It slaps you in the face, knocks you down, and tramples upon you. It is like a bad dream.

The outside pattern is a florid arabesque,[10] reminding one of a fungus. If you can imagine a toadstool in joints, an 400 interminable string of toadstools, budding and sprouting in endless convolutions—why, that is something like it.

That is, sometimes!

There is one marked peculiarity about this paper, a thing nobody seems to notice but myself, and that is that it changes as the light changes.

When the sun shoots in through the east window—I always watch for that first long, straight ray—it changes so quickly that I never can quite believe it.

That is why I watch it always.

410 By moonlight—the moon shines in all night when there is a moon—I wouldn't know it was the same paper.

At night in any kind of light, in twilight, candle light, lamplight, and worst of all by moonlight, it becomes bars!

10. **florid arabesque:** an elaborate interwoven pattern.

The outside pattern I mean, and the woman behind it is as plain as can be.

I didn't realize for a long time what the thing was that showed behind, that dim sub-pattern, but now I am quite sure it is a woman.

By daylight she is subdued, quiet. I fancy it is the pattern that keeps her so still. It is so puzzling. It keeps me quiet by the hour.

I lie down ever so much now. John says it is good for me, and to sleep all I can.

Indeed he started the habit by making me lie down for an hour after each meal.

It is a very bad habit I am convinced, for you see I don't sleep.

And that cultivates deceit, for I don't tell them I'm awake— O no!

The fact is I am getting a little afraid of John.

He seems very queer sometimes, and even Jennie has an inexplicable look.

It strikes me occasionally, just as a scientific hypothesis,— that perhaps it is the paper!

I have watched John when he did not know I was looking, and come into the room suddenly on the most innocent excuses, and I've caught him several times *looking at the paper!* And Jennie too. I caught Jennie with her hand on it once.

She didn't know I was in the room, and when I asked her in a quiet, a very quiet voice, with the most restrained manner possible, what she was doing with the paper—she turned around as if she had been caught stealing, and looked quite angry—asked me why I should frighten her so!

Then she said that the paper stained everything it touched, that she had found yellow smooches[11] on all my clothes and John's, and she wished we would be more careful!

Did not that sound innocent? But I know she was studying that pattern, and I am determined that nobody shall find it out but myself!

---

11. **smooches:** dirty marks or spots; smudges.

NOTES

....
....
....
....
....
....
....
....
....
....
....
....
....

Pause & Reflect

1. Review the phrases that you circled as you read. How does the narrator feel about the "woman" she sees in the wallpaper? **(Infer)**

_____

_____

_____

_____

2. Do you think the narrator's interpretation of Jennie's behavior is accurate? *Yes/No,* because _____

_____

_____ .

(Evaluate)

3. What do you think will happen to the narrator? **(Predict)**

_____

_____

_____

_____

FOCUS

The narrator thinks about nothing but the wallpaper. As you read, notice details that suggest the narrator is losing her mind.

Life is very much more exciting now than it used to be. You see I have something more to expect, to look forward to, to watch. I really do eat better, and am more quiet than I was.

John is so pleased to see me improve! He laughed a little the other day, and said I seemed to be flourishing in spite of my wallpaper.

I turned it off with a laugh. I had no intention of telling
460 him it was *because* of the wallpaper—he would make fun of me. He might even want to take me away.

I don't want to leave now until I have found it out. There is a week more, and I think that will be enough.

I'm feeling ever so much better! I don't sleep much at night, for it is so interesting to watch developments; but I sleep a good deal in the daytime.

In the daytime it is tiresome and perplexing.

There are always new shoots on the fungus, and new shades of yellow all over it. I cannot keep count of them,
470 though I have tried conscientiously.

It is the strangest yellow, that wallpaper! It makes me think of all the yellow things I ever saw—not beautiful ones like buttercups, but old foul, bad yellow things.

But there is something else about that paper—the smell! I noticed it the moment we came into the room, but with so much air and sun it was not bad. Now we have had a week of fog and rain, and whether the windows are open or not, the smell is here.

It creeps all over the house.
480 I find it hovering in the dining room, skulking in the parlor, hiding in the hall, lying in wait for me on the stairs.

It gets into my hair.

Even when I go to ride, if I turn my head suddenly and surprise it—there is that smell!

Such a peculiar odor, too! I have spent hours in trying to analyze it, to find what it smelled like.

It is not bad—at first, and very gentle, but quite the subtlest, most enduring odor I ever met.

In this damp weather it is awful, I wake up in the night and
490 find it hanging over me.

It used to disturb me at first. I thought seriously of burning the house—to reach the smell.

But now I am used to it. The only thing I can think of that it is like is the *color* of the paper! A yellow smell.

There is a very funny mark on this wall, low down, near the mopboard.[12] A streak that runs round the room. It goes behind every piece of furniture, except the bed, a long, straight, even *smooch*, as if it had been rubbed over and over.

500   I wonder how it was done and who did it, and what they did it for. Round and round and round—round and round and round—it makes me dizzy!

📖 READ ALOUD   Lines 496–502

The narrator wonders who made the smooch, or mark, and why. How do you think the mark got on the wall? **(Cause and Effect)**

_____

_____

_____

I really have discovered something at last.

Through watching so much at night, when it changes so, I have finally found out.

The front pattern *does* move—and no wonder! The woman behind shakes it!

Sometimes I think there are a great many women behind, and sometimes only one, and she crawls around fast, and her
510   crawling shakes it all over.

Then in the very bright spots she keeps still, and in the very shady spots she just takes hold of the bars and shakes them hard.

And she is all the time trying to climb through. But nobody could climb through that pattern—it strangles so; I think that is why it has so many heads.

They get through, and then the pattern strangles them off and turns them upside down, and makes their eyes white!

If those heads were covered or taken off it would not be
520   half so bad.

I think that woman gets out in the daytime!

And I'll tell you why—privately—I've seen her!

I can see her out of every one of my windows!

It is the same woman, I know, for she is always creeping, and most women do not creep by daylight.

I see her on that long road under the trees, creeping along, and when a carriage comes she hides under the blackberry vines.

---

12. **mopboard:** baseboard; wooden molding that covers the corner where a floor and a wall are joined.

Pause **&** **Reflect**

1. The narrator is going mad. What does she now believe about the wallpaper? Check each statement below that applies. **(Infer)**

It has a foul smell.

A woman is behind the wallpaper.

The pattern moves.

It changes color.

2. What does the narrator see when she looks out the windows of her room? **(Clarify)**

_____

_____

_____

_____

....

....

....

....

....

....

....

....

....

....

....

....

....

I don't blame her a bit. It must be very humiliating to be caught creeping by daylight!

530   I always lock the door when I creep by daylight. I can't do it at night, for I know John would suspect something at once.

And John is so queer now, that I don't want to irritate him. I wish he would take another room! Besides, I don't want anybody to get that woman out at night but myself.

I often wonder if I could see her out of all the windows at once.

But, turn as fast as I can, I can only see out of one at one time.

And though I always see her, she may be able to creep

540 faster than I can turn!

I have watched her sometimes away off in the open country, creeping as fast as a cloud shadow in a high wind.

Pause **&** **Reflect**

FOCUS
In the final part of the story, the narrator slips into complete madness. Read on to see what she finally thinks about the wallpaper.

If only that top pattern could be gotten off from the under one! I mean to try it, little by little.

I have found out another funny thing, but I shan't tell it this time! It does not do to trust people too much.

There are only two more days to get

550 this paper off, and I believe John is beginning to notice. I don't like the look in his eyes.

And I heard him ask Jennie a lot of professional questions about me. She had a very good report to give.

She said I slept a good deal in the daytime.

John knows I don't sleep very well at night, for all I'm so quiet!

He asked me all sorts of questions, too, and pretended to be very loving and kind.

As if I couldn't see through him!

560   Still, I don't wonder he acts so, sleeping under this paper for three months.

It only interests me, but I feel sure John and Jennie are secretly affected by it.

Hurrah! This is the last day,[13] but it is enough. John to stay in town over night, and won't be out until this evening.

Jennie wanted to sleep with me—the sly thing! but I told her I should undoubtedly rest better for a night all alone.

That was clever, for really I wasn't alone a bit! As soon as it was moonlight and that poor thing began to crawl and shake the pattern, I got up and ran to help her.

I pulled and she shook, I shook and she pulled, and before morning we had peeled off yards of that paper.

A strip about as high as my head and half around the room.

And then when the sun came and that awful pattern began to laugh at me, I declared I would finish it today!

We go away tomorrow, and they are moving all my furniture down again to leave things as they were before.

Jennie looked at the wall in amazement, but I told her merrily that I did it out of pure spite at the vicious thing.

She laughed and said she wouldn't mind doing it herself, but I must not get tired.

How she betrayed herself that time!

But I am here, and no person touches this paper but me,— not *alive!*

She tried to get me out of the room—it was too <u>patent</u>! But I said it was so quiet and empty and clean now that I believed I would lie down again and sleep all I could; and not to wake me even for dinner—I would call when I woke.

So now she is gone, and the servants are gone, and the things are gone, and there is nothing left but that great bedstead nailed down, with the canvas mattress we found on it.

We shall sleep downstairs tonight, and take the boat home tomorrow.

I quite enjoy the room, now it is bare again.

How those children did tear about here!

This bedstead is fairly gnawed!

But I must get to work.

---

13. **This . . . last day:** The narrator is actually speaking on the night before the last full day. The word *this* refers to the day that will begin the next morning.

WORDS
TO
KNOW

patent (păt′nt) *adj.* obvious; apparent

> ✎ **MARK IT UP** **KEEP TRACK**
>
> Remember to use these marks to keep track of your understanding.
>
> ✔ ..... I understand.
>
> ? ..... I don't understand this.
>
> ! ..... Interesting or surprising idea

600   I have locked the door and thrown the key down into the front path.

I don't want to go out, and I don't want to have anybody come in, till John comes.

I want to astonish him.

I've got a rope up here that even Jennie did not find. If that woman does get out, and tries to get away, I can tie her!

But I forgot I could not reach far without anything to stand on!

This bed will *not* move!

610   I tried to lift and push it until I was lame, and then I got so angry I bit off a little piece at one corner—but it hurt my teeth.

Then I peeled off all the paper I could reach standing on the floor. It sticks horribly and the pattern just enjoys it! All those strangled heads and bulbous eyes and waddling fungus growths just shriek with <u>derision</u>!

I am getting angry enough to do something desperate. To jump out of the window would be admirable exercise, but the bars are too strong even to try.

620   Besides I wouldn't do it. Of course not. I know well enough that a step like that is improper and might be misconstrued.

> I don't like to *look* out of the windows even—there are so many of those creeping women, and they creep so fast.
>
> I wonder if they all come out of that wallpaper as I did?
>
> But I am securely fastened now by my well-hidden rope— you don't get *me* out in the road there!
>
> I suppose I shall have to get back behind the pattern when it comes night, and that is hard!

It is so pleasant to be out in this great room and creep

630 around as I please!

I don't want to go outside. I won't, even if Jennie asks me to.

For outside you have to creep on the ground, and everything is green instead of yellow.

But here I can creep smoothly on the floor, and my shoulder just fits in that long smooch around the wall, so I cannot lose my way.

Why there's John at the door!

It is no use, young man, you can't open it!

📖 **READ ALOUD** | **Lines 622–628**

What does the narrator now believe about her own connection to the wallpaper? **(Draw Conclusions)**

WORDS TO KNOW   **derision** (dĭ-rĭzh′ən) *n.* harsh ridicule or mockery; scorn

640 How he does call and pound!

Now he's crying for an axe.

It would be a shame to break down that beautiful door!

"John dear!" said I in the gentlest voice, "the key is down by the front steps, under a plantain leaf!"

That silenced him for a few moments.

Then he said—very quietly indeed, "Open the door, my darling!"

"I can't," said I. "The key is down by the front door under a plantain leaf!"

650 And then I said it again, several times, very gently and slowly, and said it so often that he had to go and see, and he got it of course, and came in. He stopped short by the door.

"What is the matter?" he cried. "What are you doing!"

I kept on creeping just the same, but I looked at him over my shoulder.

"I've got out at last," said I, "in spite of you and Jane.[14] And I've pulled off most of the paper, so you can't put me back!"

Now why should that man have fainted? But he did, and

660 right across my path by the wall, so that I had to creep over him every time!

Pause & Reflect

Pause & Reflect

MARK IT UP 1. How do you know that the narrator is now mad? Underline details that support your answer. (Clarify)

2. The narrator is desperate to peel off all the wallpaper. Why is this so important to her? (Infer)

CHALLENGE

Who or what is to blame for the narrator's losing her mind? Mark passages that provide evidence for your conclusions. (Draw Conclusions)

Wrapping Up

If you are using *The Language of Literature,* you can now move to the questions and activities on pages 779–781 of that book.

14. **in spite of you and Jane:** This reference to a previously unmentioned Jane is a point of debate. It could be an error made by the original printer for the name of the sister-housekeeper Jennie or Cousin Julia. It is also possible, however, that Jane is the narrator. If so, the narrator has freed herself from her wifely "Jane" identity.

Active Reading SkillBuilder

Making Inferences About the Narrator

Inferences are logical guesses based on the details the narrator provides and what you know about life. When reading "The Yellow Wallpaper," try to see things as the narrator does. Use the questions in this sequence chart to figure out what is happening. Two answers are given.

1. Why is the narrator writing in secret? (p. 220)

because her husband and brother don't want her to write

2. Describe the relationship between the narrator and her husband. (pp. 220–221)

3. What do the details about the room suggest about its use? (p. 221)

6. What is the "idea" that John says the narrator should not "let . . . enter your mind"? (pp. 229–230)

5. How do you explain the figure beginning to appear in the wallpaper? (pp. 225, 228)

The narrator is imagining the figure.

4. Describe the effect the wallpaper is having on the narrator. (pp. 222–223)

7. The narrator's attitude seems to have changed. Do you think she will get better? (p. 232)

8. What is the narrator's condition? (p. 235)

9. What does the narrator now believe? (p. 237)

Literary Analysis SkillBuilder

First-Person Narrator

The **narrator** relates the story's events to the reader and, in the first-person point of view, is a character in the story. In this story, the first-person narrator begins to see **images** in the wallpaper: bars, bulbous eyes, a creeping woman, and more. If the wallpaper reflects the narrator's mental state, readers can use it as evidence to draw conclusions about her feelings and preoccupations. Use the chart below to list images from the story that describe the wallpaper. Then try to interpret each image, associating it with some aspect of the narrator's life.

Image	Interpretation
pattern that lolls like a broken neck (p. 224)	The narrator feels like her spirit and creativity are being broken.

Follow Up: With a small group, discuss conclusions you draw about the narrator's problem. What are the advantages and disadvantages of using a first-person narrator to tell this story, especially in light of the narrator's condition?

Words to Know SkillBuilder

Words to Know

atrocious	derision	impertinence	patent	querulous
basely	felicity	inanimate	perseverance	undulating

A. On each blank line, write the word from the word list that the rhyme describes.

If this is your style, you find things that are wrong.
You whine and complain as you grumble along.

_____ (1)

If something is too clear for you to miss,
You might describe that thing as being this.

_____ (2)

This is what you show when it's a long way to the top,
But, though you are exhausted, you keep on and
   will not stop.

_____ (3)

If this describes the artworks you create,
The comments of the critics won't be "Great!"

_____ (4)

If this describes the ride you choose,
Your cash may not be all you lose.

_____ (5)

This is treating folks with less respect than they deserve,
To which they may respond by saying, "What a
   lot of nerve!"

_____ (6)

This does not describe a daisy or a doctor or a dog.
It does describe a rock, a chair, a sidewalk, and a log.

_____ (7)

Is this the state of mind you're in?
No wonder you can't help but grin.

_____ (8)

This is the reaction other people show to you
When they just laugh in nasty ways at everything
   you do.

_____ (9)

This is how a cheater cheats,
Cowards lie about their feats,
Robbers rob or big kids bully,
Wolves deceive in clothing woolly.

_____ (10)

B. Write a description of the narrator of "The Yellow Wallpaper," from the point of view of her husband. Use at least **four** of the Words to Know.

PREVIEW Paul Laurence Dunbar, an African–American poet, died young—at the age of 33 in 1906. He did not live to see such **lyric poems** as "We Wear the Mask" and "Sympathy" win him lasting respect. In these poems the speakers comment on the situation of African Americans. At that time, many white Americans stereotyped blacks as grinning and happy-go-lucky. A popular theatrical event was the minstrel show. In it, white entertainers darkened their faces, pretending to be black and performing funny antics. Dunbar's poems express the misery of his people in this climate of racial prejudice.

WE WEAR THE MASK

Paul Laurence Dunbar

FOCUS

In this poem the "mask" is a false appearance that hides true feelings. Read to find out about the contrast between the way the mask looks and the feelings it hides.

MARK IT UP As you read, underline words and phrases that help you understand the pain hidden by the mask. An example is highlighted.

We wear the mask that grins and lies,
It hides our cheeks and shades our eyes,—
This debt we pay to human guile;[1]
With torn and bleeding hearts we smile,
And mouth[2] with myriad subtleties.[3]

5

---

1. **guile:** slyness and craftiness in dealing with others.
2. **mouth:** to speak without conviction.
3. **myriad subtleties:** countless misleading statements.

Before You Read

If you are using *The Language of Literature,* study the information on page 835 of that book to prepare for reading.

Reading Tips

Lyric poems express deep feelings in emotional language. These lyric poems were written in the 1890s. As you read, keep these points in mind:

- Read the poems first silently and then aloud to get a sense of the feelings the poet expresses.

- Check the footnotes for help with difficult words and phrases.

- Remember that if the word order in a line is unusual, you won't find the structure *subject-verb-object.* Instead, look for the subject and the verb after the object or at the end of a line of verse.

MARK IT UP **KEEP TRACK**

As you read, you can use these marks to keep track of your understanding.

✔ ..... I understand.

? ..... I don't understand this.

! ..... Interesting or surprising idea

Why should the world be overwise,
In counting all our tears and sighs?
Nay, let them only see us, while
    We wear the mask.

10 We smile, but, O great Christ, our cries
To Thee from tortured souls arise.
We sing, but oh, the clay is vile[4]
Beneath our feet, and long the mile;
But let the world dream otherwise,
15   We wear the mask.

Pause & Reflect

Pause & Reflect

1. Review the words and phrases you underlined as you read. Then describe the contrast between the way the mask looks and the feelings it hides. **(Compare and Contrast)**

_____

_____

_____

_____

2. Why do the speaker and his people hide their true feelings from the world? **(Infer)**

_____

_____

_____

_____

3. Do you think people gain more or lose more by hiding their true feelings? **(Connect)**

_____

_____

_____

_____

4. **vile:** disgusting or objectionable.

Sympathy

Paul Laurence Dunbar

> **FOCUS**
>
> In this poem, the speaker deeply feels the pain and longing of a bird locked in a cage. This bird stands for African Americans in Dunbar's time.
>
> **MARK IT UP** As you read, underline details that reveal the caged bird's pain.

I know what the caged bird feels, alas!
    When the sun is bright on the upland slopes;
When the wind stirs soft through the springing grass,
And the river flows like a stream of glass;
    When the first bird sings and the first bud opes,[1]
And the faint perfume from its chalice steals[2]—
I know what the caged bird feels!

I know why the caged bird beats his wing
    Till its blood is red on the cruel bars;
For he must fly back to his perch and cling
When he fain[3] would be on the bough a-swing;
    And a pain still throbs in the old, old scars
And they pulse again with a keener sting—
I know why he beats his wing!

> **MARK IT UP** **WORD POWER**
>
> Mark words that you'd like to add to your **Personal Word List.** After reading, you can record the words and their meanings beginning on page 344.

---

1. **opes:** opens.
2. **the faint perfume . . . steals:** the lovely smell from the opening bud (**its chalice**) attracts the senses.
3. **fain:** gladly or willingly.

1. Review the details you underlined as you read. Why does the caged bird struggle so fiercely? **(Infer)**

_____

_____

_____

_____

READ ALOUD **2.** Read aloud lines 15–21. What feelings does the caged bird's song express? **(Infer)**

_____

_____

_____

_____

I know why the caged bird sings, ah me,
    When his wing is bruised and his bosom sore,—
When he beats his bars and he would be free;
It is not a carol⁴ of joy or glee,
    But a prayer that he sends from his heart's deep core,
But a plea, that upward to Heaven he flings—
I know why the caged bird sings!

Pause **&** Reflect

CHALLENGE

Irony is the contrast between appearance and reality. For example, the mask in "We Wear the Mask" appears to "grin" but in fact conceals the reality of "tears and sighs." How would you describe the central irony in "Sympathy"? Mark or highlight lines that support your interpretation. What **theme**, or message, about African Americans does the irony in these poems suggest?

Wrapping Up

If you are using **The Language of Literature**, you can now move to the questions and activities on pages 838–839 of that book.

4. **carol:** song, especially for Christmas.

Active Reading SkillBuilder

Interpreting Symbols

Interpreting symbols involves discovering what they might represent. On a second reading of these poems, use the following strategies to help figure out the symbolic meanings in the poems. Identify a possible symbol; consider the qualities of the symbolic object; note the ideas or feelings the poet associates with the symbol; consider the associations the symbol seems to trigger in you; make a logical guess about what the symbol might represent. Use the chart to organize your thoughts about the symbols. The symbolic objects in each poem are shown.

	Object	Qualities	Symbol of . . .
"We Wear the Mask"	mask		
"Sympathy"	caged bird		

Literary Analysis SkillBuilder

Symbol

A **symbol** is a person, place, or object that represents something beyond itself. Symbols in literature generally have several possible interpretations rather than one precise meaning, and often communicate complex, abstract ideas. Clues to the meaning of a particular symbol are usually found within the work itself. Identify what the mask and the caged bird represent in Dunbar's poems. Then think of other symbols that could represent similar ideas. Write these symbols in the diagrams below. Two examples are given.

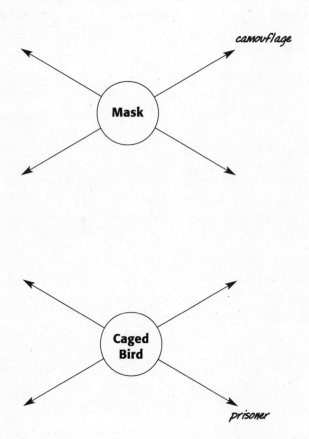

PREVIEW Langston Hughes was an African-American poet who wrote in the early and mid-20th century. In his poems, he used the rhythms of blues music and jazz to create unforgettable pictures of ordinary working people. The three poems you will read express deep feelings. They show the beauties, strengths, and hardships of African-American life.

FOCUS

In this poem, the speaker uses his own experience to show the painful effects of racial prejudice.

MARK IT UP Put a *P* next to those sentences that describe the present. Put an *F* next to those that describe the future. Examples are given on pages 247 and 248.

P I, too, sing America.

I am the darker brother.
They send me to eat in the kitchen
When company comes,
5 But I laugh,
And eat well,
And grow strong.

MARK IT UP KEEP TRACK

As you read, you can use these marks to keep track of your understanding.

✔ ..... I understand.

? ..... I don t understand this.

! ..... Interesting or surprising idea

F Tomorrow,
   I'll be at the table
10 When company comes.
   Nobody'll dare
   Say to me,
   "Eat in the kitchen,"
   Then.

15 Besides,
   They'll see how beautiful I am
   And be ashamed—

   I, too, am America.

Pause & Reflect

Pause & Reflect

✎ MARK IT UP 1. Reread lines 1–7. Circle the words that help you picture the speaker. (Visualize)

2. Why do you think the speaker is sent to eat in the kitchen? (Infer)

_____

_____

_____

_____

3. Look at the lines you marked in the poem. In what way does the speaker expect the future to be different from the present? (Compare and Contrast)

_____

_____

_____

_____

Harlem

LANGSTON HUGHES

FOCUS

This poem begins with a question about a dream deferred, or postponed. Several comparisons follow.

▶ MARK IT UP Number the five comparisons made in lines 2 through 10.

What happens to a dream deferred?

Does it dry up
like a raisin in the sun?
Or fester like a sore—
5   And then run?
Does it stink like rotten meat?
Or crust and sugar over—
like a syrupy sweet?

Maybe it just sags
10   like a heavy load.

Or does it explode?

Pause **&** **Reflect**

Pause **&** **Reflect**

1. Look back at the comparisons you numbered. Circle the sentence below that describes what the five comparisons have in common. (**Compare and Contrast**)

The comparisons show the harmful effects of a dream postponed.

The comparisons show the pleasant benefits of a dream postponed.

▶ MARK IT UP   2. Star the comparison that interests you the most. What does that comparison reveal about a dream deferred? (**Infer**)

_____
_____
_____
_____

3. What is it like to have to constantly postpone something you really want to do? (**Connect**)

_____
_____
_____
_____

The Weary Blues

LANGSTON HUGHES

Droning[1] a drowsy syncopated[2] tune,
Rocking back and forth to a mellow croon,[3]
    I heard a Negro play.
Down on Lenox Avenue the other night
By the pale dull pallor[4] of an old gas light   5
    He did a lazy sway. . . .
    He did a lazy sway. . . .
To the tune o' those Weary Blues.
With his ebony hands on each ivory key
He made that poor piano moan with melody.   10
    O Blues!
Swaying to and fro on his rickety[5] stool
He played that sad raggy tune like a musical fool.
    Sweet Blues!
Coming from a black man's soul.   15
    O Blues!

Pause & Reflect

---

1. **droning:** The piano player is singing in a low, steady voice.
2. **syncopated** (sĭng′kə-pā′tĭd): characterized by a shifting of stresses from normally strong to normally weak beats.
3. **croon:** a soft humming or singing.
4. **pallor** (păl′ər): lack of color.
5. **rickety** (rĭk′ĭ-tē): likely to break or fall apart.

Pause & Reflect

MARK IT UP **1.** Look at the passages that you circled. Star the ones that tell you something about the **setting**—the time and the place—of the blues performance. **(Clarify)**

2. Do you think the speaker enjoys the performance? *Yes/No,* because _____

_____

_____ .

(Infer)

READ ALOUD **3.** Read lines 9–16 aloud, paying close attention to the **rhythms.** Do the lines have a fast or a slow pace? Do the rhythms match the music being described? **(Detect Rhythm)**

_____

_____

_____

In the second part of the poem, the poet includes two **stanzas** of the actual blues song the musician is singing.

MARK IT UP Put brackets around the two stanzas of the song.

In a deep song voice with a melancholy[6] tone
I heard that Negro sing, that old piano moan—
    "Ain't got nobody in all this world,
20   Ain't got nobody but ma self.
    I's gwine to quit ma frownin'
    And put ma troubles on the shelf."
Thump, thump, thump, went his foot on the floor.
He played a few chords then he sang some more—
25   "I got the Weary Blues
    And I can't be satisfied.
    Got the Weary Blues
    And can't be satisfied—
    I ain't happy no mo'
30   And I wish that I had died."
And far into the night he crooned that tune.
The stars went out and so did the moon.
The singer stopped playing and went to bed
While the Weary Blues echoed through his head.
35 He slept like a rock or a man that's dead.

Pause & Reflect

Pause & Reflect

READ ALOUD **1.** Read the two stanzas of the blues song aloud. What three phrases are repeated? **(Clarify)**

_____
_____
_____
_____

2. Why do you think the blues singer sleeps so soundly? **(Infer)**

_____
_____
_____
_____

3. Do you think "The Weary Blues" is a good title for this poem? *Yes/No,* because_____

_____
_____ .

(Evaluate)

CHALLENGE

What do these three poems have in common? Use examples from the poems to support your ideas. **(Compare and Contrast)**

Wrapping Up

If you are using *The Language of Literature,* you can now move on to the questions and activities on pages 928 and 929 of that book. You may also want to review the questions on pages 925 and 926.

---

6. **melancholy** (mĕl'ən-kŏl'ē): sad or gloomy.

Active Reading SkillBuilder

Detecting Rhythm in Poetry

Inspired by the blues and jazz that he heard in Harlem nightclubs, Hughes tried to write poetry with the distinctive **rhythms** of these types of music. Try to detect the different rhythms that Hughes creates through his arrangement of stressed and unstressed syllables in a line. Read each poem aloud, listen for the rhythm, then tap it out as you read the poem silently. Imagine how the poems would sound recited over a background of blues or jazz music. On the chart below, write down lines in each poem that have a rhythm you particularly like. Mark syllables that you think should be stressed. An example is given.

Poems	Lines with Rhythm I Like
"I, Too"	"Í am the dárker bróther."
"Harlem"	
"The Weary Blues"	

Literary Analysis SkillBuilder

Mood

The **mood** of a poem is the emotional feeling or atmosphere that the poet creates
for a reader. Poets create mood through their use of imagery, figurative language,
sound devices, description, and rhythm. Use the chart below to identify the
mood of each of these poems. Then list the various elements that Hughes uses
to develop that mood. Two examples are given.

Poem	Mood of Poem	Elements That Contribute to Mood
"I, Too"	*self-confident; proud*	*word choice—"Nobody'll dare/Say to me,"*
"Harlem"		
"The Weary Blues"		

Before You Read

If you are using *The Language of Literature,* study the information on page 950 of that book to prepare for reading.

Reading Tips

Some passages in this **essay** may remind you of poetry. They contain **figurative language** that creates vivid pictures for your imagination.

Figurative language expresses ideas beyond the literal meaning of words. When you come upon figurative words and phrases, don't stop reading to figure out the meaning. Just note them so that you can return to them later for close study. You will find it easier to understand them after you have read through the entire essay.

◢ MARK IT UP KEEP TRACK

As you read, you can use these marks to keep track of your understanding.

✔ ..... I understand.

? ..... I don't understand this.

! ..... Interesting or surprising idea

How It Feels to Be Colored Me

ZORA NEALE HURSTON

PREVIEW In this **essay**, first published in 1928, the author describes her feelings about herself as an African American. She recalls her first 13 years growing up in an African-American town in Florida. She also reflects upon the times in her later life when she was most aware of her race. Finally, she describes what she and all others have in common.

FOCUS
Read to find out about Hurston's experiences with white people as a child in Eatonville.
◢ MARK IT UP As you read, circle details that tell you how she reacted to the white people traveling through town. An example is highlighted.

I am colored[1] but I offer nothing in the way of extenuating circumstances except the fact that I am the only Negro in the United States whose grandfather on the mother's side was *not* an Indian chief.

I remember the very day that I became colored. Up to my thirteenth year I lived in the little Negro town of Eatonville, Florida. It is exclusively a colored town. The only white people I knew passed through the town going to or coming from Orlando. The native whites rode dusty horses; the Northern tourists chugged down the sandy village road in automobiles. The town knew the Southerners and never stopped cane chewing when they passed. But the Northerners were something else again. They

---

1. **colored:** Hurston uses the term *colored* to refer to herself and to other African Americans. This term was in use in 1928 when Hurston wrote this essay.

WORDS
TO
KNOW

extenuating (ĭk-stĕn′yōō-ā′tĭng) *adj.* lessening a fault by serving as a partial excuse **extenuate** *v.*

were peered at cautiously from behind curtains by the timid. The more venturesome would come out on the porch to watch them go past and got just as much pleasure out of the tourists as the tourists got out of the village.

The front porch might seem a daring place for the rest of the town, but it was a gallery seat for me. My favorite place was atop the gatepost. Proscenium box² for a born first-nighter.³ Not only did I enjoy the show, but I didn't mind the actors knowing that I liked it. I usually spoke to them in passing. I'd wave at them and when they returned my salute, I would say something like this: "Howdy-do-well-I-thank-you-where-you-goin'?" Usually the automobile or the horse paused at this, and after a queer exchange of compliments, I would probably "go a piece of the way" with them, as we say in farthest Florida. If one of my family happened to come to the front in time to see me, of course negotiations would be rudely broken off. But even so, it is clear that I was the first "welcome-to-our-state" Floridian, and I hope the Miami Chamber of Commerce will please take notice.

During this period, white people differed from colored to me only in that they rode through town and never lived there. They liked to hear me "speak pieces" and sing and wanted to see me dance the parse-me-la, and gave me generously of their small silver for doing these things, which seemed strange to me, for I wanted to do them so much that I needed bribing to stop. Only they didn't know it. The colored people gave no dimes. They deplored any joyful tendencies in me, but I was their Zora nevertheless. I belonged to them, to the nearby hotels, to the county—everybody's Zora.

But changes came in the family when I was thirteen, and I was sent to school in Jacksonville. I left Eatonville, the town of the oleanders,⁴ as Zora. When I disembarked from the riverboat at Jacksonville, she was no more. It seemed that I had suffered a sea change.⁵ I was not Zora of Orange County

> **MARK IT UP** WORD POWER
> Mark words that you'd like to add to your **Personal Word List**. After reading, you can record the words and their meanings beginning on page 344.

---

2. **proscenium** (prō-sē′nē-əm) **box:** a box seat near the stage.
3. **first-nighter:** a person who attends the opening performance of a play, an opera, or a similar show.
4. **oleanders** (ō′lē-ăn′dərz): evergreen shrubs with fragrant flowers.
5. **sea change:** complete transformation.

WORDS TO KNOW — **deplore** (dĭ-plôr′) v. to feel strong disapproval of or deeply regret

1. Review the details you circled
   as you read. How does Hurston
   react to the white tourists?
   (Infer)

_____

_____

_____

_____

MARK IT UP How does
Hurston's view of herself
change when she leaves home
at 13? Write the answer below.
Then underline words and
phrases on pages 255 and 256
that led you to the answer.
(Main Idea)

_____

_____

_____

_____

any more, I was now a little colored girl. I found it out in
certain ways. In my heart as well as in the mirror, I became a
fast brown—warranted not to rub nor run.

Pause **&** Reflect

FOCUS
The word *tragic* means
"doomed or unhappy."
Hurston begins this
part by stating, "But I
am not tragically
colored." Read to find
out her feelings about
her race and about
her people's past
experience of slavery.

But I am not tragically colored. There is
no great sorrow dammed up in my soul,
nor lurking behind my eyes. I do not
mind at all. I do not belong to the
sobbing school of Negrohood who hold
that nature somehow has given them a
lowdown dirty deal and whose feelings
are all hurt about it. Even in the helter-
skelter skirmish that is my life, I have
seen that the world is to the strong
regardless of a little pigmentation[6] more or less. No, I do not
weep at the world—I am too busy sharpening my oyster knife.[7]

Someone is always at my elbow reminding me that I am the
granddaughter of slaves. It fails to register depression with
me. Slavery is sixty years in the past. The operation was
successful and the patient is doing well, thank you. The
terrible struggle that made me an American out of a potential
slave said, "On the line!" The Reconstruction said, "Get set!"
and the generation before said, "Go!" I am off to a flying
start and I must not halt in the stretch to look behind and
weep. Slavery is the price I paid for civilization, and the choice
was not with me. It is a bully[8] adventure and worth all that I
have paid through my ancestors for it. No one on earth ever
had a greater chance for glory. The world to be won and
nothing to be lost. It is thrilling to think—to know that for
any act of mine, I shall get twice as much praise or twice as
much blame. It is quite exciting to hold the center of the
national stage, with the spectators not knowing whether to
laugh or to weep.

---

6. **pigmentation:** darkness of skin coloration.

7. **oyster knife:** a reference to the saying "The world is my oyster," implying
   that the world contains treasure waiting to be taken, like the pearl in an
   oyster.

8. **bully:** excellent; splendid.

The position of my white neighbor is much more difficult. No brown <u>specter</u> pulls up a chair beside me when I sit down to eat. No dark ghost thrusts its leg against mine in bed. The game of keeping what one has is never so exciting as the game of getting.

I do not always feel colored. Even now I often achieve the unconscious Zora of Eatonville before the Hegira.[9] I feel most colored when I am thrown against a sharp white background.

For instance at Barnard.[10] "Beside the waters of the Hudson"[11] I feel my race. Among the thousand white persons, I am a dark rock surged upon, and overswept, but through it all, I remain myself. When covered by the waters, I am; and the ebb but reveals me again.

Pause & Reflect

FOCUS

Hurston describes what she experiences while listening to jazz. MARK IT UP As you read, underline the details that help you understand her reaction to this music.

Sometimes it is the other way around. A white person is set down in our midst, but the contrast is just as sharp for me. For instance, when I sit in the drafty basement that is The New World Cabaret with a white person, my color comes. We enter chatting about any little nothing that we have in common and are seated by the jazz waiters. In the abrupt way that jazz orchestras have, this one plunges into a number. It loses no time in circumlocutions,[12] but gets right down to business. It constricts the thorax and splits the heart with its tempo and narcotic harmonies. This orchestra grows rambunctious, rears on its hind legs and attacks the tonal veil with primitive fury, <u>rending</u> it, clawing it until it breaks through to the jungle

---

9. **Hegira** (hĭ-jī′rə): journey (from the name given to Mohammed's journey from Mecca to Medina in 622).

10. **Barnard:** the college in New York City from which Hurston graduated in 1928.

11. **"Beside the waters of the Hudson":** a reference to the first line of Barnard's school song.

12. **circumlocutions** (sûr′kəm-lō-kyōō′shənz): unnecessary elaboration or "beating around the bush."

WORDS TO KNOW
specter (spĕk′tər) *n.* a ghostly vision; phantom
rend (rĕnd) *v.* to tear or split apart violently

Pause & Reflect

1. How does Hurston feel about her race? **(Clarify)**

_____

_____

_____

MARK IT UP 2. Why is Hurston not depressed about her people's past experience of slavery? Write the answer below. Then underline details on pages 256 and 257 that helped you reach your conclusion. **(Infer)**

_____

_____

_____

_____

3. Hurston is most aware of her race when _____

_____

_____

(Cause and Effect)

1. Look at the details you
underlined as you read. Then
write a sentence to **summarize**
Hurston's reaction to jazz.

_____

_____

_____

_____

READ ALOUD   2. Read aloud
the boxed passage on this page.
How does Hurston's reaction to
jazz differ from her white
companion's reaction?
(Compare and Contrast)

_____

_____

_____

beyond. I follow those heathen—follow them exultingly. I
dance wildly inside myself; I yell within, I whoop; I shake my
assegai[13] above my head, I hurl it true to the mark
yeeeeooww! I am in the jungle and living in the jungle way.
My face is painted red and yellow and my body is painted
blue. My pulse is throbbing like a war drum. I want to
slaughter something—give pain, give death to what, I do not
know. But the piece ends. The men of the orchestra wipe their
lips and rest their fingers. I creep back slowly to the <u>veneer</u> we
call civilization with the last tone and find the white friend
sitting motionless in his seat, smoking calmly.

"Good music they have here," he remarks, drumming the
table with his fingertips.

Music. The great blobs of purple and red emotion have not
touched him. He has only heard what I felt. He is far away
and I see him but dimly across the ocean and the continent
that have fallen between us. He is so pale with his whiteness
then and I am *so* colored.

Pause & Reflect

FOCUS
Read to find out how
Hurston sums up her
feelings about race.

At certain times I have no race. I am *me*.
When I set my hat at a certain angle
and saunter down Seventh Avenue,
Harlem City, feeling as snooty as the
lions in front of the Forty-Second Street
Library, for instance. So far as my feelings are concerned,
Peggy Hopkins Joyce on the Boule Mich with her gorgeous
raiment, stately carriage,[14] knees knocking together in a most
aristocratic manner, has nothing on me. The cosmic[15] Zora
emerges. I belong to no race nor time. I am the eternal
feminine with its string of beads.

---

13. **assegai** (ăs′ə-gī′): a light spear, especially one with a short shaft and long
    blade, used in southern Africa.
14. **Peggy Hopkins Joyce . . . carriage:** one of the richest women of Hurston's
    day, walking along the Boulevard Saint-Michel in Paris, dressed in beautiful
    clothes, carrying herself like a queen.
15. **cosmic:** of or belonging to the universe.

WORDS TO KNOW	**veneer** (və-nîr′) *n.* a thin surface layer that conceals what is below

(140) I have no separate feeling about being an American citizen and colored. I am merely a fragment of the Great Soul that surges within the boundaries. My country, right or wrong.

Sometimes, I feel discriminated against, but it does not make me angry. It merely astonishes me. How *can* any deny themselves the pleasure of my company? It's beyond me.

But in the main, I feel like a brown bag of miscellany[16] propped against a wall. Against a wall in company with other bags, white, red, and yellow. Pour out the contents, and there is discovered a jumble of small things priceless and worthless. (150) A first-water[17] diamond, an empty spool, bits of broken glass, lengths of string, a key to a door long since crumbled away, a rusty knife blade, old shoes saved for a road that never was and never will be, a nail bent under the weight of things too heavy for any nail, a dried flower or two still a little fragrant. In your hand is the brown bag. On the ground before you is the jumble it held—so much like the jumble in the bags, could they be emptied, that all might be dumped in a single heap and the bags refilled without altering the content of any greatly. A bit of colored glass more or less would not matter. (160) Perhaps that is how the Great Stuffer of Bags filled them in the first place—who knows?

Pause & Reflect

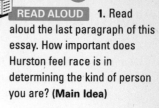
Pause & Reflect

READ ALOUD **1.** Read aloud the last paragraph of this essay. How important does Hurston feel race is in determining the kind of person you are? **(Main Idea)**

_____

_____

_____

_____

2. If you had met Zora Neale Hurston, would you have liked her? Explain. **(Connect)**

_____

_____

_____

_____

CHALLENGE

Tone is the writer's attitude toward his or her subject. For example, Hurston conveys a breezy, optimistic tone in describing her childhood zest for interacting with the tourists. Reread Hurston's description of her experience listening to jazz. How would you describe the **tone** of this passage? What words and phrases help to convey this tone? **(Analyze)**

Wrapping Up

If you are using **_The Language of Literature,_** you can now move to the questions and activities on pages 957–958 of that book.

16. **miscellany** (mĭs′ə-lā′nē): a collection of various parts, items, or ingredients.

17. **first-water:** of the highest quality or purity.

Active Reading SkillBuilder

Drawing Conclusions About Author's Purposes

A writer usually writes for one or more **purposes**—to inform, to entertain, to express himself or herself, or to persuade readers to believe or do something. When reading this essay, identify passages from each part that affect you strongly. For each passage, consider the kinds of experiences Hurston relates, descriptive details she provides, and her direct statements and comparisons. Use the following chart to record data about the selected passages. Then use the data to draw conclusions about Hurston's purposes for writing each passage. Record these conclusions on the chart. An example is shown.

Hurston's Essay	
Passages	**Purposes**
1. Childhood in Eatonville *Hurston describes growing up in an African-American town in Florida where she "was everybody's Zora" and enjoyed entertaining Northern white tourists who rode through town.*	
2. Experiencing Live Jazz	
3. Comparison of People to Stuffed Bags	

Literary Analysis SkillBuilder

Autobiographical Essay

An **autobiographical essay** is a short work of nonfiction that focuses on an aspect of the writer's life. One of the challenges for the writer of an autobiographical essay is to combine objective description with the expression of subjective feelings. Use the following chart to analyze Hurston's account of listening to jazz at The New World Cabaret. Identify examples of both objective description and Hurston's expression of subjective feelings. An example is shown.

Objective Description	Subjective Expression
The club is located in a drafty basement.	physical effect of listening to jazz—"constricts the thorax and splits the heart"

Words to Know SkillBuilder

Words to Know

deplore   extenuating   rend   specter   veneer

A. On each blank line, write the word from the word list that the clue describes.

1. This word is most commonly used to modify *circumstances.* A lawyer might use it to explain why a defendant should receive mercy.

   _____ (1)

2. To do this is to separate or tear something, but forcefully and destructively. Lightning bolts do it to trees, predators to their prey.

   _____ (2)

3. This is the visible form of something not actually present, always mysterious and usually frightening. It is often used figuratively to describe something dreaded, such as war.

   _____ (3)

4. To do this is to be very sorry about something or to find a lot of fault with it. People tend to disapprove of rudeness but do this to murder.

   _____ (4)

5. This is a surface, and only a surface, appearance. It can be a layer of fine oak on top of plywood or a friendly smile that hides jealousy or hate.

   _____ (5)

B. Fill in each blank with the correct word from the word list.

1. Under her _____ of sternness is a soft heart. You could describe her as a cement-covered marshmallow.

2. Are past hardships and injustices _____ conditions for a crime committed in the present? People disagree, to put it mildly.

3. I remain haunted by the _____ of poverty. It looms in my pantry, waiting for me to waste a bite of food.

4. Most people _____ the poverty that large numbers of families live in. How many do something about it?

5. I'll _____ this dress right up the back the first time I bend over. What ever possessed me to buy a garment so much too small?

C. Imagine that you are listening to a piece of music that strongly affects you as the music at The New World Cabaret affects Hurston. Write a description of the music and your reaction to it, similar in nature to how Hurston describes the jazz she listens to. Use at least **two** of the Words to Know.

The DEATH of the HIRED MAN

ROBERT FROST

PREVIEW "The Death of the Hired Man" is one of Robert Frost's best known poems. It is set on a farm in New England in the early years of the 20th century. At that time, much of the work on a farm had to be done by hand. Farmers needed extra workers at certain times, especially during the fall harvest. The hired man, mentioned in this poem, is a wandering laborer. He works on farms in exchange for room and board. As the poem begins, he has just returned to the farm he left during the last harvest.

Before You Read

If you are using *The Language of Literature,* study the information on page 1006 of that book to prepare for reading.

Reading Tips

Much of the poem is written in the form of a **dialogue** between two characters: a wife and her husband.

- Figuring out who is speaking can be tricky at times. Not all of the speeches are marked "he said" or "she said." Pay attention to the quotation marks and line breaks. They indicate when one character stops talking and the other takes over.

- These characters express different views about the hired man. Think about the contrast between their points of view.

FOCUS

Mary waits to tell her husband, Warren, about the return of Silas, the hired man. Read to find out how Warren feels about Silas.

MARK IT UP As you read, circle words or phrases that help you understand Warren's feelings about Silas. An example is highlighted on page 264.

MARK IT UP **KEEP TRACK**

As you read, you can use these marks to keep track of your understanding.

✔ ..... I understand.

? ..... I don't understand this.

! ..... Interesting or surprising idea

Mary sat musing on the lamp-flame[1] at the table,
Waiting for Warren. When she heard his step,
She ran on tiptoe down the darkened passage
To meet him in the doorway with the news
And put him on his guard. "Silas is back."

---

1. **musing on the lamp-flame:** looking thoughtfully at the flame of an oil lamp.

She pushed him outward with her through the door
And shut it after her. "Be kind," she said.
She took the market things from Warren's arms
And set them on the porch, then drew him down
10 To sit beside her on the wooden steps.

"When was I ever anything but kind to him?
But I'll not have the fellow back," he said.
"I told him so last haying,[2] didn't I?
If he left then, I said, that ended it.
What good is he? Who else will <u>harbor</u> him
At his age for the little he can do?
What help he is there's no depending on.
Off he goes always when I need him most.
He thinks he ought to earn a little pay,
20 Enough at least to buy tobacco with,
So he won't have to beg and be <u>beholden</u>.
'All right,' I say, 'I can't afford to pay
Any fixed wages,[3] though I wish I could.'
'Someone else can.' 'Then someone else will have to.'
I shouldn't mind his bettering himself
If that was what it was. You can be certain,
When he begins like that, there's someone at him
Trying to coax him off with pocket money—
In haying time, when any help is scarce.
30 In winter he comes back to us. I'm done."

Pause & Reflect

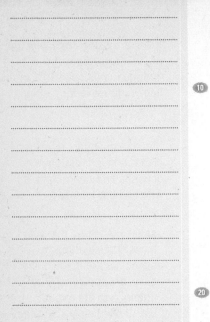
2. **haying:** the time of the year when hay is cut.

3. **fixed wages:** a specified sum of money given by an employer to a worker.

WORDS TO KNOW	**harbor** (här′bər) *v.* to shelter; protect **beholden** (bǐ hōl′ dən) *adj.* obliged to feel grateful; indebted

Mary describes her impressions of Silas on his return. Her feelings for Silas are different from her husband's.

MARK IT UP As you read, underline words or phrases that suggest her feelings for Silas.

"Sh! not so loud: he'll hear you," Mary said.

"I want him to: he'll have to soon or late."[4]

"He's worn out. He's asleep beside the stove.
When I came up from Rowe's I found him here,
Huddled against the barn door fast asleep,
A miserable sight, and frightening, too—
You needn't smile—I didn't recognize him—
I wasn't looking for him—and he's changed.
Wait till you see."

        "Where did you say he'd been?"

40 "He didn't say. I dragged him to the house,
And gave him tea and tried to make him smoke.
I tried to make him talk about his travels.
Nothing would do: he just kept nodding off."

"What did he say? Did he say anything?"

"But little."

        "Anything? Mary, confess
He said he'd come to ditch the meadow[5] for me."

"Warren!"

        "But did he? I just want to know."

"Of course he did. What would you have him say?
Surely you wouldn't grudge the poor old man
50 Some humble way to save his self-respect.
He added, if you really care to know,
He meant to clear the upper pasture, too.
That sounds like something you have heard before?"

---

4. **soon or late:** sooner or later; eventually.

5. **ditch the meadow:** to dig one or more channels in a field in order to drain off excess water.

1. Review the words and phrases
you underlined as you read.
Then check the two words
below that indicate Mary's
feelings for Silas. **(Evaluate)**

pity   anger

disgust   sympathy

2. If you were in Warren's position,
would you take Silas back
again? *Yes / No,* because_____

_____

_____

_____ .

(Connect)

Warren, I wish you could have heard the way
He jumbled everything. I stopped to look
Two or three times—he made me feel so queer—
To see if he was talking in his sleep.

Pause & Reflect

> **FOCUS**
> Mary recalls Silas's relationship with
> Harold Wilson. He was a college student
> who worked on the farm four years ago.
> Read to find out what Silas thinks of
> Harold.

He ran on[6] Harold Wilson—you remember—
The boy you had in haying four years since.[7]
60   He's finished school, and teaching in his college.
Silas declares you'll have to get him back.
He says they two will make a team for work:
Between them they will lay this farm as smooth!
The way he mixed that in with other things.
He thinks young Wilson a likely lad, though daft
On[8] education—you know how they fought
All through July under the blazing sun,
Silas up on the cart to build the load,
Harold along beside to pitch it on."

70   "Yes, I took care to keep well out of earshot."

"Well, those days trouble Silas like a dream.
You wouldn't think they would. How such things
     linger!
Harold's young college-boy's <u>assurance</u> piqued[9] him.

---

6. **ran on:** kept talking about.

7. **since:** ago.

8. **daft on:** crazy about; obsessed with.

9. **piqued** (pēkt): aroused resentment in.

WORDS
TO   **assurance** (ə-shŏŏr′əns) *n.* self-confidence
KNOW

After so many years he still keeps finding
Good arguments he sees he might have used.
I sympathize. I know just how it feels
To think of the right thing to say too late.
Harold's associated in his mind with Latin.[10]
He asked me what I thought of Harold's saying
He studied Latin, like the violin,
Because he liked it—that an argument!
He said he couldn't make the boy believe
He could find water with a hazel prong—[11]
Which showed how much good school had ever done
    him.
He wanted to go over that. But most of all
He thinks if he could have another chance
To teach him how to build a load of hay—"

"I know, that's Silas' one accomplishment.
He bundles every forkful in its place.
And tags and numbers it for future reference,
So he can find and easily dislodge it
In the unloading. Silas does that well.
He takes it out in bunches like big birds' nests.
You never see him standing on the hay
He's trying to lift, straining to lift himself."
"He thinks if he could teach him that, he'd be
Some good perhaps to someone in the world.
He hates to see a boy the fool of books.[12]
Poor Silas, so concerned for other folk,
And nothing to look backward to with pride,
And nothing to look forward to with hope,
So now and never any different."

Pause & Reflect

10. **Harold's associated . . . with Latin:** To Silas, Harold's love of the Latin language stands for all knowledge with no practical use.

11. **find . . . prong:** refers to the practice of dowsing, in which a person uses a forked stick made of hazel wood to try to find underground water.

12. **the fool of books:** a person with much education but no common sense.

Pause & Reflect

MARK IT UP **1.** What does Silas think of Harold Wilson? Write the answer below. Then circle details on pages 266 and 267 that led you to your conclusion. **(Draw Conclusions)**

_____

_____

_____

_____

2. Reread lines 88–95. How would you evaluate Silas as a worker? **(Evaluate)**

_____

_____

_____

_____

READ ALOUD **3.** Read aloud lines 99–102. How do these lines make you feel about Silas? **(Connect)**

_____

_____

_____

_____

The narrator describes the moonlight flowing upon Mary. Mary and Warren then tell what home means to each of them.

✎ MARK IT UP   As you read, mark Warren's definition of home with a *W*. Mark Mary's definition of home with an *M*.

Part of a moon was falling down the west,
Dragging the whole sky with it to the hills.
Its light poured softly in her lap. She saw it
And spread her apron to it. She put out her hand
Among the harplike morning-glory strings,
<u>Taut</u> with the dew from garden bed to eaves,
As if she played unheard some tenderness
110   That wrought on[13] him beside her in the night.

"Warren," she said, "he has come home to die:
You needn't be afraid he'll leave you this time."

"Home," he mocked gently.
                              "Yes, what else but home?
It all depends on what you mean by home.
Of course he's nothing to us, any more
Than was the hound that came a stranger to us
Out of the woods, worn out upon the trail."

"Home is the place where, when you have to go there,
They have to take you in."

                              "I should have called it
120   Something you somehow haven't to deserve."

Pause **&** *Reflect*

Pause **&** **Reflect**

📖 READ ALOUD   **1.** Read aloud lines 103–110. These lines associate Mary with moonlight, flowers, and music. What do these lines suggest about her character? **(Infer)**

_____

_____

_____

_____

2. Review the definitions you marked as you read. Which definition do you prefer? *Warren's / Mary's* because ____

_____

_____

_____

_____

(Compare and Contrast)

13. **wrought** (rôt) **on:** worked on.

WORDS
TO
KNOW   **taut** (tôt) *adj.* pulled tight; straight

Warren leaned out and took a step or two,
Picked up a little stick, and brought it back
And broke it in his hand and tossed it by.
"Silas has better claim on us you think
Than on his brother? Thirteen little miles
As the road winds would bring him to his door.
Silas has walked that far no doubt today.
Why doesn't he go there? His brother's rich,
A somebody—director in the bank."

130   "He never told us that."

               "We know it, though."

"I think his brother ought to help, of course.
I'll see to that if there is need. He ought of right
To take him in, and might be willing to—
He may be better than appearances.[14]
But have some pity on Silas. Do you think
If he had any pride in claiming kin
Or anything he looked for from his brother,
He'd keep so still about him all this time?"

"I wonder what's between them."

               "I can tell you.

140   Silas is what he is—we wouldn't mind him—
But just the kind that kinsfolk[15] can't <u>abide</u>.
He never did a thing so very bad.
He don't know why he isn't quite as good
As anybody. Worthless though he is,
He won't be made ashamed to please his brother."

Pause **&** **Reflect**

---

14. **better than appearances:** better than he looks.
15. **kinsfolk:** relatives.

Pause & **Reflect**

1. Why does Mary ask Warren to
   go in and see Silas? (**Clarify**)

_____

_____

_____

READ ALOUD   **2.** Read aloud
lines 164–166. What reactions do
you have to the poem's ending?
(**Connect**)

_____

_____

_____

....

....

....

....

....

....

CHALLENGE

In describing how poetry affects
the reader, Frost wrote that a
poem "begins in delight and
ends in wisdom." The beginning
of this poem sets up a **conflict**
between a wife and her
husband over how to treat the
hired man. What **theme,** or
nugget of "wisdom," does the
end of this poem convey to you?

Wrapping Up

If you are using **The Language
of Literature,** you can now
move to the questions and
activities on pages 1013–1015 of
that book.

FOCUS

Read to find out what happens to the hired
man at the end of the poem.

"I can't think Si ever hurt anyone."

"No, but he hurt my heart the way he lay
And rolled his old head on the sharp-edged chair-back.
He wouldn't let me put him on the lounge.[16]
You must go in and see what you can do.
I made the bed up for him there tonight.
You'll be surprised at him—how much he's broken.[17]
His working days are done; I'm sure of it."

"I'd not be in a hurry to say that."

"I haven't been. Go, look, see for yourself.
But, Warren, please remember how it is:
He's come to help you ditch the meadow.
He has a plan. You mustn't laugh at him.
He may not speak of it, and then he may.
I'll sit and see if that small sailing cloud
Will hit or miss the moon."

          It hit the moon.
Then there were three there, making a dim row,
The moon, the little silver cloud, and she.

Warren returned—too soon, it seemed to her—
Slipped to her side, caught up her hand and waited.

"Warren?" she questioned.
          "Dead," was all he answered.

Pause & **Reflect**

---

16. **lounge:** couch.
17. **broken:** weakened.

Active Reading SkillBuilder

Understanding Form in Poetry

Form is the placement of a poem's lines on the page and the grouping of those lines into stanzas. The blank-verse form of "The Death of the Hired Man" may make it difficult to keep track of the dialogue. Frost uses several devices to help the reader. Two of these devices are quotation marks and line breaks. A third device is point of view—the narrator always speaks in the third person. On the chart below, record any parts of the poem that cause you to pause to identify the speaker.

Line(s) from Poem	Who I Think Is Speaking	Why I Think So

Literary Analysis SkillBuilder

Blank Verse

"The Death of the Hired Man" is written in **blank verse,** lines of unrhymed iambic pentameter. Well-written blank verse imitates natural rhythms of English speech and sounds very much like the way people talk. A line of blank verse has five iambic feet, each consisting of an unstressed syllable followed by a stressed syllable. In each box below, write a line from the poem that sounds to you like natural speech. Mark the syllables as unstressed (˘) or stressed (´). An example is shown.

Line A

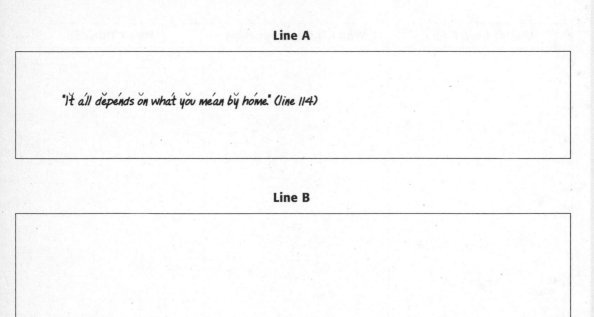

"Ĭt áll dĕpénds ŏn whát yŏu méan bў hóme." (line 114)

Line B

Line C

Words to Know SkillBuilder

Words to Know

abide   assurance   beholden   harbor   taut

A. Decide which Word to Know is described by each clue. Write the word on the blank line next to the clue.

1. If you hold your head up and act with confidence, people will think you know what you are doing.

_____
(1)

2. Keep the clothesline pulled tight to keep the clothing from sagging to the ground.

_____
(2)

3. If you accept that favor, you might feel that you owe something in return.

_____
(3)

4. My little brother can be an awful pest, but I have to put up with him.

_____
(4)

5. This term is usually used in connection with ships or boats, but it can be used for people, too.

_____
(5)

B. Circle the word in each group that is a synonym for the boldfaced word.

1. **abide**   home   endure   brick   leave

2. **assurance** intelligence   reluctance   confidence   influence

3. **beholden**   indebted   excluded   upset   disinterested

4. **harbor**   exclude   refute   display   protect

5. **taut**   loose   smooth   tight   educated

C. "The Death of the Hired Man" includes a famous definition of *home*. Write your description of an ideal home. Include details about both the physical environment and the people who share this home. Use at least **two** Words to Know in your description.

The End of Something

Ernest Hemingway

PREVIEW This story takes place in the summer of 1919, after the end of World War I. The two main characters are Nick, a former soldier, and his girlfriend, Marjorie. They are going fishing near the ruins of an old lumber mill on Lake Michigan, a place they know well. Nick is trying to sort out his life now that the war is over. As he and Marjorie fish and talk, a change in their relationship becomes clear.

FOCUS
The story opens with a brief history of the town of Hortons Bay and then introduces the two **main characters**. As you read, look for hints about the kind of relationship the two characters have.

In the old days Hortons Bay was a lumbering town. No one who lived in it was out of sound of the big saws in the mill by the lake. Then one year there were no more logs to make lumber. The lumber schooners came into the bay and were loaded with the cut of the mill that stood stacked in the yard. All the piles of lumber were carried away. The big

10

mill building had all its machinery that was removable taken out and hoisted on board one of the schooners by the men who had worked in the mill. The schooner moved out of the bay toward the open lake carrying the two great saws, the travelling carriage that hurled the logs against the revolving, circular saws and all the rollers, wheels, belts, and iron piled on a hull-deep load of lumber. Its open hold covered with canvas and lashed tight, the sails of the schooner filled and it moved out into the open lake, carrying with it everything that had made the mill a mill and

20 Hortons Bay a town.

The one-story bunk houses, the eating-house, the company store, the mill offices, and the big mill itself stood deserted in the acres of sawdust that covered the swampy meadow by the shore of the bay.

Ten years later there was nothing of the mill left except the broken white limestone of its foundations showing through the swampy second growth[1] as Nick and Marjorie rowed along the shore. They were trolling[2] along the edge of the channel-bank where the bottom dropped off suddenly from sandy shallows to twelve feet of dark water. They were trolling on their way to the point to set night lines for rainbow trout.

"There's our old ruin, Nick," Marjorie said.

Nick, rowing, looked at the white stone in the green trees.

"There it is," he said.

"Can you remember when it was a mill?" Marjorie asked.

"I can just remember," Nick said.

"It seems more like a castle," Marjorie said.

Nick said nothing. They rowed on out of sight of the mill, following the shore line. Then Nick cut across the bay.

"They aren't striking," he said.

"No," Marjorie said. She was intent on the rod all the time they trolled, even when she talked. She loved to fish. She loved to fish with Nick.

Close beside the boat a big trout broke the surface of the water. Nick pulled hard on one oar so the boat would turn and the bait spinning far behind would pass where the trout was feeding. As the trout's back came up out of the water the minnows jumped wildly. They sprinkled the surface like a handful of shot[3] thrown into the water. Another trout broke water, feeding on the other side of the boat.

"They're feeding," Marjorie said.

"But they won't strike," Nick said.

He rowed the boat around to troll past both the feeding fish, then headed it for the point. Marjorie did not reel in until the boat touched the shore.

---

1. **swampy second growth:** new trees and other plants growing in swampy area surrounding the ruins of the mill.

2. **trolling:** a method of fishing in which a line and baited hook trail along behind a slow-moving boat.

3. **shot:** the tiny metal pellets used as ammunition in a shotgun.

READ ALOUD Lines 33–39

Read these lines of dialogue aloud. How would you describe this conversation between Nick and Marjorie? (Evaluate)

_____

_____

_____

_____

MARK IT UP WORD POWER

Mark words that you'd like to add to your **Personal Word List.** After reading, you can record the words and their meanings beginning on page 344.

1. What happened to the old lumber mill in Hortons Bay? **(Clarify)**

_____

_____

_____

_____

 MARK IT UP 2. Circle at least three details on pages 275–276 that show Nick and Marjorie's fishing skills. **(Visualize)**

3. Check two words or phrases below that you think describe the relationship between Nick and Marjorie at this point. **(Infer)**

are often together

angry

very romantic

matter-of-fact

talk a lot

They pulled the boat up the beach and Nick lifted out a pail of live perch. The perch swam in the water in the pail. Nick caught three of them with his hands and cut their heads 60 off and skinned them while Marjorie chased with her hands in the bucket, finally caught a perch, cut its head off and skinned it. Nick looked at her fish.

"You don't want to take the ventral fin[4] out," he said. "It'll be all right for bait but it's better with the ventral fin in."

He hooked each of the skinned perch through the tail. There were two hooks attached to a leader[5] on each rod. Then Marjorie rowed the boat out over the channel-bank, holding the line in her teeth, and looking toward Nick, who stood on the shore holding the rod and letting the line run out from 70 the reel.

"That's about right," he called.

"Should I let it drop?" Marjorie called back, holding the line in her hand.

"Sure. Let it go." Marjorie dropped the line overboard and watched the baits go down through the water.

Pause & Reflect

FOCUS
In this part of the story, Nick and Marjorie's relationship is about to go through a major change. **MARK IT UP** As you read, underline passages that show what is happening to the relationship. An example is highlighted on page 277.

80 **She came in with the boat** and ran the second line out the same way. Each time Nick set a heavy slab of driftwood across the butt of the rod to hold it solid and propped it up at an angle with a small slab. He reeled in the slack line so the line ran taut out to where the bait rested on the sandy floor of the channel and set the click on the reel. When a trout, feeding on the bottom, took the bait it would run with it, taking line out of the reel in a rush and making the reel sing with the click on.

Marjorie rowed up the point a little way so she would not disturb the line. She pulled hard on the oars and the boat

---

4. **ventral fin:** fin on the underside of a fish.

5. **leader:** short length of line by which a hook is fastened to a fishing line.

90 went way up the beach. Little waves came in with it. Marjorie stepped out of the boat and Nick pulled the boat high up the beach.

"What's the matter, Nick?" Marjorie asked.

"I don't know," Nick said, getting wood for a fire.

They made a fire with driftwood. Marjorie went to the boat and brought a blanket. The evening breeze blew the smoke toward the point, so Marjorie spread the blanket out between the fire and the lake.

Marjorie sat on the blanket with her back to the fire and 100 waited for Nick. He came over and sat down beside her on the blanket. In back of them was the close second-growth timber[6] of the point and in front was the bay with the mouth of Hortons Creek. It was not quite dark. The fire-light went as far as the water. They could both see the two steel rods at an angle over the dark water. The fire glinted on the reels.

Marjorie unpacked the basket of supper.

"I don't feel like eating," said Nick.

"Come on and eat, Nick."

"All right."

110 They ate without talking, and watched the two rods and the fire-light in the water.

"There's going to be a moon tonight," said Nick. He looked across the bay to the hills that were beginning to sharpen against the sky. Beyond the hills he knew the moon was coming up.

"I know it," Marjorie said happily.

"You know everything," Nick said.

"Oh, Nick, please cut it out! Please, please don't be that way!"

120 "I can't help it," Nick said. "You do. You know everything. That's the trouble. You know you do."

Marjorie did not say anything.

"I've taught you everything. You know you do. What don't you know, anyway?"

"Oh, shut up," Marjorie said. "There comes the moon."

They sat on the blanket without touching each other and watched the moon rise.

"You don't have to talk silly," Marjorie said. "What's really the matter?"

---

6. **second-growth timber:** trees that cover an area after the original, "old growth" trees have been cut or burned.

1. Look back at the passages that you underlined as you read. Describe what happens to Nick and Marjorie's relationship. **(Infer)**

_____

_____

_____

_____

MARK IT UP **2.** How is Nick feeling at the end of the story? Circle phrases on this page that help you know. **(Infer)**

_____

_____

3. Think of one question that you would like to ask about the ending of the story. Write it below. **(Question)**

_____

_____

_____

_____

CHALLENGE

How does the history of Hortons Bay reflect the relationship between Nick and Marjorie? Mark words and phrases in the description of Hortons Bay that relate to what happens to the two characters. **(Evaluate)**

Wrapping Up

If you are using **_The Language of Literature,_** you can now move to the questions and activities on pages 1023–1024 of that book.

130 "I don't know."

"Of course you know."

"No I don't."

"Go on and say it."

Nick looked on at the moon, coming up over the hills.

"It isn't fun any more."

He was afraid to look at Marjorie. Then he looked at her. She sat there with her back toward him. He looked at her back. "It isn't fun any more. Not any of it."

She didn't say anything. He went on. "I feel as though 140 everything was gone to hell inside of me. I don't know, Marge. I don't know what to say."

He looked on at her back.

"Isn't love any fun?" Marjorie said.

"No," Nick said. Marjorie stood up. Nick sat there his head in his hands.

"I'm going to take the boat," Marjorie called to him. "You can walk back around the point."

"All right," Nick said. "I'll push the boat off for you."

"You don't need to," she said. She was afloat in the boat 150 on the water with the moonlight on it. Nick went back and lay down with his face in the blanket by the fire. He could hear Marjorie rowing on the water.

He lay there for a long time. He lay there while he heard Bill come into the clearing walking around through the woods. He felt Bill coming up to the fire. Bill didn't touch him, either.

"Did she go all right?" Bill said.

"Yes," Nick said, lying, his face on the blanket.

"Have a scene?"

160 "No, there wasn't any scene."

"How do you feel?"

"Oh, go away, Bill! Go away for a while."

Bill selected a sandwich from the lunch basket and walked over to have a look at the rods.

Pause & Reflect

Active Reading SkillBuilder

Making Inferences

The scenes in "The End of Something" are made up almost entirely of dialogue between Nick and Marjorie. As they speak, the narrator gives little direct information about how they feel or think. Hemingway's plain style challenges readers to **make inferences,** or logical guesses, to discover the meanings behind the characters' spoken words. Their remarks give clues about their relationship. On the chart below, record lines of dialogue that seem especially meaningful. Then explain what you think these remarks show. An example has been done for you.

Dialogue Clues	What They Show
Nick's Comments "You know everything."	He is feeling critical of Marjorie.
Marjorie's Comments	

Literary Analysis SkillBuilder

Style

Style is the distinctive way in which a piece of literature is written. "The End of Something" reflects the simple, direct style of a newspaper reporter and journalist. It has short sentences, attention to detail, simple descriptions, clear language, and a matter-of-fact tone. In the chart below, identify an example of each of these characteristics of Hemingway's style. An example has been done for you.

Characteristics of Style	Example
Short Sentences	
Attention to Detail	
Simple Descriptions	*They made a fire with driftwood.*
Clear Language	
Matter-of-Fact Tone	

Follow Up: Work with a small group of classmates to rewrite a passage of the story to include Nick's feelings and thoughts. Discuss differences between Hemingway's style and the style of your rewrite.

Before You Read

If you are using **The Language of Literature,** study the information on page 1025 of that book to prepare for reading.

Reading Tips

This poem goes into the mind of the main character, J. Alfred Prufrock. This technique is known as **stream of consciousness.** Because Prufrock's thoughts are often rambling and disconnected, you will be confused at first. The following strategies may help:

• As you read, note places in the poem that seem disconnected. Try to figure out what is going on before and after the break in thought.

• Look for repeated words or lines. They may give you clues to what is happening.

• Use the information in the Guide for Reading to help you with difficult words and passages.

MARK IT UP **KEEP TRACK**

As you read, you can use these marks to keep track of your understanding.

✔ ..... I understand.

? ..... I don't understand this.

! ..... Interesting or surprising idea

The Love Song of J. Alfred Prufrock

T. S. Eliot

PREVIEW This poem, written in the early 20th century, follows the inner thoughts and feelings of the speaker, J. Alfred Prufrock. Prufrock is going to a high society party and is worrying about asking a woman an "overwhelming question." The more he thinks about his decision, the more insecure he becomes. Prufrock's thoughts reveal his fears, dreams, and limitations.

FOCUS
Prufrock is walking through city streets on his way to a tea party.
MARK IT UP As you read, underline details that help you picture the streets. Two examples are highlighted.

S'io credessi che mia risposta fosse
a persona che mai tornasse al mondo,
questa fiamma staria senza più scosse.
Ma per ciò che giammai di questo fondo
non tornò vivo alcun, s'i'odo il vero,
senza tema d'infamia ti rispondo.

Let us go then, you and I,
When the evening is spread out against the sky
Like a patient etherized upon a table;
Let us go, through certain half-deserted streets,
The muttering retreats
Of restless nights in one-night cheap hotels
And sawdust restaurants with oyster-shells:

5

GUIDE FOR READING

Use this guide for help with unfamiliar words
and difficult passages.

> **✎ MARK IT UP WORD POWER**
>
> Mark words that you'd like to add to your
> **Personal Word List.** After reading, you
> can record the words and their meanings
> beginning on page 344.

This is a quotation in Italian from Dante's
Inferno. One of the people in hell is speaking
to a visitor. The speaker says that he will
describe his torment only because the visitor
cannot return alive to the world to repeat it.

1 you and I: Prufrock may be addressing a
companion, the reader, or possibly part of
himself.
3 Ether was used to make a patient unconscious during an operation.

7 Cheap seafood restaurants sprinkled
sawdust on the floor to absorb moisture.
Customers also dropped oyster shells on the
floor.

> **✎ JOT IT DOWN   Reread Lines 4–7**
>
> What do these lines suggest to you about
> this section of the city? **(Infer)**
> _____
> _____
> _____

Streets that follow like a tedious argument
Of insidious intent
To lead you to an overwhelming question . . .
Oh, do not ask, "What is it?"
Let us go and make our visit.

In the room the women come and go
Talking of Michelangelo.

The yellow fog that rubs its back upon the window-
    panes,
The yellow smoke that rubs its muzzle on the window-
    panes,
Licked its tongue into the corners of the evening,
Lingered upon the pools that stand in drains,
Let fall upon its back the soot that falls from chimneys,
Slipped by the terrace, made a sudden leap,
And seeing that it was a soft October night,
Curled once about the house, and fell asleep.

Pause & *Reflect*

FOCUS

Read on to learn why Prufrock worries
about the party.

MARK IT UP Underline the words or
phrases that are repeated in these lines.

And indeed there will be time
For the yellow smoke that slides along the street
Rubbing its back upon the window-panes;
There will be time, there will be time
To prepare a face to meet the faces that you meet;
There will be time to murder and create,
And time for all the works and days of hands
That lift and drop a question on your plate;
Time for you and time for me,
And time yet for a hundred indecisions,
And for a hundred visions and revisions,
Before the taking of a toast and tea.

In the room the women come and go
Talking of Michelangelo.

8 **tedious** (tē'dē-əs): tiresome.

9 **insidious** (ĭn-sĭd'ē-əs): harmful.

10–12 Prufrock appears reluctant to say what his "overwhelming question" is.

13–14 The women mentioned in these lines may be those at the party Prufrock is going to attend, or they may be women at other parties Prufrock has attended. These lines also appear later in the poem.

14 **Michelangelo** (mī'kəl-ăn'jə-lō'): a famous 16th-century Italian painter and sculptor.

JOT IT DOWN   **Reread Lines 13–14**

Do you think this is a serious discussion of the great artist or simply party talk? **(Infer)**

_____

_____

Pause & Reflect

1. Look at the details you underlined as you read. What do these city streets look like? **(Visualize)**

_____

_____

_____

2. Prufrock compares the fog to a cat in lines 15 to 22. How would you feel if you found yourself in this kind of fog? **(Connect)**

_____

_____

_____

_____

23–34 This stanza reveals part of Prufrock's problem—he has trouble making up his mind and taking action.

27 This line suggests that Prufrock and the people at the tea party are not sincere or open.

And indeed there will be time
To wonder, "Do I dare?" and, "Do I dare?"
Time to turn back and descend the stair,
With a bald spot in the middle of my hair—
(They will say: "How his hair is growing thin!")
My morning coat, my collar mounting firmly to
    the chin,
My necktie rich and modest, but asserted by a
    simple pin—
(They will say: "But how his arms and legs are thin!")
Do I dare
Disturb the universe?
In a minute there is time
For decisions and revisions which a minute will reverse.

Pause & Reflect

FOCUS
Prufrock imagines trying to ask the "overwhelming question." He wonders if he can
do it.
MARK IT UP As you read, circle the
phrases Prufrock uses to describe himself
and his life.

For I have known them all already, known them all—
Have known the evenings, mornings, afternoons,
I have measured out my life with coffee spoons;
I know the voices dying with a dying fall
Beneath the music from a farther room.
    So how should I <u>presume</u>?

And I have known the eyes already, known them all—
The eyes that fix you in a formulated phrase,
And when I am formulated, sprawling on a pin,
When I am pinned and wriggling on the wall,
Then how should I begin
To spit out all the butt-ends of my days and ways?
    And how should I presume?

WORDS
TO
KNOW

presume (prĭ-zōōm′) *v.* to act overconfidently; go beyond
    the proper limits; dare

42 morning coat: man's formal dress coat, cut high at the waist and tapering to tails at the back.

51 coffee spoons: small spoons about half the size of teaspoons.

55–58 Prufrock recalls being stared at by women at other parties. The image of himself is one of a live insect that has been classified, labeled, and mounted for display.
56 formulated: reduced to a formula or prepared according to a formula.

Pause **&** *Reflect*

1. Look at the repeated words and phrases that you underlined as you read. What do they tell you about Prufrock's worries? **(Infer)**

_____
_____
_____
_____

2. The question "Do I dare?" suggests that Prufrock wants to do something amazing at the party. What do you think he wants to do? **(Predict)**

_____
_____
_____
_____

MARK IT UP **3.** Prufrock wonders about the impression he will make at the party. Star lines on page 286 in which Prufrock imagines what people will say about him. **(Clarify)**

4. Reread lines 42 and 43, where Prufrock describes what he is wearing. What do you learn about Prufrock from his clothing? **(Visualize/Infer)**

_____
_____
_____
_____

READ ALOUD **Lines 49–54**

As you read these lines aloud, listen for the repeated vowel sounds ī, ō, and ōō. They help to express Prufrock's sadness.

And I have known the arms already, known them all—
Arms that are braceleted and white and bare
(But in the lamplight, downed with light brown hair!)
65 Is it perfume from a dress
That makes me so <u>digress</u>?
Arms that lie along a table, or wrap about a shawl.
   And should I then presume?
   And how should I begin?

                 • • • • •

70 Shall I say, I have gone at dusk through narrow streets
And watched the smoke that rises from the pipes
Of lonely men in shirt-sleeves, leaning out
   of windows? . . .
I should have been a pair of ragged claws
Scuttling across the floors of silent seas.

                 • • • • •

Pause & Reflect

FOCUS

In lines 75–110, Prufrock considers his "overwhelming question" further. As you read, note Prufrock's fears.

MARK IT UP Underline lines that are repeated in this section, which will help you identify his fears.

75 And the afternoon, the evening, sleeps so peacefully!
Smoothed by long fingers,
Asleep . . . tired . . . or it <u>malingers</u>,
Stretched on the floor, here beside you and me.
Should I, after tea and cakes and ices,
80 Have the strength to force the moment to its crisis?
But though I have wept and fasted, wept and prayed,
Though I have seen my head (grown slightly bald)
   brought in upon a platter,
I am no prophet—and here's no great matter;

WORDS
TO
KNOW

digress (dĭ-grĕs′) v. to wander away from the main subject in a conversation or in writing; ramble

malinger (mə-lĭng′gər) v. to pretend illness in order to avoid duty or work

62–69 Prufrock is talking about the women at the party. He finds them attractive, but he doesn't know how to talk to them.

73–74 Prufrock has presented an image of himself as an insect (lines 57–58) and, here, as a crab or lobster; **scuttling:** running in a hurried way.

75 Note that Prufrock earlier compared the evening to a cat that fell asleep.

81–83 These lines refer to the biblical story of John the Baptist, who is imprisoned by King Herod (Matthew 14; Mark 6). To please his stepdaughter Salome, Herod orders the Baptist's head cut off and brought to him on a platter; **fasted:** for religious reasons, did not eat for a long period; **prophet:** an important religious figure who delivers messages from God.

Pause **&** **Reflect**

1. Look at the phrases that you circled as you read. On a scale of 1 to 10 (1 is lowest), how would you rate Prufrock's level of self-confidence? **(Evaluate)**

_____

2. Why does Prufrock keep saying that he has "known them all" (lines 49, 55, and 62)? Does Prufrock have positive or negative feelings about these people? **(Infer)**

_____

_____

_____

_____

3. In lines 68 to 74, Prufrock seems on the verge of asking the "overwhelming question." Does he do it? *Yes/No,* because _____

_____

_____

_____

(Infer)

....
....
....
....
....
....
....
....

MARK IT UP **KEEP TRACK**

Remember to use these marks to keep track of your understanding.

✔ ..... I understand.

? ..... I don't understand this.

! ..... Interesting or surprising idea

I have seen the moment of my greatness flicker,
And I have seen the eternal Footman hold my coat, and
    snicker,
And in short, I was afraid.

And would it have been worth it, after all,
After the cups, the marmalade, the tea,
Among the porcelain, among some talk of you and me,
Would it have been worth while,
To have bitten off the matter with a smile,
To have squeezed the universe into a ball
To roll it towards some overwhelming question,
To say: "I am Lazarus, come from the dead,
Come back to tell you all, I shall tell you all"—
If one, settling a pillow by her head,
    Should say: "That is not what I meant at all.
    That is not it, at all."

And would it have been worth it, after all,
Would it have been worth while,
After the sunsets and the dooryards and the sprinkled
    streets,
After the novels, after the teacups, after the skirts that
    trail along the floor—
And this, and so much more?—
It is impossible to say just what I mean!
But as if a magic lantern threw the nerves in patterns
    on a screen:
Would it have been worth while
If one, settling a pillow or throwing off a shawl,
And turning toward the window, should say:
"That is not it at all,
That is not what I meant, at all."

Pause & Reflect

85 eternal Footman: The image here is of Prufrock being mocked by a servant. The "eternal Footman" may represent Death, who waits for all and knows the hidden weaknesses of each person.

87–110 In these two stanzas, Prufrock rationalizes his failure to ask the "overwhelming question."

89 porcelain: expensive china dishes.

94 Lazarus: In the biblical story (John 11:17–44), Lazarus lay dead in his tomb for four days before Jesus brought him back to life. By comparing himself to Lazarus, Prufrock shows his desire for recognition. He wants other people to think he is important. He also wants to come alive again emotionally.

105 The magic lantern was a forerunner of the slide projector. In this image, the "nerves" may be Prufrock's inner self exposed for all to see.

107 shawl: a large piece of cloth, often woven of wool or silk, that can be worn around the shoulders or used as a light covering.

Pause & Reflect

1. What is the "crisis" Prufrock refers to in line 80? **(Infer)**

_____

_____

_____

_____

2. Look back at the lines you underlined as you read. What is Prufrock afraid of? **(Infer)**

_____

_____

_____

_____

3. Prufrock says, "I have seen the moment of my greatness flicker" (line 84). In your own words, explain what you think he means. **(Paraphrase)**

_____

_____

_____

_____

4. Why would Prufrock be like Lazarus if he asked the "overwhelming question"? **(Compare and Contrast)**

_____

_____

_____

_____

FOCUS

At this point, Prufrock gives up on the possibility of asking the question. As you read, think about what Prufrock's life will be like in the future.

No! I am not Prince Hamlet, nor was meant to be;
Am an attendant lord, one that will do
To swell a progress, start a scene or two,
Advise the prince; no doubt, an easy tool,
115   Deferential, glad to be of use,
Politic, cautious, and <u>meticulous</u>;
Full of high sentence, but a bit <u>obtuse</u>;
At times, indeed, almost ridiculous—
Almost, at times, the Fool.

120   I grow old . . . I grow old . . .
I shall wear the bottoms of my trousers rolled.

Shall I part my hair behind? Do I dare to eat a peach?
I shall wear white flannel trousers, and walk upon the
    beach.
I have heard the mermaids singing, each to each.

125   I do not think that they will sing to me.

I have seen them riding seaward on the waves
Combing the white hair of the waves blown back
When the wind blows the water white and black.

We have lingered in the chambers of the sea
130   By sea-girls wreathed with seaweed red and brown
Till human voices wake us, and we drown.

Pause **&** **Reflect**

WORDS
TO
KNOW

meticulous (mĭ-tĭk′yə-ləs) *adj.* extremely careful and precise about details
obtuse (ŏb-tōōs′) *adj.* slow to understand; dull

111–119 Notice that Prufrock resigns himself to playing a supporting role rather than a starring one in life.

111 Prince Hamlet: the tragic hero in Shakespeare's drama *Hamlet.*

113 progress: a ceremonial journey made by a king or queen ; to "swell a progress" was to join it and so help increase its size.

115 deferential (děf′ə-rěn′shəl): yielding to someone else's opinion.

116 politic (pŏl′ĭ-tĭk): skillful in dealing with others; diplomatic.

117 high sentence: lofty thoughts and opinions.

124–128 In mythology, mermaids attract men by their beauty and their singing, sometimes allowing men to live with them in the sea.

129–131 Prufrock continues his fantasy of seeing mermaids. However, his fantasy image ends in drowning. The "we" here might refer to different parts of Prufrock himself (see line 1) or to Prufrock and others who, like him, have retreated to a fantasy world.

Pause & Reflect

1. Briefly **summarize** Prufrock's description of himself in lines 111 to 121.

_____

_____

_____

_____

2. How would you describe Prufrock's attitude about his life? **(Infer)**

_____

_____

_____

_____

3. Prufrock imagines a fantasy world inhabited by mermaids. Circle two phrases below that describe how this fantasy makes him feel. **(Infer)**

separated from   sad about his life
other people

hopeful about   satisfied with his life
the future

CHALLENGE

This poem is full of **irony**—for example, the poem is called a love song, but Prufrock does not speak even one word of love. What other examples of irony can you find? **(Analyze)**

Wrapping Up

If you are using *The Language of Literature,* you can now move to the questions and activities on pages 1030–1032 of that book.

Active Reading SkillBuilder

Understanding Stream of Consciousness

Stream of consciousness writing presents the flow of thoughts, responses, and sensations as they occur in a character's mind. Eliot uses this technique to reveal the jumble of images, ideas, feelings, and daydreams that flow through Prufrock's mind. To help you follow Prufrock's random thoughts and feelings, fill in the chart below with key details about a decision that he is trying to make. One example is done for you.

	Details
Part 1: Prufrock's musings about asking the "overwhelming question" (lines 1–83)	*"Oh, do not ask, 'What is it?'"*
Part 2: Prufrock's decision (lines 84–86)	
Part 3: Prufrock's justification for his decision (lines 87–110)	

Literary Analysis SkillBuilder

Imagery

Imagery consists of words and phrases that appeal to any of the five senses. Imagery helps the reader imagine precisely what the writer is describing. In "The Love Song of J. Alfred Prufrock," Eliot uses imagery to describe Prufrock and to picture details of the setting in the poem, such as the city streets and the tea party. On the chart below, list three images that describe Prufrock and three images that give some detail of the setting. Examples are given.

Images That Describe Prufrock	Images That Picture the Setting
1. *his hair is growing thin (line 41)*	1. *yellow smoke that slides along the street (line 24)*
2.	2.
3.	3.
4.	4.

Follow Up: What do the images of Prufrock tell you about him?

Words to Know SkillBuilder

Words to Know

digress   malinger   meticulous   obtuse   presume

A. Find familiar words in the puzzle below. Circle all the ones you can find that go from left to right or top to bottom in the puzzle. Write them down to the right of the puzzle or on a separate sheet of paper.

S	U	S	T	F	A	K	E	C
D	O	P	E	U	H	W	O	R
S	N	O	B	S	A	E	F	A
A	C	R	A	S	V	A	F	B
B	U	L	L	Y	E	K	S	O
O	R	U	B	O	L	D	H	U
U	E	M	I	L	A	Z	Y	T

Use five words from the puzzle to fill in the blanks in the following sentences. If you cannot find a word that makes sense and has the correct meaning, look at the puzzle again. Don't use the same word more than once.

1. A meticulous person may seem _____ to other people.

2. You might tell an obtuse person not to be such a _____ .

3. When you digress, you say things that are _____ the subject.

4. People who malinger _____ an illness.

5. When you presume, you are being _____ .

B. Fill in each blank with the correct word from the word list.

"I hate it when people _____ ," said my boss. "Half

of the staff have 'stomach aches' today? How _____

do they think I am? I'll fire them! Which reminds me, where are the matches?"

"Don't _____ ," I said. "The problem has to do with

needing a lunchroom chef who's a little more _____

about sanitary conditions. I didn't eat there yesterday and neither did you, Fred."

"That's Mr. Fritzel to you, young lady. Don't _____ ."

C. Write a brief stream-of-consciousness narrative that Prufrock might write as an old man looking back on his life. Use at least **three** of the Words to Know.

The JILTING of *Granny Weatherall*

Katherine Anne Porter

PREVIEW In her writing, Katherine Anne Porter was able to say little and suggest much. She does exactly that in this **short story**. Its main character, Granny Weatherall, is nearly 80 years old and near death. As she lies in her sickroom, she recalls key moments and relationships in her life. A terrible event still haunts her memory. Sixty years ago, her bridegroom-to-be did not show up for the wedding. This jilting hurt Granny's pride, and time has not healed the wound.

Before You Read

If you are using *The Language of Literature* . . .

• Use the information on page 1034 of that book to prepare for reading.

• Look at the art on page 1035 to help you **visualize** the **main character**.

Reading Tips

Most of this **short story** takes place in the mind of the **main character**. Her mind wanders from present to past and back again. To take you inside her mind, the author uses a technique called **stream-of-consciousness**. This technique presents the flow of thoughts in a character's mind.

• Be aware that sometimes the main character gets confused about where she is and what is happening.

• Watch out for time jumps in the story. Ask yourself whether an event is happening now in the sickroom or in the past.

• As you read each section, try to put the major events in a time **sequence**. Consider whether an event tells about the main character as a young girl, as a wife and mother, or as an old widow.

FOCUS

As Granny Weatherall lies in bed, Doctor Harry examines her. The first sentence shows her reaction as he takes her pulse. The second sentence takes you into her mind to reveal her feelings about Doctor Harry.

MARK IT UP As you read, circle details that help you form impressions of Granny. An example is highlighted.

She flicked her wrist neatly out of Doctor Harry's pudgy careful fingers and pulled the sheet up to her chin. The brat ought to be in knee breeches.[1] Doctoring around the country with spectacles on his nose! "Get along now, take your schoolbooks and go. There's nothing wrong with me."

Doctor Harry spread a warm paw like a cushion on her forehead where the forked green vein danced and made her eyelids twitch. "Now, now, be a good girl, and we'll have you up in no time."

"That's no way to speak to a woman nearly eighty years old just because she's down. I'd have you respect your elders, young man."

"Well, Missy, excuse me." Doctor Harry patted her cheek. "But I've got to warn you, haven't I? You're a marvel, but you must be careful or you're going to be good and sorry."

---

1. **knee breeches:** short pants or knickers worn by young boys.

....
....
....
....
....
....
....
....
....
....
....
....

....
....
....
....

20   "Don't tell me what I'm going to be. I'm on my feet now, morally speaking. It's Cornelia. I had to go to bed to get rid of her."

Her bones felt loose, and floated around in her skin, and Doctor Harry floated like a balloon around the foot of the bed. He floated and pulled down his waistcoat and swung his glasses on a cord. "Well, stay where you are, it certainly can't hurt you."

"Get along and doctor your sick," said Granny Weatherall. "Leave a well woman alone. I'll call for you when I want you.

30   . . . Where were you forty years ago when I pulled through milk-leg[2] and double pneumonia? You weren't even born. Don't let Cornelia lead you on," she shouted, because Doctor Harry appeared to float up to the ceiling and out. "I pay my own bills, and I don't throw my money away on nonsense!"

She meant to wave good-by, but it was too much trouble. Her eyes closed of themselves, it was like a dark curtain drawn around the bed. The pillow rose and floated under her, pleasant as a hammock in a light wind. She listened to the leaves rustling outside the window. No, somebody was

40 swishing newspapers: no, Cornelia and Doctor Harry were whispering together. She leaped broad awake, thinking they whispered in her ear.

"She was never like this, *never* like this!" "Well, what can we expect?" "Yes, eighty years old. . . ."

Well, and what if she was? She still had ears. It was like Cornelia to whisper around doors. She always kept things secret in such a public way. She was always being <u>tactful</u> and kind. Cornelia was dutiful; that was the trouble with her. Dutiful and good: "So good and dutiful," said Granny, "that

50 I'd like to spank her." She saw herself spanking Cornelia and making a fine job of it.

"What'd you say, Mother?"

Granny felt her face tying up in hard knots.

"Can't a body think, I'd like to know?"

"I thought you might want something."

"I do. I want a lot of things. First off, go away and don't whisper."

---

2. **milk-leg:** a painful swelling of the leg experienced by some women after giving birth.

She lay and drowsed, hoping in her sleep that the children
would keep out and let her rest a minute. It had been a long
60 day. Not that she was tired. It was always pleasant to snatch a
minute now and then. There was always so much to be done,
let me see: tomorrow.

Pause **&** **Reflect**

FOCUS

Granny plans for the
next day and recalls
the time when she
thought she was going
to die.

MARK IT UP As you
read, circle details that
help you understand
her feelings about
70 death.

Tomorrow was far away and there was
nothing to trouble about. Things were
finished somehow when the time came;
thank God there was always a little
margin over for peace: then a person
could spread out the plan of life and
tuck in the edges orderly. It was good to
have everything clean and folded away,
with the hair brushes and tonic bottles
sitting straight on the white underbroidered

linen: the day started without fuss and the pantry shelves laid
out with rows of jelly glasses and brown jugs and white stone-
china jars with blue whirligigs[3] and words painted on them:
coffee, tea, sugar, ginger, cinnamon, allspice: and the bronze
clock with the lion on top nicely dusted off. The dust that lion
could collect in twenty-four hours! The box in the attic with
all those letters tied up, well, she'd have to go through that
80 tomorrow. All those letters—George's letters and John's letters
and her letters to them both—lying around for the children to
find afterwards made her uneasy. Yes, that would be tomorrow's
business. No use to let them know how silly she had been once.

While she was underrummaging around she found death in her
mind and it felt clammy and unfamiliar. She had spent so
much time preparing for death there was no need for bringing
it up again. Let it take care of itself now. When she was sixty
she had felt very old, finished, and went around making
farewell trips to see her children and grandchildren, with a
90 secret in her mind: This is the very last of your mother,
children! Then she made her will and came down with a long

Pause **&** **Reflect**

1. Review the details you circled
as you read. Based on these
details, describe your
impressions of Granny. **(Infer)**

_____

_____

_____

_____

MARK IT UP 2. What does
Granny think of her daughter
Cornelia? Write the answer
below. Then underline the clues
on page 298 that led you to it.
(Infer)

_____

_____

_____

_____

3. If you were in Granny's
situation, what might you think
about as you lay dying?
(Connect)

_____

_____

_____

_____

---

3. **stone-china jars with blue whirligigs** (hwûr′lĭ-gĭgz′): jars made of thick
pottery with blue spiral designs.

WORDS
TO
KNOW

embroidered (ĕm-broi′dərd) *adj.* decorated with stitched
designs **embroider** *v.*
rummage (rŭm′ĭj) *v.* to search through a confusion of
objects

1. Granny does not want her
children to read the letters in the
box in the attic. What do you
suppose those letters contain?
(Infer)

_____

_____

_____

_____

2. Review the details you circled as
you read. How would you
describe Granny's feelings about
death? (Infer)

_____

_____

_____

_____

fever. That was all just a notion like a lot of other things, but it was lucky too, for she had once for all got over the idea of dying for a long time. Now she couldn't be worried. She hoped she had better sense now. Her father had lived to be one hundred and two years old and had drunk a noggin of strong hot toddy[4] on his last birthday. He told the reporters it was his daily habit, and he owed his long life to that. He had made quite a scandal and was very pleased about it. She believed she'd just <u>plague</u> Cornelia a little.

"Cornelia! Cornelia!" No footsteps, but a sudden hand on her cheek. "Bless you, where have you been?"

"Here, Mother."

"Well, Cornelia, I want a noggin of hot toddy."

"Are you cold, darling?"

"I'm chilly, Cornelia. Lying in bed stops the circulation. I must have told you that a thousand times."

Pause & Reflect

FOCUS
Granny thinks about
her children and her
dead husband John.
Read to find out about
Granny as a wife and a
mother.

Well, she could just hear Cornelia telling her husband that Mother was getting a little childish and they'd have to humor her. The thing that most annoyed her was that Cornelia thought she was deaf, dumb, and blind. Little hasty glances and tiny gestures tossed around her and over her head saying, "Don't cross her, let her have her way, she's eighty years old," and she sitting there as if she lived in a thin glass cage. Sometimes Granny almost made up her mind to pack up and move back to her own house where nobody could remind her every minute that she was old. Wait, wait, Cornelia, till your own children whisper behind your back!

In her day she had kept a better house and had got more work done. She wasn't too old yet for Lydia to be driving eighty miles for advice when one of the children jumped the track, and Jimmy still dropped in and talked things over: "Now, Mammy, you've a good business head, I want to know what you think of this? . . ." Old. Cornelia couldn't change

---

4. **noggin of strong hot toddy:** mug of a strong, hot alcoholic drink.

WORDS
TO
KNOW
    plague (plāg) *v.* to annoy; harass

the furniture around without asking. Little things, little things! They had been so sweet when they were little. Granny wished the old days were back again with the children young and

130 everything to be done over. It had been a hard pull, but not too much for her. When she thought of all the food she had cooked, and all the clothes she had cut and sewed, and all the gardens she had made—well, the children showed it. There they were, made out of her, and they couldn't get away from that. Sometimes she wanted to see John again and point to them and say, Well, I didn't do so badly, did I? But that would have to wait. That was for tomorrow. She used to think of him as a man, but now all the children were older than their father, and he would be a child beside her if she saw him

140 now.[5] It seemed strange and there was something wrong in the idea. Why, he couldn't possibly recognize her. She had fenced in a hundred acres once, digging the post holes herself and clamping the wires with just a negro boy to help. That changed a woman. John would be looking for a young woman with the peaked Spanish comb in her hair and the painted fan. Digging post holes changed a woman. Riding country roads in the winter when women had their babies was another thing: sitting up nights with sick horses and sick negroes and sick children and hardly ever losing one. John, I

150 hardly ever lost one of them! John would see that in a minute, that would be something he could understand, she wouldn't have to explain anything!

It made her feel like rolling up her sleeves and putting the whole place to rights again. No matter if Cornelia was determined to be everywhere at once, there were a great many things left undone on this place. She would start tomorrow and do them. It was good to be strong enough for everything, even if all you made melted and changed and slipped under your hands, so that by the time you finished you almost

160 forgot what you were working for. What was it I set out to do? she asked herself <u>intently</u>, but she could not remember. A fog rose over the valley, she saw it marching across the creek swallowing the trees and moving up the hill like an army of ghosts. Soon it would be at the near edge of the orchard, and

READ ALOUD **Lines 128–133**

Read aloud the boxed sentences. What was Granny like as a mother? **(Evaluate)**

---

5. **She used to think of him . . . now:** Granny's husband, John, died at a younger age than his children have reached.

WORDS
TO
KNOW

intently (ĭn-tĕnt′lē) *adv.* with concentrated attention

Granny Weatherall   **301**

Pause & Reflect

1. Circle the phrase below that is *not* true of Granny's dead husband. **(Clarify)**

died at a young age

helped Granny fence in 100 acres

would no longer recognize Granny

would admire how Granny took care of the sick

MARK IT UP **2.** Circle details on page 301 that tell you about some hardships Granny has faced. What do you learn about Granny from the way she dealt with her hardships? **(Infer)**

_____

_____

_____

_____

then it was time to go in and light the lamps. Come in, children, don't stay out in the night air.

Lighting the lamps had been beautiful. The children huddled up to her and breathed like little calves waiting at the bars in the twilight. Their eyes followed the match and 170 watched the flame rise and settle in a blue curve, then they moved away from her. The lamp was lit, they didn't have to be scared and hang on to mother any more. Never, never, never more. God, for all my life I thank Thee. Without Thee, my God, I could never have done it. Hail, Mary, full of grace.[6]

I want you to pick all the fruit this year and see that nothing is wasted. There's always someone who can use it. Don't let good things rot for want of using. You waste life when you waste good food. Don't let things get lost. It's bitter to lose things. Now, don't let me get to thinking, not when I 180 am tired and taking a little nap before supper. . . .

Pause & Reflect

FOCUS
Granny recalls her jilting by George, the man she was supposed to marry. Read to find out whether or not she has forgiven him.

The pillow rose about her shoulders and pressed against her heart and the memory was being squeezed out of it: oh, push down the pillow, somebody: it would smother her if she tried to hold it. Such a fresh breeze blowing and such a green day with no threats in it. But he had not come, just the same. What does a woman do when she has put on the white veil and set out the white cake for a man and he doesn't come? She 190 tried to remember. No, I swear he never harmed me but in that. He never harmed me but in that. . .and what if he did? There was the day, the day, but a whirl of dark smoke rose and covered it, crept up and over into the bright field where everything was planted so carefully in orderly rows. That was hell, she knew hell when she saw it. For sixty years she had prayed against remembering him and against losing her soul in the deep pit of hell, and now the two things were mingled in one and the thought of him was a smoky cloud from hell that moved and crept in her head when she had just got rid of 200 Doctor Harry and was trying to rest a minute. Wounded vanity,[7] Ellen, said a sharp voice in the top of her mind.

---

6. **Hail . . . grace:** the beginning of a Roman Catholic prayer to the Virgin Mary.

7. **vanity:** pride.

Don't let your wounded vanity get the upper hand of you. Plenty of girls get jilted. You were jilted, weren't you? Then stand up to it. Her eyelids wavered and let in streamers of blue-gray light like tissue paper over her eyes. She must get up and pull the shades down or she'd never sleep. She was in bed again and the shades were not down. How could that happen? Better turn over, hide from the light, sleeping in the light gave you nightmares. "Mother, how do you feel now?"

210 and a stinging wetness on her forehead. But I don't like having my face washed in cold water!

Hapsy? George? Lydia? Jimmy? No, Cornelia, and her features were swollen and full of little puddles. "They're coming, darling, they'll all be here soon." Go wash your face, child, you look funny.

Instead of obeying, Cornelia knelt down and put her head on the pillow. She seemed to be talking but there was no sound. "Well, are you tongue-tied? Whose birthday is it? Are you going to give a party?"

220 Cornelia's mouth moved urgently in strange shapes. "Don't do that, you bother me, daughter."

"Oh, no, Mother. Oh, no. . . ."

Nonsense. It was strange about children. They disputed your every word. "No what, Cornelia?"

"Here's Doctor Harry."

"I won't see that boy again. He just left five minutes ago."

"That was this morning, Mother. It's night now. Here's the nurse."

"This is Doctor Harry, Mrs. Weatherall. I never saw you

230 look so young and happy!"

"Ah, I'll never be young again—but I'd be happy if they'd let me lie in peace and get rested."

She thought she spoke up loudly, but no one answered. A warm weight on her forehead, a warm bracelet on her wrist, and a breeze went on whispering, trying to tell her something. A shuffle of leaves in the everlasting hand of God, He blew on them and they danced and rattled. "Mother, don't mind, we're going to give you a little hypodermic."[8] "Look here, daughter, how do ants get in this bed? I saw sugar ants yesterday." Did

240 you send for Hapsy too?

Pause **&** *Reflect*

---

8. **hypodermic** (hī′pə-dûr′mĭk): injection.

Pause **&** **Reflect**

✏️ **MARK IT UP** **1.** Review the boxed passage on page 302. Do you think Granny has forgiven George for jilting her? Write your answer below. Then circle details in the passage that led you to your conclusion. **(Draw Conclusions)**

_____

_____

_____

2. Do you think people should forgive those who have hurt them deeply? Why or why not? **(Connect)**

_____

_____

_____

✏️ **MARK IT UP** **3.** What details on this page suggest that Granny's condition is getting worse? Underline these details, starting with the moment when Cornelia puts cold water on Granny's face (line 210). **(Analyze)**

Read to find out how
Granny feels about
Hapsy, her dead
daughter, and John,
her late husband.

It was Hapsy she really wanted. She had to go a long way back through a great many rooms to find Hapsy standing with a baby on her arm.[9] She seemed to herself to be Hapsy also, and the baby on Hapsy's arm was Hapsy and himself and herself, all at once, and there was no surprise in the meeting. Then Hapsy melted from within and turned flimsy as gray gauze and the baby was a gauzy shadow, and Hapsy came up close and said, "I thought you'd never come," and looked at her very searchingly and said, "You haven't changed a bit!" They leaned forward to kiss, when Cornelia began whispering from a long way off, "Oh, is there anything you want to tell me? Is there anything I can do for you?"

Yes, she had changed her mind after sixty years and she would like to see George. I want you to find George. Find him and be sure to tell him I forgot him. I want him to know I had my husband just the same and my children and my house like any other woman. A good house too and a good husband that I loved and fine children out of him. Better than I hoped for even. Tell him I was given back everything he took away and more. Oh, no, oh, God, no, there was something else besides the house and the man and the children. Oh, surely they were not all? What was it? Something not given back. . . . Her breath crowded down under her ribs and grew into a monstrous frightening shape with cutting edges; it bored up into her head, and the agony was unbelievable: Yes, John, get the Doctor now, no more talk, my time has come.[10]

When this one was born it should be the last. The last. It should have been born first, for it was the one she had truly wanted. Everything came in good time. Nothing left out, left over. She was strong, in three days she would be as well as ever. Better. A woman needed milk in her to have her full health.

"Mother, do you hear me?"

READ ALOUD **Lines 261–265**
Read aloud the boxed sentences. What do you suppose George took from Granny that she never got back? **(Infer)**

_____

_____

_____

---

9. **Hapsy standing with a baby on her arm:** This detail may suggest that Hapsy died in childbirth.

10. **Her breath . . . my time has come:** The memory of George triggers a horrible pain, and Granny relives a moment at the beginning of childbirth, perhaps the birth of Hapsy.

304 The InterActive Reader

"I've been telling you—"

"Mother, Father Connolly's here."

"I went to Holy Communion only last week. Tell him I'm
not so sinful as all that."

"Father just wants to speak to you."

He could speak as much as he pleased. It was like him to
drop in and inquire about her soul as if it were a teething
baby, and then stay on for a cup of tea and a round of cards
and gossip. He always had a funny story of some sort, usually
about an Irishman who made his little mistakes and confessed
them, and the point lay in some absurd thing he would blurt
out in the confessional showing his struggles between native
piety and original sin. Granny felt easy about her soul.
Cornelia, where are your manners? Give Father Connolly a
chair. She had her secret comfortable understanding with a
few favorite saints who cleared a straight road to God for her.
All as surely signed and sealed as the papers for the new Forty
Acres. Forever. . . . heirs and assigns[11] forever. Since the day
the wedding cake was not cut, but thrown out and wasted.
The whole bottom dropped out of the world, and there she
was blind and sweating with nothing under her feet and the
walls falling away. His hand had caught her under the breast,
she had not fallen, there was the freshly polished floor with
the green rug on it, just as before. He had cursed like a sailor's
parrot and said, "I'll kill him for you." Don't lay a hand on
him, for my sake leave something to God. "Now, Ellen, you
must believe what I tell you. . . ."

Pause & Reflect

FOCUS
Granny slips closer and
closer to death. Read
to find out what hap-
pens to her at the end
of the story.

So there was nothing, nothing to worry
about any more, except sometimes in
the night one of the children screamed
in a nightmare, and they both hustled
out shaking and hunting for the
matches and calling, "There, wait a
minute, here we are!" John, get the doctor now, Hapsy's time
has come. But there was Hapsy standing by the bed in a

---

11. **assigns:** people to whom property is transferred in a will or other
legal document.

Pause & Reflect

1. Check the phrase below that
describes Granny's attitude
toward her dead daughter,
Hapsy. (**Infer**)

loves her deeply

cares for her only a little

never wants to see her again

 MARK IT UP   2. Whom do
you think Granny loved more—
her husband, John, or George,
the man who jilted her? Write
down your answer on the lines
below. Then circle any details
on page 304 that support your
answer. (**Compare and
Contrast**)

_____

_____

_____

_____

READ ALOUD   3. Read
aloud the boxed passage on this
page (lines 289–294). What does
Granny think will happen to her
after she dies? (**Infer**)

_____

_____

_____

_____

Granny Weatherall   **305**

white cap.[12] "Cornelia, tell Hapsy to take off her cap. I can't see her plain."

Her eyes opened very wide and the room stood out like a picture she had seen somewhere. Dark colors with the shadows rising towards the ceiling in long angles. The tall black dresser gleamed with nothing on it but John's picture, enlarged from a little one, with John's eyes very black when they should have been blue. You never saw him, so
320 how do you know how he looked? But the man insisted the copy was perfect, it was very rich and handsome. For a picture, yes, but it's not my husband. The table by the bed had a linen cover and a candle and a crucifix.[13] The light was blue from Cornelia's silk lampshades. No sort of light at all, just frippery. You had to live forty years with kerosene lamps to appreciate honest electricity. She felt very strong and she saw Doctor Harry with a rosy nimbus[14] around him.

"You look like a saint, Doctor Harry, and I vow that's as
330 near as you'll ever come to it."

"She's saying something."

"I heard you, Cornelia. What's all this carrying-on?"

"Father Connolly's saying—"

Cornelia's voice staggered and bumped like a cart in a bad road. It rounded corners and turned back again and arrived nowhere. Granny stepped up in the cart very lightly and reached for the reins, but a man sat beside her and she knew him by his hands, driving the cart. She did not look in his face, for she knew without seeing, but looked instead down
340 the road where the trees leaned over and bowed to each other and a thousand birds were singing a Mass. She felt like singing too, but she put her hand in the bosom of her dress and pulled out a rosary,[15] and Father Connolly murmured Latin in a very solemn voice and tickled her feet.[16] My God,

MARK IT UP **KEEP TRACK**

Remember to use these marks to keep track of your understanding.

✔ ..... I understand.

? ..... I don't understand this.

! ..... Interesting or surprising idea

12. **Hapsy . . . in a white cap:** Granny mistakenly thinks she sees Hapsy in the white cap. She actually sees the nurse whom Cornelia mentioned.

13. **crucifix** (kro͞o′sə-fĭks′): a cross bearing a sculptured representation of the crucified Christ.

14. **nimbus:** halo of light.

15. **rosary** (rō′zə-rē): a string of beads used by Roman Catholics to count their prayers.

16. **Father Connolly . . . tickled her feet:** Father Connolly puts oil on Granny's feet as part of the ritual for anointing the sick and dying.

will you stop that nonsense? I'm a married woman. What if he did run away and leave me to face the priest by myself? I found another a whole world better. I wouldn't have exchanged my husband for anybody except St. Michael himself, and you may tell him that for me with a thank you in
350 the bargain.

Light flashed on her closed eyelids, and a deep roaring shook her. Cornelia, is that lightning? I hear thunder. There's going to be a storm. Close all the windows. Call the children in. . . . "Mother, here we are, all of us." "Is that you, Hapsy?" "Oh, no, I'm Lydia. We drove as fast as we could."

Their faces drifted above her, drifted away. The rosary fell out of her hands and Lydia put it back. Jimmy tried to help, their hands fumbled together, and Granny closed two fingers around Jimmy's thumb. Beads wouldn't do, it must be
360 something alive. She was so amazed her thoughts ran round and round. So, my dear Lord, this is my death and I wasn't even thinking about it. My children have come to see me die. But I can't, it's not time. Oh, I always hated surprises.
I wanted to give Cornelia the amethyst set—Cornelia, you're to have the amethyst set, but Hapsy's to wear it when she wants, and, Doctor Harry, do shut up. Nobody sent for you. Oh, my dear Lord, do wait a minute. I meant to do something about the Forty Acres, Jimmy doesn't need it and Lydia will later on, with that worthless husband of hers. I
370 meant to finish the altar cloth and send six bottles of wine to Sister Borgia for her dyspepsia.[17] I want to send six bottles of wine to Sister Borgia, Father Connolly, now don't let me forget.

Cornelia's voice made short turns and tilted over and crashed. "Oh, Mother, oh, Mother, oh, Mother . . . ."

"I'm not going, Cornelia. I'm taken by surprise. I can't go."
You'll see Hapsy again. What about her? "I thought you'd never come." Granny made a long journey outward, looking for Hapsy. What if I don't find her? What then?
380 Her heart sank down and down, there was no bottom to death, she couldn't come to the end of it. The blue light from Cornelia's lampshade drew into a tiny point in the center of her brain, it flickered and winked like an eye, quietly it fluttered and dwindled. Granny lay curled down

READ ALOUD   **Lines 356–363**

Granny realizes she is about to die. She tells herself she "always hated surprises." On what other occasion was she given a terrible surprise? (**Compare and Contrast**)

_____

_____

_____

_____

---

17. dyspepsia (dĭs-pĕp′shə): indigestion.

Pause & Reflect

READ ALOUD **1.** Read aloud the boxed sentences. Then circle the *two* words below that describe Granny's attitude at the moment of death. **(Infer)**

peaceful   bitter

happy   disappointed

2. What did you find most memorable about Granny? **(Connect)**

_____

_____

_____

_____

CHALLENGE

In the **third-person limited point of view,** the narrator stands outside the action and focuses on one character's thoughts, observations, and feelings. In the **third-person omniscient** point of view, the narrator relates the thoughts and feelings of different characters. What did Porter gain by using the third-person limited point of view in this story? What would be different if she had used the third-person omniscient point of view? **(Analyze)**

Wrapping Up

If you are using **The Language of Literature,** you can now move to the questions and activities on pages 1043–1044 of that book.

within herself, amazed and watchful, staring at the point of light that was herself; her body was now only a deeper mass of shadow in an endless darkness and this darkness would curl around the light and swallow it up. God, give a sign!

For the second time there was no sign. Again no bridegroom and the priest in the house. She could not remember any other sorrow because this grief wiped them all away. Oh, no, there's nothing more cruel than this—I'll never forgive it. She stretched herself with a deep breath and blew out the light.

Pause & Reflect

Active Reading SkillBuilder

Sequencing

In this stream-of-consciousness narrative, Porter shuffles the past and the present to show the distorted way that a dying person perceives the **sequence,** or time order, of events. The reader experiences Granny's sense of time as she imaginatively travels backward and forward through her life, re-creating dramatic moments. Complete the time line below, sequencing additional important events in Granny's life in chronological order. An example is shown.

Jilting   *Marriage*   **Examination**
by George   *to John*   **by Dr. Harry**

Literary Analysis SkillBuilder

Stream of Consciousness

Stream of consciousness is a literary technique developed by modernist writers to present the flow of a character's unconnected thoughts, responses, and sensations. A stream-of-consciousness narrative is not structured into a coherent, logical presentation of events. Rather, one event triggers thoughts of another. In the chart below, write three events in the story that take place in Granny's sickroom shortly before her death and three events that take place in her mind. An example is shown.

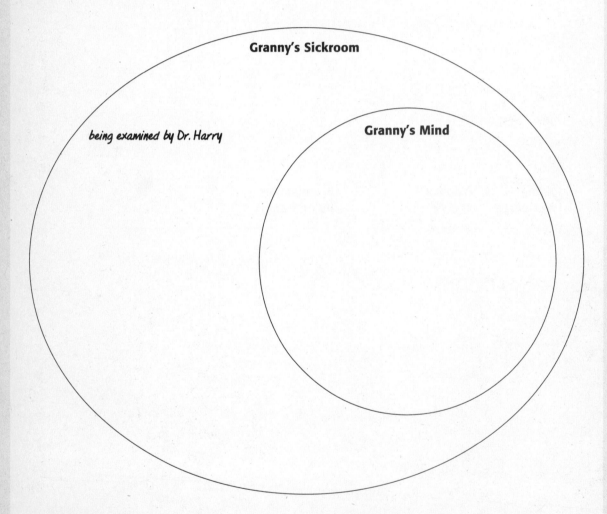

Granny's Sickroom

being examined by Dr. Harry

Granny's Mind

Follow Up: Write a short stream-of-consciousness narrative in which George lies on his deathbed and recalls jilting Granny. Share your narrative with classmates.

Words to Know SkillBuilder

Words to Know

embroidered   intently   plague   rummage   tactful

A. Decide which Word to Know best completes each sentence below. Then write the word on the blank line on the right.

I like to watch Grandma (1) through the contents of her trunk. She pulls out all sorts of knickknacks and letters.

_____ (1)

I am amazed by her (2) pillowcases. The detail in the stitching is wonderful.

_____ (2)

I try not to bother her with constant interruptions. I do not want to (3) her with questions while she is searching.

_____ (3)

She is looking (4) for a particular letter. Her attention never wanders; eventually she finds the letter she has saved for so long.

_____ (4)

I would like to know what the letter says. Maybe if I am (5) and ask in a diplomatic way, she will read the letter to me.

_____ (5)

B. For each phrase in the first column, find the phrase in the second column that is closest in meaning. Write the letter of that phrase in the blank.

1. search in the salvage   A. a tactful trainer

2. fiercely focused   B. plague the policeman

3. a considerate coach   C. rummage in the wreckage

4. beautifully embroidered   D. intently interested

5. annoy the cop   E. stunningly stitched

C. Write a letter that Granny Weatherall might write to George. Use at least **three** Words to Know in your letter.

Before You Read

If you are using **The Language of Literature** . . .

- Use the information on page 1136 of that book to prepare for reading.

- Look at the photographs on pages 1137, 1139, 1140, and 1144. What do they tell you about the struggle Martin Luther King, Jr., was involved in?

Reading Tips

This piece of writing is a **persuasive essay** as well as a **personal letter**. It will be easier to understand if you do the following:

- Pay close attention to the first sentence or two in each paragraph. That's usually where King states his **main idea**.

- Try to identify the major reasons that King gives to support his actions and beliefs.

- For now, don't worry about names or details that are unfamiliar. Keep in mind that you don't have to understand everything to get a general sense of King's meaning.

MARK IT UP KEEP TRACK

As you read, you can use these marks to keep track of your understanding.

✔ ..... I understand.

? ..... I don't understand this.

! ..... Interesting or surprising idea

from LETTER FROM BIRMINGHAM JAIL

APRIL 16, 1963

Martin Luther King, Jr.

PREVIEW Martin Luther King, Jr., was put in jail several times when he was campaigning for civil rights in Birmingham, Alabama, in 1963. During one of those imprisonments, eight local white clergymen published a letter in which they criticized King's methods. King responded with a long letter defending his actions. Here he explains why civil disobedience—breaking unjust laws—is necessary in the struggle for justice.

FOCUS

In the first part of his letter, King defends his presence in Birmingham, Alabama.

MARK IT UP Underline the reasons that King gives for being in Birmingham. An example is highlighted on page 313.

My Dear Fellow Clergymen:

While confined here in the Birmingham city jail, I came across your recent statement calling my present activities "unwise and untimely." Seldom do I pause to answer criticism of my work and ideas. If I sought to answer all the criticisms that cross my desk, my secretaries would have little

10 time for anything other than such correspondence in the course of the day, and I would have no time for constructive work. But since I feel that you are men of genuine goodwill and that your criticisms are sincerely set forth, I want to try to answer your statement in what I hope will be patient and reasonable terms.

I think I should indicate why I am here in Birmingham, since you have been influenced by the view which argues against "outsiders coming in." I have the honor of serving as president of the Southern Christian Leadership Conference, an

20 organization operating in every Southern state, with

headquarters in Atlanta, Georgia. We have some eighty-five affiliated organizations across the South, and one of them is the Alabama Christian Movement for Human Rights. Frequently we share staff, educational, and financial resources with our affiliates. Several months ago the <u>affiliate</u> here in Birmingham asked us to be on call to engage in a nonviolent direct-action program if such were deemed necessary. We readily consented, and when the hour came, we lived up to our promise. So I, along with several members of my staff, am

30 here because I was invited here. I am here because I have organizational ties here.

But more basically, I am in Birmingham because injustice is here. Just as the prophets of the eighth century B.C. left their villages and carried their "thus saith the Lord" far beyond the boundaries of their hometowns,[1] and just as the Apostle Paul left his village of Tarsus and carried the gospel of Jesus Christ to the far corners of the Greco-Roman world, so am I compelled to carry the gospel of freedom beyond my own hometown. Like Paul, I must constantly respond to the

40 Macedonian call for aid.[2]

Moreover, I am <u>cognizant</u> of the interrelatedness of all communities and states. I cannot sit idly by in Atlanta and not be concerned about what happens in Birmingham. Injustice anywhere is a threat to justice everywhere. We are caught in an inescapable network of mutuality,[3] tied in a single garment of destiny. Whatever affects one directly, affects all indirectly. Never again can we afford to live with the narrow, provincial "outside agitator" idea. Anyone who lives inside the United States can never be considered an outsider anywhere within its

50 bounds.

Pause & Reflect

---

1. **prophets . . . hometowns:** Hebrew religious figures, including Amos, Hosea, and Micah, who traveled from village to village with messages from God for the Hebrew people.

2. **Macedonian** (măs′ĭ-dō′nē-ən) **call for aid:** According to the Bible (Acts 16), a man appeared to the Apostle Paul in a vision, calling him to preach in Macedonia (at that time a Roman province north of Greece).

3. **inescapable network of mutuality:** King makes the point that people must depend on one another in this world.

WORDS	**affiliate** (ə-fĭl′ē-ĭt) *n.* a person or organization associated
TO	with another
KNOW	**cognizant** (kŏg′nĭ-zənt) *adj.* aware

Pause & Reflect

1. Look at the passages that you underlined. King is in Birmingham because_____

_____

_____

_____.

(Logical Argument)

2. An agitator is someone who stirs up people to take action. Why was King called an "outside agitator" (line 48) by some people in Birmingham? **(Infer)**

_____

_____

_____

_____

3. How would you feel if you were put in jail for doing what you thought was right? **(Connect)**

_____

_____

_____

_____

You deplore the demonstrations taking place in Birmingham. But your statement, I am sorry to say, fails to express a similar concern for the conditions that brought about the demonstrations. I am sure that none of you would want to rest content with the superficial kind of social analysis that deals merely with effects and does not grapple with underlying causes. It is unfortunate that demonstrations are taking place in Birmingham, but it is even more unfortunate that the city's white power structure left the Negro community with no alternative.

In any nonviolent campaign there are four basic steps: collection of the facts to determine whether injustices exist; negotiation; self-purification; and direct action. We have gone through all these steps in Birmingham. There can be no gainsaying[4] the fact that racial injustice engulfs this community. Birmingham is probably the most thoroughly <u>segregated</u> city in the United States. Its ugly record of brutality is widely known. Negroes have experienced grossly unjust treatment in the courts. There have been more unsolved bombings of Negro homes and churches in Birmingham than in any other city in the nation. These are the hard, brutal facts of the case. On the basis of these conditions, Negro leaders sought to negotiate with the city fathers. But the latter consistently refused to engage in good-faith negotiations.

Then, last September, came the opportunity to talk with leaders of Birmingham's economic community. In the course of the negotiations, certain promises were made by the merchants—for example, to remove the stores' humiliating racial signs.[5] On the basis of these promises, The Reverend Fred Shuttlesworth and the leaders of the Alabama Christian Movement for Human Rights agreed to a moratorium[6] on all demonstrations. As the weeks and months went by, we

---

MARK IT UP Lines 67–75

Underline examples of racial injustice in Birmingham that King mentions in this passage. **(Clarify)**

---

4. **gainsaying:** denying.

5. **racial signs:** signs marking segregated buildings and other facilities.

6. **moratorium** (môr′ə-tôr′ē-əm): temporary stoppage.

WORDS TO KNOW

segregated (sĕg′rĭ-gā′tĭd) *adj.* separated according to race
segregate *v.*

realized that we were the victims of a broken promise. A few signs, briefly removed, returned; the others remained.

As in so many past experiences, our hopes had been

90 blasted, and the shadow of deep disappointment settled upon us. We had no alternative except to prepare for direct action, whereby we would present our very bodies as a means of laying our case before the conscience of the local and the national community. Mindful of the difficulties involved, we decided to undertake a process of self-purification. We began a series of workshops on nonviolence, and we repeatedly asked ourselves: "Are you able to accept blows without retaliating?" "Are you able to endure the ordeal of jail?" We decided to schedule our direct-action program for the Easter

100 season, realizing that except for Christmas, this is the main shopping period of the year. Knowing that a strong economic-withdrawal program[7] would be the by-product of direct action, we felt that this would be the best time to bring pressure to bear on the merchants for the needed change.

Then it occurred to us that Birmingham's mayoral election was coming up in March, and we speedily decided to postpone action until after election day. When we discovered that the Commissioner of Public Safety, Eugene "Bull" Connor, had piled up enough votes to be in the runoff, we

110 decided again to postpone action until the day after the runoff so that the demonstrations could not be used to cloud the issues. Like many others, we waited to see Mr. Connor defeated, and to this end we endured postponement after postponement. Having aided in this community need, we felt that our direct-action program could be delayed no longer.

You may well ask: "Why direct action? Why sit-ins,[8] marches, and so forth? Isn't negotiation a better path?" You are quite right in calling for negotiation. Indeed, this is the very purpose of direct action. Nonviolent direct action seeks

120 to create such a crisis and foster such a tension that a community which has constantly refused to negotiate is forced to confront the issue. It seeks so to dramatize the issue that it

MARK IT UP WORD POWER

Mark words that you'd like to add to your **Personal Word List**. After reading, you can record the words and their meanings beginning on page 344.

---

7. **a strong economic-withdrawal program:** King knew that demonstrations would result in fewer customers for the merchants.

8. **sit-ins:** peaceful demonstrations in which protesters occupied, and refused to leave, seats in segregated lunch counters and other places of business.

WORDS
TO
KNOW

retaliating (rĭ-tăl′ē-ā′tĭng) *n.* taking revenge **retaliate** *v.*

Pause & Reflect

1. What was the result of negotiations with the merchants, or businessmen? Circle the correct statement below. **(Clarify)**

   The merchants refused to make any changes.

   The merchants promised some changes, but didn't keep their promises.

2. According to King, the purpose of direct action, such as sit-ins and marches, is to _____ _____ _____ _____ .
   (Clarify)

3. Review the four steps of the Birmingham campaign that you numbered. Do you think the campaign was justified? *Yes/No*, because _____ _____ _____ _____ _____ .
   (Evaluate)

can no longer be ignored. My citing the creation of tension as part of the work of the nonviolent-resister may sound rather shocking. But I must confess that I am not afraid of the word "tension." I have earnestly opposed violent tension, but there is a type of constructive, nonviolent tension which is necessary for growth. Just as Socrates[9] felt that it was necessary to create a tension in the mind so that individuals could rise from the bondage of myths and half-truths to the unfettered realm of creative analysis and objective appraisal, so must we see the need for nonviolent gadflies[10] to create the kind of tension in society that will help men rise from the dark depths of prejudice and racism to the majestic heights of understanding and brotherhood.[11]

The purpose of our direct-action program is to create a situation so crisis-packed that it will inevitably open the door to negotiation. I therefore concur with you in your call for negotiation. Too long has our beloved Southland been bogged down in a tragic effort to live in monologue rather than dialogue.

Pause & Reflect

FOCUS

King now responds to the criticism that his demonstrations are "untimely." He explains why he thinks action cannot be delayed.

MARK IT UP As you read, look for passages that support King's position. Mark the passages with an *S*.

One of the basic points in your statement is that the action that I and my associates have taken in Birmingham is untimely. Some have asked: "Why didn't you give the new city administration time to act?" The only answer that I can give to this query is that the new Birmingham administration must be prodded about as much as the outgoing one before it will act. . . . My friends, I

---

9. **Socrates** (sŏk′rə-tēz′): a Greek philosopher of the fifth century B.C.—one of the major influences in the development of Western thought. Socrates taught people through the use of questions. He made people uncomfortable so that they could discover truth for themselves.

10. **gadflies:** critics.

11. King compares the civil-rights protesters to Socrates. They must create tension so that people can be led to new ways of thinking and living.

WORDS
TO
KNOW
    appraisal (ə-prā′zəl) *n.* evaluation

must say to you that we have not made a single gain in civil rights without determined legal and nonviolent pressure. Lamentably, it is a historical fact that privileged groups seldom give up their privileges voluntarily. Individuals may see the moral light and voluntarily give up their unjust posture; but, as Reinhold Niebuhr[12] has reminded us, groups tend to be more immoral than individuals.

We know through painful experience that freedom is never voluntarily given by the oppressor; it must be demanded by the oppressed. Frankly, I have yet to engage in a direct-action campaign that was "well-timed" in the view of those who have not suffered unduly from the disease of segregation. For years now I have heard the word "Wait!" It rings in the ear of every Negro with piercing familiarity. This "Wait" has almost always meant "Never." We must come to see, with one of our distinguished jurists,[13] that "justice too long delayed is justice denied."

We have waited for more than 340 years for our constitutional and God-given rights. The nations of Asia and Africa are moving with jetlike speed toward gaining political independence, but we still creep at horse-and-buggy pace toward gaining a cup of coffee at a lunch counter. Perhaps it is easy for those who have never felt the stinging darts of segregation to say, "Wait." But when you have seen vicious mobs lynch your mothers and fathers at will and drown your sisters and brothers at whim; when you have seen hate-filled policemen curse, kick, and even kill your black brothers and sisters; when you see the vast majority of your twenty million Negro brothers smothering in an airtight cage of poverty in the midst of an affluent society; when you suddenly find your tongue twisted and your speech stammering as you seek to explain to your six-year-old daughter why she can't go to the public amusement park that has just been advertised on television, and see tears welling up in her eyes when she is told that Funtown is closed to colored children, and see ominous[14] clouds of inferiority beginning to form in her little mental sky, and see her beginning to distort her personality by developing an unconscious bitterness toward white people;

READ ALOUD Lines 163–166

Read aloud the boxed passage. Why does King say "Wait!" almost always means "Never" for African Americans? **(Paraphrase)**

---

12. **Reinhold Niebuhr** (rĭn′hōld′ nē′bŏŏr′): a 20th-century American theologian whose writings deal mainly with moral and social problems.

13. **distinguished jurists:** outstanding judges or legal scholars.

14. **ominous** (ŏm′ə-nəs): threatening.

1. In lines 171–208, King describes the painful effects of racial injustice. Which of the items below is *not* mentioned by King? Circle it. **(Clarify)**

poverty

segregation of public facilities

lynching

lack of education

lack of respect

✎ **MARK IT UP** 2. Look back at the passages that you marked with an *S*. Star that passage that you find most convincing. **(Evaluate)**

3. If you had lived during the early 1960s, how do you think you would have responded to King's call for action? **(Connect)**

_____

_____

_____

_____

190 when you have to concoct an answer for a five-year-old son who is asking: "Daddy, why do white people treat colored people so mean?"; when you take a cross-country drive and find it necessary to sleep night after night in the uncomfortable corners of your automobile because no motel will accept you; when you are humiliated day in and day out by nagging signs reading "white" and "colored"; when your first name becomes "nigger," your middle name becomes "boy" (however old you are) and your last name becomes "John," and your wife and mother are never given the respected title "Mrs."; when you are

200 harried by day and haunted by night by the fact that you are a Negro, living constantly at tiptoe stance, never quite knowing what to expect next, and are plagued with inner fears and outer resentments; when you are forever fighting a degenerating sense of "nobodiness"—then you will understand why we find it difficult to wait. There comes a time when the cup of endurance runs over, and men are no longer willing to be plunged into the abyss of despair. I hope, sirs, you can understand our legitimate and unavoidable impatience.

Pause & Reflect

FOCUS
210 King now talks about just and unjust laws. He explains the differences between these kinds of laws.

✎ **MARK IT UP** As you read, underline the qualities of a just law.

You express a great deal of anxiety over our willingness to break laws. This is certainly a legitimate concern. Since we so <u>diligently</u> urge people to obey the Supreme Court's decision of 1954 outlawing segregation in the public schools,[15] at first glance it may seem rather paradoxical[16] for us consciously to break laws. One may well ask: "How can you advocate breaking some laws and obeying others?" The answer lies in the fact that there are two types of laws: just and unjust. I would be

220 the first to advocate obeying just laws. One has not only a legal

---

15. **the Supreme Court's . . . public schools:** the U.S. Supreme Court's decision in the case *Brown v. Board of Education of Topeka, Kansas.*

16. **paradoxical** (păr′ə-dŏk′sĭ-kəl): self-contradictory.

WORDS TO KNOW	**diligently** (dĭl′ə-jənt-lē) *adv.* in a persevering, painstaking manner

(Handwritten notes in margin:)

"when you are..."
- HISTORICAL ALLUSION
PAINFUL SORROW

"then you will understand"
- CLOSING ARGUMENT

"when you"
- ANAPHORA

but a moral responsibility to obey just laws. Conversely, one has a moral responsibility to disobey unjust laws. I would agree with St. Augustine[17] that "an unjust law is no law at all."

Now, what is the difference between the two? How does one determine whether a law is just or unjust? A just law is a man-made code that squares with the moral law or the law of God. An unjust law is a code that is out of harmony with the moral law. To put it in the terms of St. Thomas Aquinas:[18] An unjust law is a human law that is not rooted in eternal law

230 and natural law. Any law that uplifts human personality is just. Any law that degrades human personality is unjust. All segregation statutes are unjust because segregation distorts the soul and damages the personality. It gives the segregator a false sense of superiority and the segregated a false sense of inferiority. Segregation, to use the terminology of the Jewish philosopher Martin Buber,[19] substitutes an "I-it" relationship for an "I-thou" relationship and ends up relegating persons to the status of things. Hence segregation is not only politically, economically, and sociologically unsound, it is morally wrong

240 and sinful. Paul Tillich[20] has said that sin is separation. Is not segregation an existential[21] expression of man's tragic separation, his awful estrangement, his terrible sinfulness? Thus it is that I can urge men to obey the 1954 decision of the Supreme Court, for it is morally right; and I can urge them to disobey segregation ordinances, for they are morally wrong.

Let us consider a more concrete example of just and unjust laws. An unjust law is a code that a numerical or power majority group compels a minority group to obey but does not make binding on itself. This is *difference* made legal. By

250 the same token, a just law is a code that a majority compels a minority to follow and that it is willing to follow itself. This is *sameness* made legal.

---

17. **St. Augustine** (ô′gə-stēn′): a North African bishop, whose writings have influenced the history of Christianity.

18. **St. Thomas Aquinas** (ə-kwī′nəs): a noted philosopher and theologian in the Middle Ages.

19. **Martin Buber** (bōō′bər): an influential 20th-century Jewish philosopher.

20. **Paul Tillich** (tĭl′ĭk): a German-born American theologian of the 20th century.

21. **existential** (ĕg′zĭ-stĕn′shəl): existing in the real world.

READ ALOUD Lines 231–235

Read aloud the boxed passage. What type of laws relating to African Americans does King give as an example of unjust laws? **(Clarify)**

_____

_____

WORDS TO KNOW

statute (stăch′ōōt) *n.* a law
estrangement (ĭ-strānj′mənt) *n.* separation; alienation

Let me give another explanation. A law is unjust if it is inflicted on a minority that, as a result of being denied the right to vote, had no part in enacting or devising the law. Who can say that the legislature of Alabama which set up that state's segregation laws was democratically elected? Throughout Alabama all sorts of devious[22] methods are used to prevent Negroes from becoming registered voters, and there are some counties in which, even though Negroes constitute a majority of the population, not a single Negro is registered. Can any law enacted under such circumstances be considered democratically structured?

Sometimes a law is just on its face and unjust in its application. For instance, I have been arrested on a charge of parading without a permit. Now, there is nothing wrong in having an ordinance which requires a permit for a parade. But such an ordinance becomes unjust when it is used to maintain segregation and to deny citizens the First Amendment privilege of peaceful assembly and protest.

I hope you are able to see the distinction I am trying to point out. In no sense do I advocate evading or defying the law, as would the rabid segregationist. That would lead to anarchy.[23] One who breaks an unjust law must do so openly, lovingly, and with a willingness to accept the penalty. I submit that an individual who breaks a law that conscience tells him is unjust, and who willingly accepts the penalty of imprisonment in order to arouse the conscience of the community over its injustice, is in reality expressing the highest respect for law.

Of course, there is nothing new about this kind of civil disobedience. It was evidenced sublimely in the refusal of Shadrach, Meshach, and Abednego to obey the laws of Nebuchadnezzar,[24] on the ground that a higher moral law was at stake. It was practiced superbly by the early Christians, who were willing to face hungry lions and the excruciating pain of chopping blocks rather than submit to certain unjust laws of the Roman Empire. To a degree, academic freedom is a reality today because Socrates practiced civil disobedience.

READ ALOUD **Lines 274–279**

As you read this passage aloud, notice the respect that King shows for the law.

---

22. **devious:** tricky; indirect.

23. **anarchy** (ăn′ər-kē): an absence of law and order in a society.

24. **the refusal . . . Nebuchadnezzar** (nĕb′ə-kəd-nĕz′ər): In the Bible (Daniel 3), Shadrach (shăd′răk), Meshach (mē′shăk), and Abednego (ə-bĕd′nĭ-gō′) are three Hebrews condemned to death for refusing to worship an idol set up by Nebuchadnezzar, king of Babylon. When cast into a fiery furnace, they are miraculously protected from the fire and emerge unharmed.

In our own nation, the Boston Tea Party represented a
massive act of civil disobedience.

We should never forget that everything Adolf Hitler did in
Germany was "legal" and everything the Hungarian freedom
fighters[25] did in Hungary was "illegal." It was "illegal" to aid
and comfort a Jew in Hitler's Germany. Even so, I am sure
that, had I lived in Germany at the time, I would have aided
and comforted my Jewish brothers. If today I lived in a
Communist country where certain principles dear to the
Christian faith are suppressed, I would openly advocate
disobeying that country's antireligious laws.

Pause & *Reflect*

FOCUS
Read to find out why
King is disappointed
with "white moderates"
who criticize his
nonviolent direct
action.

I must make two honest confessions to
you, my Christian and Jewish brothers.
First, I must confess that over the past
few years I have been gravely
disappointed with the white moderate. I
have almost reached the regrettable
conclusion that the Negro's great
stumbling block in his stride toward freedom is not the White
Citizen's Counciler or the Ku Klux Klanner,[26] but the white
moderate, who is more devoted to "order" than to justice;
who prefers a negative peace which is the absence of tension
to a positive peace which is the presence of justice; who
constantly says: "I agree with you in the goal you seek, but I
cannot agree with your methods of direct action"; who
paternalistically[27] believes he can set the timetable for another
man's freedom; who lives by a mythical concept of time and
who constantly advises the Negro to wait for a "more
convenient season." Shallow understanding from people of
goodwill is more frustrating than absolute misunderstanding
from people of ill will. Lukewarm acceptance is much more
bewildering than outright rejection.

---

25. **Hungarian freedom fighters:** Hungarians who participated in a 1956
    rebellion against the Communist government of their homeland. (The
    uprising was crushed by troops sent into Hungary by the Soviet Union.)

26. **the White . . . Klanner:** a member of either of two hate groups which claim
    that white people are superior to African Americans and other minorities.

27. **paternalistically** (pə-tûr′nə-lĭs′tĭ-klē): in a manner that suggests the way a
    father deals with his children.

Pause & *Reflect*

1. Review what you underlined
   about the qualities of a just law.
   Star the quotes below from
   King's letter that apply to a just
   law. **(Clarify)**

   "moral responsibility to obey"

   "uplifts human personality"

   "*sameness* made legal"

   "out of harmony with the moral
   law"

MARK IT UP   2. Review
the examples that King gives of
breaking the law for a just
cause (lines 280–299). What are
King's most powerful examples?
Circle them. **(Evaluate)**

"Isn't this like" –
ANAPHORA

"But is this..."
RHETORICAL
QUESTION

"Like A BOIL..."
SIMILE

I had hoped that the white moderate would understand that law and order exist for the purpose of establishing justice and that when they fail in this purpose, they become the dangerously structured dams that block the flow of social progress. I had hoped that the white moderate would understand that the present tension in the South is a necessary phase of the transition from an obnoxious negative peace, in which the Negro passively accepted his unjust plight, to a substantive and positive peace, in which all men will respect the dignity and worth of human personality. Actually, we who engage in nonviolent direct action are not the creators of tension. We merely bring to the surface the hidden tension that is already alive. We bring it out in the open, where it can be seen and dealt with. Like a boil that can never be cured so long as it is covered up but must be opened with all its ugliness to the natural medicines of air and light, injustice must be exposed, with all the tension its exposure creates, to the light of human conscience and the air of national opinion before it can be cured.

In your statement you assert that our actions, even though peaceful, must be condemned because they precipitate violence. But is this a logical assertion? Isn't this like condemning a robbed man because his possession of money precipitated[28] the evil act of robbery? Isn't this like condemning Socrates because his unswerving commitment to truth and his philosophical inquiries precipitated the act by the misguided populace in which they made him drink hemlock?[29] Isn't this like condemning Jesus because his unique God-consciousness and never-ceasing devotion to God's will precipitated the evil act of crucifixion? We must come to see that, as the federal courts have consistently affirmed, it is wrong to urge an individual to cease his efforts to gain his basic constitutional rights because the quest may precipitate violence. Society must protect the robbed and punish the robber. . . .

Oppressed people cannot remain oppressed forever. The yearning for freedom eventually manifests itself, and that is what has happened to the American Negro. Something within has reminded him of his birthright of freedom, and something

MARK IT UP KEEP TRACK

Remember to use these marks to keep track of your understanding.

✔ ..... I understand.

? ..... I don't understand this.

! ..... Interesting or surprising idea

---

28. **precipitated** (prĭ-sĭp′ĭ-tā′tĭd): brought about; caused.

29. **Socrates . . . hemlock:** Socrates was tried for ruining the minds of the youth of Athens. He was condemned to die by drinking hemlock, a poison.

360 without has reminded him that it can be gained. Consciously or unconsciously, he has been caught up by the *Zeitgeist*,[30] and with his black brothers of Africa and his brown and yellow brothers of Asia, South America, and the Caribbean, the United States Negro is moving with a sense of great urgency toward the promised land of racial justice. If one recognizes this vital urge that has engulfed the Negro community, one should readily understand why public demonstrations are taking place. The Negro has many pent-up resentments and <u>latent</u> frustrations, and he must release them.

370 So let him march; let him make prayer pilgrimages to the city hall; let him go on freedom rides—and try to understand why he must do so. If his repressed emotions are not released in nonviolent ways, they will seek expression through violence; this is not a threat but a fact of history. So I have not said to my people: "Get rid of your discontent." Rather, I have tried to say that this normal and healthy discontent can be channeled into the creative outlet of nonviolent direct action. And now this approach is being termed extremist.

Pause & Reflect

FOCUS

380 King answers those who call him an extremist. Then he goes on to point out the "real heroes" of the South.

✎ MARK IT UP Circle some of the names King gives as examples of extremists.

But though I was initially disappointed at being categorized as an extremist, as I continued to think about the matter, I gradually gained a measure of satisfaction from the label. Was not Jesus an extremist for love: "Love your enemies, bless them that curse you, do good to them that hate you, and pray for them which despitefully use you, and persecute you." Was not Amos[31] an

---

30. *Zeitgeist* (tsīt′gīst′) *German*: spirit of the time—the beliefs and attitudes shared by most of the people living in a particular period.

31. *Amos*: a Hebrew prophet whose words are recorded in the Old Testament book bearing his name.

WORDS
TO
KNOW   **latent** (lāt′nt) *adj.* existing in a hidden form

Pause **&** *Reflect*

1. King regards the white moderates as "the Negro's great stumbling block in his stride toward freedom" (lines 306–307). Star the phrases below that identify reasons King gives for his opinion. (**Logical Argument**)

more interested in "order" than in justice

don't approve of direct action

openly reject African-Americans

prefer an absence of tension to the presence of justice

2. Reread the boxed paragraph on page 322. Circle the sentence below that best expresses the **main idea** of this passage.

Condemning peaceful protests is like treating the victims of crimes as though they had caused the crimes.

Peaceful protests should be condemned because they lead to violence.

extremist for justice: "Let justice roll down like waters and righteousness like an ever-flowing stream." Was not Paul an extremist for the Christian gospel: "I bear in my body the marks of the Lord Jesus." Was not Martin Luther[32] an extremist: "Here I stand; I cannot do otherwise, so help me God." And John Bunyan:[33] "I will stay in jail to the end of my days before I make a butchery of my conscience." And Abraham Lincoln: "This nation cannot survive half slave and half free." And Thomas Jefferson: "We hold these truths to be self-evident, that all men are created equal. . . ." So the question is not whether we will be extremists, but what kind of extremists we will be. Will we be extremists for hate or for love? Will we be extremists for the preservation of injustice or for the extension of justice? In that dramatic scene on Calvary's hill[34] three men were crucified. We must never forget that all three were crucified for the same crime—the crime of extremism. Two were extremists for immorality, and thus fell below their environment. The other, Jesus Christ, was an extremist for love, truth, and goodness, and thereby rose above his environment. Perhaps the South, the nation and the world are in dire need of creative extremists. . . .

I wish you had commended the Negro sit-inners and demonstrators of Birmingham for their sublime courage, their willingness to suffer, and their amazing discipline in the midst of great <u>provocation</u>. One day the South will recognize its real heroes. They will be the James Merediths,[35] with the noble sense of purpose that enables them to face jeering and hostile mobs, and with the agonizing loneliness that characterizes the life of the pioneer.

---

32. **Martin Luther:** a German monk who started the Protestant Reformation. Luther condemned the wealth and corruption of the 16th-century Roman Catholic Church.

33. **John Bunyan:** a 17th-century English preacher and author of the famous religious work *The Pilgrim's Progress*. He was twice imprisoned for preaching without a license.

34. **Calvary's hill:** the site of Jesus's crucifixion.

35. **James Merediths:** people like James Meredith, who endured violent opposition from whites to become the first African American to attend the University of Mississippi.

WORDS TO KNOW

provocation (prŏv′ə-kā′shən) *n.* something that arouses anger

They will be old, oppressed, battered Negro women, symbolized in a seventy-two-year-old woman in Montgomery, Alabama, who rose up with a sense of dignity and with her people decided not to ride segregated buses, and who responded with ungrammatical profundity to one who inquired about her weariness: "My feets is tired, but my soul is at rest." They will be the young high school and college students, the young ministers of the gospel and a host of their elders, courageously and nonviolently sitting in at lunch counters and willingly going to jail for conscience' sake. One day the South will know that when these disinherited children of God sat down at lunch counters, they were in reality standing up for what is best in the American dream and for the most sacred values in our Judaeo-Christian heritage, thereby bringing our nation back to those great wells of democracy which were dug deep by the founding fathers in their formulation of the Constitution and the Declaration of Independence.

Pause **&** *Reflect*

FOCUS

The ending of the letter returns to a more personal tone. Read to find out about King's feelings and hopes.

Never before have I written so long a letter. I'm afraid it is much too long to take your precious time. I can assure you that it would have been much shorter if I had been writing from a comfortable desk, but what else can one do when he is alone in a narrow jail cell, other than write long letters, think long thoughts, and pray long prayers?

If I have said anything in this letter that overstates the truth and indicates an unreasonable impatience, I beg you to forgive me. If I have said anything that understates the truth and indicates my having a patience that allows me to settle for anything less than brotherhood, I beg God to forgive me.

READ ALOUD Lines 419–425

As you read these lines aloud, listen to what the elderly woman says about herself.

Pause **&** *Reflect*

1. Look back at the names you circled as you read. Who are some of the extremists King identifies in lines 383–398? **(Clarify)**

_____

_____

_____

2. Why does King say in lines 381–383 that he "gained a measure of satisfaction" from being called an extremist? **(Infer)**

_____

_____

_____

3. King identifies several groups of people as the "real heroes" of the South (lines 411–437). Do you agree with King that these people are heroic? *Yes/No,* because _____

_____

_____

_____ .

(Evaluate)

1. King expresses his hopes in the final paragraph of his letter. What is his goal? **(Infer)**

_____

_____

_____

2. Based on this letter, what is your impression of King? **(Connect)**

_____

_____

_____

_____

I hope this letter finds you strong in the faith. I also hope that circumstances will soon make it possible for me to meet each of you, not as an integrationist or a civil-rights leader but as a fellow clergyman and a Christian brother. Let us all hope that the dark clouds of racial prejudice will soon pass away and the deep fog of misunderstanding will be lifted from our fear-drenched communities, and in some

460 not too distant tomorrow the radiant stars of love and brotherhood will shine over our great nation with all their scintillating[36] beauty.

Yours for the cause of Peace and Brotherhood,

Martin Luther King, Jr.

Pause & Reflect

CHALLENGE

How would you describe King's attitude toward the eight clergymen he is writing to? Mark words and phrases in the letter that tell something about his attitudes. **(Recognizing Tone)**

Wrapping Up

If you are using **The Language of Literature,** you can now move to the questions and activities on pages 1146–1147 of that book.

36. **scintillating** (sĭn′tl-āt′ĭng): sparkling.

Active Reading SkillBuilder

Logical Argument: Induction and Deduction

Writers often use different processes of reasoning in one nonfiction work. **Induction** is a process of reasoning in which a writer begins with specific facts and then reaches a general conclusion based on these facts. **Deduction** is a process of reasoning in which a writer begins with a general statement and then infers specific statements from it. Read King's letter, then use the diagram below to analyze a passage that appeals to you. One example is given.

Passage: _pages 312-313, lines 16–31_

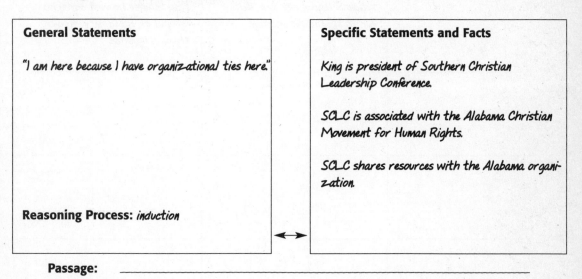

General Statements

"I am here because I have organizational ties here."

Reasoning Process: *induction*

Specific Statements and Facts

King is president of Southern Christian Leadership Conference.

SCLC is associated with the Alabama Christian Movement for Human Rights.

SCLC shares resources with the Alabama organization.

Passage: _____

General Statements

Reasoning Process:

Specific Statements and Facts

Literary Analysis SkillBuilder

Allusion

An **allusion** is a reference to a historical or literary person, place, or event with which the reader is assumed to be familiar. By using allusions, writers draw upon associations already in the reader's mind. On the chart below, list allusions to people, places, or events that King makes in this selection. Then explain the meaning that each allusion suggests to you. Briefly explain why you think King includes the allusion in his argument. An example has been done for you.

Allusion	Possible Meaning	Why Included
Apostle Paul	religious leader who traveled far to spread his message	King believes he must carry his "gospel of freedom" wherever there is injustice.

Words to Know SkillBuilder

Words to Know

affiliate	cognizant	estrangement	provocation	segregated
appraisal	diligently	latent	retaliating	statute

A. Fill in each blank with the correct Word to Know.

1. During the early 1960s there was more than one _____ that enforced segregation.

2. The _____ between the races led to misunderstanding and violence.

3. The civil rights movement made many more people _____ of the evils of racism.

4. Dr. King discouraged his supporters from _____ when provoked.

5. We can all benefit from a frequent _____ of the status of civil rights in this country.

B. Write the Word to Know that best completes each of the following analogies.

1. threat : intimidation : : insult : _____

2. acceptance : rejection : : integrated : _____

3. walk : purposefully : : labor : _____

4. obvious : overt : : hidden : _____

5. teacher : instructor : : associate : _____

C. Write a letter to Martin Luther King, Jr. Describe two or three things about the status of African Americans in 1963 that you learned from his writings. Use at least **three** of the Words to Know in your letter.

Before You Read

If you are using **The Language of Literature,** study the information on page 1194 of that book to prepare for reading.

Reading Tips

• Read "Mexicans Begin Jogging" and "Legal Alien" silently and then aloud to get a sense of what these poems are about. Hearing the sounds of a poem makes the meaning clearer and may add to your enjoyment.

• As you read each poem, try to imagine each situation that is described. Put yourself in the speaker's situation and try to relate to his or her feelings.

• After reading each poem a few times, zero in on the **figurative language,** or imaginative comparisons. For each comparison, identify the things compared and think about how they are alike.

MARK IT UP KEEP TRACK

As you read, you can use these marks to keep track of your understanding.

✔..... I understand.

?..... I don't understand this.

!..... Interesting or surprising idea

PREVIEW Gary Soto and Pat Mora are Mexican-American poets who are widely read. The poems "Mexicans Begin Jogging" and "Legal Alien" explore what happens when someone is prejudged or is treated differently because of his or her ethnic background. The speaker in "Mexicans Begin Jogging" is a United States citizen who is mistaken for an "illegal alien"— an immigrant who has unlawfully entered the country. "Legal Alien" is a term applied to an immigrant who, though not a U. S. citizen, is allowed to live in the United States.

MEXICANS BEGIN JOGGING

GARY SOTO

FOCUS

The speaker of this poem works in a factory. Read to find out what happens to the speaker when the police arrive to arrest illegal aliens.

At the factory I worked
In the fleck[1] of rubber, under the press
Of an oven yellow with flame,
Until the border patrol[2] opened
Their vans and my boss waved for us to run.   5
"Over the fence, Soto," he shouted,
And I shouted that I was American.
"No time for lies," he said, and pressed
A dollar in my palm, hurrying me
Through the back door.   10

---

1. **fleck:** a small bit or flake.
2. **border patrol:** a group of guards who watch the border between Mexico and the United States and arrest illegal aliens.

Since I was on his time, I ran
And became the wag to a short tail of Mexicans—
Ran past the amazed crowds that lined
The street and blurred like photographs, in rain.
I ran from that industrial road to the soft
Houses where people paled at the turn of an
    autumn sky.
What could I do but yell *vivas*³
To baseball, milkshakes, and those sociologists⁴
Who would clock me
As I jog into the next century
On the power of a great, silly grin.

Pause **&** Reflect

Pause **&** Reflect

1. What happens to the speaker in this poem? **(Summarize)**

2. How would you feel if you were in the speaker's situation? **(Connect)**

READ ALOUD 3. Read aloud lines 17–21. Cross out the sentence below that does *not* apply to the speaker. **(Clarify)**

He cheers American culture, as if to prove that he belongs.

He no longer wants to live in the United States.

He feels that his actions are being watched.

3. *vivas* (vē′väs): *Spanish*: cheers.
4. sociologists (sō′sē-ŏl′ə-jists): people who study group behavior.

LEGAL ALIEN

PAT MORA

Bi-lingual, Bi-cultural,
able to slip from "How's life?"
to *"Me'stan volviendo loca,"*[1]
able to sit in a paneled office
5 drafting memos in smooth English,
able to order in fluent Spanish
at a Mexican restaurant,
American but hyphenated,[2]
viewed by Anglos as perhaps exotic,[3]
10 perhaps inferior, definitely different,
viewed by Mexicans as alien,
(their eyes say, "You may speak
Spanish but you're not like me")
an American to Mexicans
15 a Mexican to Americans
a handy token
sliding back and forth
between the fringes of both worlds
by smiling
20 by masking the discomfort
of being pre-judged
Bi-laterally.[4]

---

1. *"Me'stan volviendo loca"* (mĕ-stän' vôl-vē-ĕn'dô lô'kä) *Spanish:* "They're making me crazy."

2. **American but hyphenated:** viewed as a Mexican-American, rather than just an American.

3. **exotic:** foreign; strange.

4. **Bi-laterally:** in a way that is undertaken by two sides equally.

Active Reading SkillBuilder

Comparing Writers' Attitudes

Tone is a **writer's attitude** toward the subject that he or she is writing about. Read "Mexicans Begin Jogging," and then identify on the chart below Soto's attitude toward being prejudged. Copy down a word, phrase, or line from Soto's poem that suggests his tone to you. When reading "Legal Alien," compare or contrast its tone with that of the first poem. Identify Mora's tone on the chart, then copy onto the chart a word, phrase, or line in the poem that you think conveys this tone.

"Mexicans Begin Jogging"

Tone: _____

_____

_____

Suggested by: _____

_____

_____

"Legal Alien"

Tone: _____

_____

_____

Suggested by: _____

_____

_____

Literary Analysis SkillBuilder

Tone

Tone is a writer's attitude toward the subject that he or she is writing about. In these two poems, the poets convey their attitudes toward being prejudged through their diction—their choice of words—their direct statements of their positions, and their use of imagery. On the chart below, list specific words, statements, and images that you think convey Soto's tone in "Mexicans Begin Jogging," and Mora's tone in "Legal Alien." Examples are shown.

	Diction	Direct Statements	Imagery
"Mexicans Begin Jogging"	*wag*	*"I shouted that I was American."*	
"Legal Alien"			

Straw into Gold:
The Metamorphosis of the Everyday

Sandra Cisneros

PREVIEW Sandra Cisneros is a Mexican-American writer who has earned many awards. One of her famous works is *The House on Mango Street*. It tells about a young girl's coming of age in inner-city Chicago. In this essay Cisneros relates some of her own recollections of growing up. The title "Straw into Gold" refers to the incredible task faced by the heroine of the folk tale "Rumpelstiltskin." She had to spin gold out of straw or be put to death. The word *metamorphosis* (mĕt´ə-môr´fə-sĭs) in the subtitle means "a change in form."

FOCUS
Cisneros begins her essay with an anecdote, or a brief story. Read to find out what happens when she is asked to cook at a dinner party in France.

When I was living in an artists' colony in the south of France, some fellow Latin-Americans who taught at the university in Aix-en-Provence invited me to share a home-cooked meal with them. I had been living abroad almost a year then on an NEA[1] grant, subsisting mainly on French bread and lentils so that my money could last longer. So when the invitation to dinner arrived, I accepted without hesitation. Especially since they had promised Mexican food.

What I didn't realize when they made this invitation was that I was supposed to be involved in preparing the meal. I guess they assumed I knew how to cook Mexican food because I am Mexican. They wanted specifically tortillas, though I'd never made a tortilla[2] in my life.

10

---

1. **NEA:** National Endowment for the Arts—a federal agency that funds artistic projects of organizations and individuals.
2. **tortilla** (tôr-tē´yə): A flat thin disk of bread made from corn meal or flour.

ESSAY

Before You Read
If you are using *The Language of Literature,* study the information on page 1227 of that book to prepare for reading.

Reading Tips
The author's style in this **essay** is personal, informal, and conversational. You might feel as though she is speaking directly to you. As you read, keep these points in mind:

- Look for the places where the author refers to the **title** of this essay. How does the title help you to understand the **main idea** of the essay?

- Remember the author's situation as a girl growing up in a Mexican-American family. Her culture had strong beliefs about the proper roles of females. She was expected to get married and devote herself to her home and family.

MARK IT UP KEEP TRACK

As you read, you can use these marks to keep track of your understanding.

✔ ..... I understand.

? ..... I don't understand this.

! ..... Interesting or surprising idea

It's true I had witnessed my mother rolling the little armies of dough into perfect circles, but my mother's family is from Guanajuato; they are *provincianos*, country folk. They only know how to make flour tortillas. My father's family, on the other hand, is *chilango*[3] from Mexico City. We ate corn tortillas but we didn't make them. Someone was sent to the corner tortilleria to buy some. I'd never seen anybody make corn tortillas. Ever.

Somehow my Latino hosts had gotten a hold of a packet of corn flour, and this is what they tossed my way with orders to produce tortillas. *Así como sea.* Any ol' way, they said and went back to their cooking.

Why did I feel like the woman in the fairy tale who was locked in a room and ordered to spin straw into gold? I had the same sick feeling when I was required to write my critical essay for the MFA[4] exam—the only piece of noncreative writing necessary in order to get my graduate degree. How was I to start? There were rules involved here, unlike writing a poem or story, which I did <u>intuitively</u>. There was a step by step process needed and I had better know it. I felt as if making tortillas—or writing a critical paper, for that matter— were tasks so impossible I wanted to break down into tears.

Somehow though, I managed to make tortillas—crooked and burnt, but <u>edible</u> nonetheless. My hosts were absolutely ignorant when it came to Mexican food; they thought my tortillas were delicious. (I'm glad my mama wasn't there.) Thinking back and looking at an old photograph documenting the three of us consuming those lopsided circles I am amazed. Just as I am amazed I could finish my MFA exam.

Pause & Reflect

Pause & Reflect

1. Why did making corn tortillas seem to be an impossible task to Cisneros? **(Main Idea)**

_____

_____

_____

_____

2. Cisneros compares making corn tortillas to writing a critical essay. What does she find similar about these challenges? **(Compare and Contrast)**

_____

_____

_____

_____

3. **chilango** (chē-län′gō): *Mexican slang:* native to Mexico City.

4. **MFA:** master of fine arts (an academic degree).

WORDS TO KNOW	**intuitively** (ĭn-tōō′ĭ-tĭv-lē) *adv.* without thinking; instinctively
	edible (ĕd′ə-bəl) *adj.* fit to eat

I've managed to do a lot of things in my life I didn't think I was capable of and which many others didn't think I was capable of either. Especially because I am a woman, a Latina,[5] an only daughter in a family of six men. My father would've liked to have seen me married long ago. In our culture men and women don't leave their father's house except by way of marriage. I crossed my father's threshold with nothing carrying me but my own two feet. A woman whom no one came for and no one chased away.

60 To make matters worse, I left before any of my six brothers had <u>ventured</u> away from home. I broke a terrible taboo.[6] Somehow, looking back at photos of myself as a child, I wonder if I was aware of having begun already my own quiet war.

I like to think that somehow my family, my Mexicanness, my poverty, all had something to do with shaping me into a writer. I like to think my parents were preparing me all along for my life as an artist even though they didn't know it. From my father I inherited a love of wandering. He was born in Mexico City but as a young man he traveled into the U.S. 70 vagabonding. He eventually was drafted and thus became a citizen. Some of the stories he has told about his first months in the U.S. with little or no English surface in my stories in *The House on Mango Street* as well as others I have in mind to write in the future. From him I inherited a sappy heart. (He still cries when he watches Mexican soaps—especially if they deal with children who have forsaken their parents.)

My mother was born like me—in Chicago but of Mexican descent. It would be her tough street-wise voice that would haunt all my stories and poems. An amazing woman who 80 loves to draw and read books and can sing an opera. A smart cookie.

When I was a little girl we traveled to Mexico City so much I thought my grandparents' house on La Fortuna, number 12,

---

5. **Latina:** a woman or girl from a Spanish-speaking culture.

6. **taboo:** a strict cultural rule forbidding something.

WORDS
TO
KNOW
   venture (vĕn′chər) *v.* to dare to go

1. What cultural taboo, or rule, did Cisneros break? **(Clarify)**

_____

_____

_____

2. Review the details you circled as you read. What two traits did Cisneros get from her father? **(Clarify)**

_____

_____

_____

3. Circle the *one* phrase below that is true of Cisneros's mother. **(Infer)**

born in Mexico

raised in wealth

artistically talented

sheltered as a child

was home. It was the only constant in our nomadic[7] ramblings from one Chicago flat to another. The house on Destiny Street, number 12, in the colonia Tepeyac would be perhaps the only home I knew, and that nostalgia[8] for a home would be a theme that would obsess me.

My brothers also figured greatly in my art. Especially the older two; I grew up in their shadows. Henry, the second oldest and my favorite, appears often in poems I have written and in stories which at times only borrow his nickname, Kiki. He played a major role in my childhood. We were bunk-bed mates. We were co-conspirators. We were pals. Until my oldest brother came back from studying in Mexico and left me odd woman out for always.

Pause & Reflect

What would my teachers say if they knew I was a writer now? Who would've guessed it? I wasn't a very bright student. I didn't much like school because we moved so much and I was always new and funny looking. In my fifth-grade report card I have nothing but an <u>avalanche</u> of C's and D's, but I don't remember being that stupid. I was good at art and I read plenty of library books and Kiki laughed at all my jokes. At home I was fine, but at school I never opened my mouth except when the teacher called on me.

When I think of how I see myself it would have to be at age eleven. I know I'm thirty-two on the outside, but inside I'm eleven. I'm the girl in the picture with skinny arms and a crumpled skirt and crooked hair. I didn't like school because all they saw was the outside me. School was lots of rules and sitting with your hands folded and being very afraid all the time. I liked looking out the window and thinking. I liked staring at the girl across the way writing her name over and over again in red ink. I wondered why the boy with the dirty

---

7. **nomadic:** moving from home to home; wandering.

8. **nostalgia** (nŏ-stăl′jə): a longing for things or people in the past.

WORDS
TO
KNOW

avalanche (ăv′ə-lănch′) *n.* an overwhelming amount

collar in front of me didn't have a mama who took better care of him.

I think my mama and papa did the best they could to keep
120 us warm and clean and never hungry. We had birthday and graduation parties and things like that, but there was another hunger that had to be fed. There was a hunger I didn't even have a name for. Was this when I began writing?

In 1966 we moved into a house, a real one, our first real home. This meant we didn't have to change schools and be the new kids on the block every couple of years. We could make friends and not be afraid we'd have to say goodbye to them and start all over. My brothers and the flock of boys they brought home would become important characters
130 eventually for my stories—Louie and his cousins, Meme Ortiz and his dog with two names, one in English and one in Spanish.

My mother flourished in her own home. She took books out of the library and taught herself to garden—to grow flowers so envied we had to put a lock on the gate to keep out the midnight flower thieves. My mother has never quit gardening.

This was the period in my life, that slippery age when you are both child and woman and neither, I was to record in *The*
140 *House on Mango Street*. I was still shy. I was a girl who couldn't come out of her shell.

How was I to know I would be recording and <u>documenting</u> the women who sat their sadness on an elbow and stared out a window? It would be the city streets of Chicago I would later record, as seen through a child's eyes.

I've done all kinds of things I didn't think I could do since then. I've gone to a prestigious[9] university, studied with famous writers, and taken an MFA degree. I've taught poetry in schools in Illinois and Texas. I've gotten an NEA grant and
150 run away with it as far as my courage would take me. I've seen the bleached and bitter mountains of the Peloponnesus.[10]

---

9. **prestigious** (prĕ-stē′jəs): respected.
10. **Peloponnesus** (pĕl′ə-pə-nē′səs): the peninsula forming the southern part of mainland Greece.

READ ALOUD Lines 142–145

As you read these lines aloud, imagine yourself in Cisneros's place, observing people in your new neighborhood. What questions might you ask about the women "who sat their sadness on an elbow"? (Connect)

_____

_____

_____

_____

WORDS TO KNOW

document (dŏk′yə-mənt) *v.* to provide a detailed account of

MARK IT UP **1.** Cisneros faced many struggles as a child. Underline details on pages 338 and 339 that tell you about them. In your opinion, what was her greatest challenge? **(Evaluate)**

_____

_____

_____

_____

2. As a writer, Cisneros must turn straw into gold. Put an *S* next to the phrases below that describe her straw. Put a *G* next to the phrase that describes her gold. **(Infer)**

everyday events

stories and poems

ordinary people

CHALLENGE

The **theme** is the main idea or opinion that the writer wants the reader to understand. Mark details or passages in this essay that reveal or hint at the writer's main idea or opinion. How would you state the theme of this essay? **(Analyze)**

Wrapping Up

If you are using *The Language of Literature,* you can now move to the questions and activities on pages 1232–1233 of that book.

I've lived on an island. I've been to Venice twice. I've lived in Yugoslavia. I've been to the famous Nice[11] flower market behind the opera house. I've lived in a village in the pre-Alps and witnessed the daily parade of promenaders.

I've moved since Europe to the strange and wonderful country of Texas, land of polaroid-blue skies and big bugs. I met a mayor with my last name. I met famous Chicana and Chicano artists and writers and *políticos*.[12]

160 Texas is another chapter in my life. It brought with it the Dobie-Paisano Fellowship, a six-month residency on a 265-acre ranch. But most important, Texas brought Mexico back to me.

In the days when I would sit at my favorite people-watching spot, the snakey Woolworth's counter across the street from the Alamo[13] (the Woolworth's which has since been torn down to make way for progress), I couldn't think of anything else I'd rather be than a writer. I've traveled and lectured from Cape Cod to San Francisco, to Spain, 170 Yugoslavia, Greece, Mexico, France, Italy, and now today to Texas. Along the way there has been straw for the taking. With a little imagination, it can be spun into gold.

Pause & Reflect

11. **Nice** (nēs): a port city in southern France.

12. *políticos* (pô-lē′tē-kôs): *Spanish:* politicians.

13. **Alamo:** a mission chapel in San Antonio, Texas—site of a famous battle in Texas's war for independence from Mexico.

Active Reading SkillBuilder

Analyzing Structure

The **structure** of an essay—the way in which its parts are arranged—is related to its purpose. For example, Cisneros's purpose in her essay is to share some of her formative experiences. Her essay, organized around recollections of growing up, begins with a story about making tortillas. In the first box below, write a summary of this opening anecdote. Write summaries of Cisneros's other recollections in the second box. On the lines between the boxes, write connections between the anecdote and the rest of the essay. An example is shown.

Connections

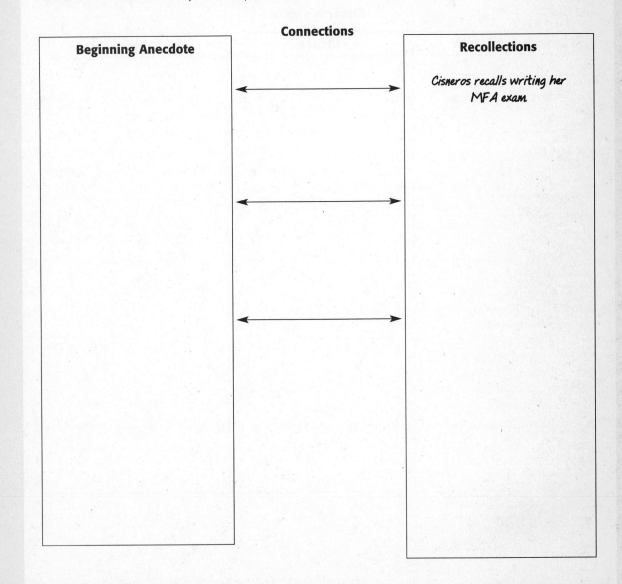

Beginning Anecdote

Recollections

Cisneros recalls writing her
MFA exam.

Literary Analysis SkillBuilder

Voice

Voice refers to a writer's unique use of language that allows a reader to "hear" a human personality in his or her writing. The elements that work together to create a writer's voice include sentence structure, diction, and tone. Use the following chart to analyze Cisneros's anecdote about making tortillas. Record information about sentence length, diction, and the writer's attitude toward her subject. An example is shown.

Cisneros's Voice

Sentence Length	Diction	Tone
short, simple sentences		

Words to Know SkillBuilder

Words to Know

avalanche   document   edible   intuitively   venture

A. Fill in each blank with the correct Word to Know.

1. Cisneros broke a terrible taboo when she decided to

   _____ away from home before any of her brothers did.

2. In her writing, Cisneros tries to _____ the lives of the
   people with whom she grew up.

3. Sometimes Cisneros can write a poem or story _____,
   almost without thinking.

4. In school Cisneros earned so many C's and D's that it seemed like an

   _____ in the Alps.

5. Cisneros was relieved when the tortillas she made turned out to be

   _____ .

B. Write the Word to Know that best complete each book title.

1. An _____ in the Mountains

2. A Childhood to Remember: My Attempt to _____ the Past

3. Speaking _____ : How to Communicate Quickly and Insightfully

4. All Things _____ : An All-Purpose Cookbook

5. My _____ into Freedom: A Daring Escapade

C. Write an anecdote about a time in your life when you succeeded at something
that you thought you could not do. Use at least **three** of the Words to Know in
your anecdote.

Personal Word List

Use these pages to build your personal vocabulary. As you read the selections take time to mark unfamiliar words. These should be words that seem interesting or important enough to add to your permanent vocabulary. After reading, look up the meanings of these words and record the information below. For each word, write a sentence that shows its correct use.

Review your list from time to time. Try to put these words into use in your writing and conversation.

Word: _____

Selection: _____

Page/Line: _____ / _____

Part of Speech: _____

Definition: _____

_____

_____

Sentence: _____

_____

Word: _____

Selection: _____

Page/Line: _____ / _____

Part of Speech: _____

Definition: _____

_____

_____

Sentence: _____

_____

Word: _____

Selection: _____

Page/Line: _____ / _____

Part of Speech: _____

Definition: _____

_____

_____

Sentence: _____

_____

Word: _____

Selection: _____

Page/Line: _____ / _____

Part of Speech: _____

Definition: _____

_____

_____

Sentence: _____

_____

Word: _____

Selection: _____

Page/Line: _____ / _____

Part of Speech: _____

Definition: _____

_____

_____

Sentence: _____

_____

Word: _____

Selection: _____

Page/Line: _____ / _____

Part of Speech: _____

Definition: _____

_____

_____

Sentence: _____

_____

Word:_____

Selection: _____

Page/Line: _____ / _____

Part of Speech: _____

Definition: _____
_____
_____

Sentence: _____
_____

Word:_____

Selection: _____

Page/Line: _____ / _____

Part of Speech: _____

Definition: _____
_____
_____

Sentence: _____
_____

Word:_____

Selection: _____

Page/Line: _____ / _____

Part of Speech: _____

Definition: _____
_____
_____

Sentence: _____
_____

Word:_____

Selection: _____

Page/Line: _____ / _____

Part of Speech: _____

Definition: _____
_____
_____

Sentence: _____
_____

Word:_____

Selection: _____

Page/Line: _____ / _____

Part of Speech: _____

Definition: _____
_____
_____

Sentence: _____
_____

Word:_____

Selection: _____

Page/Line: _____ / _____

Part of Speech: _____

Definition: _____
_____
_____

Sentence: _____
_____

Word:_____

Selection: _____

Page/Line: _____ / _____

Part of Speech: _____

Definition: _____
_____
_____

Sentence: _____
_____

Word:_____

Selection: _____

Page/Line: _____ / _____

Part of Speech: _____

Definition: _____
_____
_____

Sentence: _____
_____

Personal Word List (continued)

Word:_____

Selection: _____

Page/Line: _____ / _____

Part of Speech: _____

Definition: _____

_____

Sentence: _____

_____

Word:_____

Selection: _____

Page/Line: _____ / _____

Part of Speech: _____

Definition: _____

_____

Sentence: _____

_____

Word:_____

Selection: _____

Page/Line: _____ / _____

Part of Speech: _____

Definition: _____

_____

Sentence: _____

_____

Word:_____

Selection: _____

Page/Line: _____ / _____

Part of Speech: _____

Definition: _____

_____

Sentence: _____

_____

Word:_____

Selection: _____

Page/Line: _____ / _____

Part of Speech: _____

Definition: _____

_____

Sentence: _____

_____

Word:_____

Selection: _____

Page/Line: _____ / _____

Part of Speech: _____

Definition: _____

_____

Sentence: _____

_____

Word:_____

Selection: _____

Page/Line: _____ / _____

Part of Speech: _____

Definition: _____

_____

Sentence: _____

_____

Word:_____

Selection: _____

Page/Line: _____ / _____

Part of Speech: _____

Definition: _____

_____

Sentence: _____

_____

Word:_____

Selection: _____

Page/Line: _____ / _____

Part of Speech: _____

Definition: _____
_____
_____

Sentence: _____
_____

Word:_____

Selection: _____

Page/Line: _____ / _____

Part of Speech: _____

Definition: _____
_____
_____

Sentence: _____
_____

Word:_____

Selection: _____

Page/Line: _____ / _____

Part of Speech: _____

Definition: _____
_____
_____

Sentence: _____
_____

Word:_____

Selection: _____

Page/Line: _____ / _____

Part of Speech: _____

Definition: _____
_____
_____

Sentence: _____
_____

Word:_____

Selection: _____

Page/Line: _____ / _____

Part of Speech: _____

Definition: _____
_____
_____

Sentence: _____
_____

Word:_____

Selection: _____

Page/Line: _____ / _____

Part of Speech: _____

Definition: _____
_____
_____

Sentence: _____
_____

Word:_____

Selection: _____

Page/Line: _____ / _____

Part of Speech: _____

Definition: _____
_____
_____

Sentence: _____
_____

Word:_____

Selection: _____

Page/Line: _____ / _____

Part of Speech: _____

Definition: _____
_____
_____

Sentence: _____
_____

Personal Word List (continued)

Word: _____

Selection: _____

Page/Line: _____ / _____

Part of Speech: _____

Definition: _____

_____

_____

Sentence: _____

_____

Word: _____

Selection: _____

Page/Line: _____ / _____

Part of Speech: _____

Definition: _____

_____

_____

Sentence: _____

_____

Word: _____

Selection: _____

Page/Line: _____ / _____

Part of Speech: _____

Definition: _____

_____

_____

Sentence: _____

_____

Word: _____

Selection: _____

Page/Line: _____ / _____

Part of Speech: _____

Definition: _____

_____

_____

Sentence: _____

_____

Word: _____

Selection: _____

Page/Line: _____ / _____

Part of Speech: _____

Definition: _____

_____

_____

Sentence: _____

_____

Word: _____

Selection: _____

Page/Line: _____ / _____

Part of Speech: _____

Definition: _____

_____

_____

Sentence: _____

_____

Word: _____

Selection: _____

Page/Line: _____ / _____

Part of Speech: _____

Definition: _____

_____

_____

Sentence: _____

_____

Word: _____

Selection: _____

Page/Line: _____ / _____

Part of Speech: _____

Definition: _____

_____

_____

Sentence: _____

_____

Word:_____

Selection: _____

Page/Line: _____ / _____

Part of Speech: _____

Definition: _____

_____

_____

Sentence: _____

_____

Word:_____

Selection: _____

Page/Line: _____ / _____

Part of Speech: _____

Definition: _____

_____

_____

Sentence: _____

_____

Word:_____

Selection: _____

Page/Line: _____ / _____

Part of Speech: _____

Definition: _____

_____

_____

Sentence: _____

_____

Word:_____

Selection: _____

Page/Line: _____ / _____

Part of Speech: _____

Definition: _____

_____

_____

Sentence: _____

_____

Word:_____

Selection: _____

Page/Line: _____ / _____

Part of Speech: _____

Definition: _____

_____

_____

Sentence: _____

_____

Word:_____

Selection: _____

Page/Line: _____ / _____

Part of Speech: _____

Definition: _____

_____

_____

Sentence: _____

_____

Word:_____

Selection: _____

Page/Line: _____ / _____

Part of Speech: _____

Definition: _____

_____

_____

Sentence: _____

_____

Word:_____

Selection: _____

Page/Line: _____ / _____

Part of Speech: _____

Definition: _____

_____

_____

Sentence: _____

_____

Personal Word List (continued)

Word: _____

Selection: _____

Page/Line: _____ / _____

Part of Speech: _____

Definition: _____

_____

_____

Sentence: _____

_____

Word: _____

Selection: _____

Page/Line: _____ / _____

Part of Speech: _____

Definition: _____

_____

_____

Sentence: _____

_____

Word: _____

Selection: _____

Page/Line: _____ / _____

Part of Speech: _____

Definition: _____

_____

_____

Sentence: _____

_____

Word: _____

Selection: _____

Page/Line: _____ / _____

Part of Speech: _____

Definition: _____

_____

_____

Sentence: _____

_____

Word: _____

Selection: _____

Page/Line: _____ / _____

Part of Speech: _____

Definition: _____

_____

_____

Sentence: _____

_____

Word: _____

Selection: _____

Page/Line: _____ / _____

Part of Speech: _____

Definition: _____

_____

_____

Sentence: _____

_____

Word: _____

Selection: _____

Page/Line: _____ / _____

Part of Speech: _____

Definition: _____

_____

_____

Sentence: _____

_____

Word: _____

Selection: _____

Page/Line: _____ / _____

Part of Speech: _____

Definition: _____

_____

_____

Sentence: _____

_____

Word:_____

Selection: _____

Page/Line: _____ / _____

Part of Speech: _____

Definition: _____

_____

_____

Sentence: _____

_____

Word:_____

Selection: _____

Page/Line: _____ / _____

Part of Speech: _____

Definition: _____

_____

_____

Sentence: _____

_____

Word:_____

Selection: _____

Page/Line: _____ / _____

Part of Speech: _____

Definition: _____

_____

_____

Sentence: _____

_____

Word:_____

Selection: _____

Page/Line: _____ / _____

Part of Speech: _____

Definition: _____

_____

_____

Sentence: _____

_____

Word:_____

Selection: _____

Page/Line: _____ / _____

Part of Speech: _____

Definition: _____

_____

_____

Sentence: _____

_____

Word:_____

Selection: _____

Page/Line: _____ / _____

Part of Speech: _____

Definition: _____

_____

_____

Sentence: _____

_____

Word:_____

Selection: _____

Page/Line: _____ / _____

Part of Speech: _____

Definition: _____

_____

_____

Sentence: _____

_____

Word:_____

Selection: _____

Page/Line: _____ / _____

Part of Speech: _____

Definition: _____

_____

_____

Sentence: _____

_____

Personal Word List (continued)

Word:_____   Word:_____

Selection: _____   Selection: _____

Page/Line: _____ / _____   Page/Line: _____ / _____

Part of Speech: _____   Part of Speech: _____

Definition: _____   Definition: _____

_____   _____

_____   _____

Sentence: _____   Sentence: _____

_____   _____

Word:_____   Word:_____

Selection: _____   Selection: _____

Page/Line: _____ / _____   Page/Line: _____ / _____

Part of Speech: _____   Part of Speech: _____

Definition: _____   Definition: _____

_____   _____

_____   _____

Sentence: _____   Sentence: _____

_____   _____

Word:_____   Word:_____

Selection: _____   Selection: _____

Page/Line: _____ / _____   Page/Line: _____ / _____

Part of Speech: _____   Part of Speech: _____

Definition: _____   Definition: _____

_____   _____

_____   _____

Sentence: _____   Sentence: _____

_____   _____

Word:_____   Word:_____

Selection: _____   Selection: _____

Page/Line: _____ / _____   Page/Line: _____ / _____

Part of Speech: _____   Part of Speech: _____

Definition: _____   Definition: _____

_____   _____

_____   _____

Sentence: _____   Sentence: _____

_____   _____

Word:_____

Selection: _____

Page/Line: _____ / _____

Part of Speech: _____

Definition: _____

_____

_____

Sentence: _____

_____

Word:_____

Selection: _____

Page/Line: _____ / _____

Part of Speech: _____

Definition: _____

_____

_____

Sentence: _____

_____

Word:_____

Selection: _____

Page/Line: _____ / _____

Part of Speech: _____

Definition: _____

_____

_____

Sentence: _____

_____

Word:_____

Selection: _____

Page/Line: _____ / _____

Part of Speech: _____

Definition: _____

_____

_____

Sentence: _____

_____

Word:_____

Selection: _____

Page/Line: _____ / _____

Part of Speech: _____

Definition: _____

_____

_____

Sentence: _____

_____

Word:_____

Selection: _____

Page/Line: _____ / _____

Part of Speech: _____

Definition: _____

_____

_____

Sentence: _____

_____

Word:_____

Selection: _____

Page/Line: _____ / _____

Part of Speech: _____

Definition: _____

_____

_____

Sentence: _____

_____

Word:_____

Selection: _____

Page/Line: _____ / _____

Part of Speech: _____

Definition: _____

_____

_____

Sentence: _____

_____

Personal Word List (continued)

Word:_____

Selection: _____

Page/Line: _____ / _____

Part of Speech: _____

Definition: _____

_____

_____

Sentence: _____

_____

Word:_____

Selection: _____

Page/Line: _____ / _____

Part of Speech: _____

Definition: _____

_____

_____

Sentence: _____

_____

Word:_____

Selection: _____

Page/Line: _____ / _____

Part of Speech: _____

Definition: _____

_____

_____

Sentence: _____

_____

Word:_____

Selection: _____

Page/Line: _____ / _____

Part of Speech: _____

Definition: _____

_____

_____

Sentence: _____

_____

Word:_____

Selection: _____

Page/Line: _____ / _____

Part of Speech: _____

Definition: _____

_____

_____

Sentence: _____

_____

Word:_____

Selection: _____

Page/Line: _____ / _____

Part of Speech: _____

Definition: _____

_____

_____

Sentence: _____

_____

Word:_____

Selection: _____

Page/Line: _____ / _____

Part of Speech: _____

Definition: _____

_____

_____

Sentence: _____

_____

Word:_____

Selection: _____

Page/Line: _____ / _____

Part of Speech: _____

Definition: _____

_____

_____

Sentence: _____

_____

Word:_____

Selection: _____

Page/Line: _____ / _____

Part of Speech: _____

Definition: _____

_____

_____

Sentence: _____

_____

Word:_____

Selection: _____

Page/Line: _____ / _____

Part of Speech: _____

Definition: _____

_____

_____

Sentence: _____

_____

Word:_____

Selection: _____

Page/Line: _____ / _____

Part of Speech: _____

Definition: _____

_____

_____

Sentence: _____

_____

Word:_____

Selection: _____

Page/Line: _____ / _____

Part of Speech: _____

Definition: _____

_____

Sentence: _____

Word:_____

Selection: _____

Page/Line: _____ / _____

Part of Speech: _____

Definition: _____

_____

_____

Sentence: _____

_____

Word:_____

Selection: _____

Page/Line: _____ / _____

Part of Speech: _____

Definition: _____

_____

_____

Sentence: _____

Word:_____

Selection: _____

Page/Line: _____ / _____

Part of Speech: _____

Definition: _____

_____

_____

Sentence: _____

Acknowledgments *(Continued from page ii)*

Estate of Zora Neale Hurston: "How It Feels to Be Colored Me" by Zora Neale Hurston, from *I Love Myself When I Am Laughing: A Zora Neale Hurston Reader,* edited by Alice Walker. Reprinted by permission of the Estate of Zora Neale Hurston.

Faber & Faber: "The Love Song of J. Alfred Prufrock," from *Collected Poems, 1909–1962* by T. S. Eliot. Reprinted by permission of Faber and Faber Ltd.

Harcourt Brace & Company: "The Jilting of Granny Weatherall," from *Flowering Judas and Other Stories* by Katherine Anne Porter. Copyright 1930 and renewed 1958 by Katherine Anne Porter. Reprinted by permission of Harcourt Brace & Company.

Henry Holt & Company: "The Death of the Hired Man" by Robert Frost, from *The Poetry of Robert Frost,* edited by Edward Connery Lathem. Copyright © 1958 by Robert Frost, copyright © 1967 by Lesley Frost Ballantine. Copyright 1930, 1939, © 1969 by Henry Holt & Company. Reprinted by permission of Henry Holt and Company, Inc.

Alfred A. Knopf: Excerpts from *Of Plymouth Plantation, 1620–1647* by William Bradford, edited by Samuel Eliot Morison. Copyright © 1952 by Samuel Eliot Morison, renewed 1980 by Emily M. Beck. / "I, Too," from *Collected Poems* by Langston Hughes. Copyright © 1994 by the Estate of Langston Hughes. / "Dream Deferred" ("Harlem"), from *Collected Poems* by Langston Hughes. Copyright © 1994 by the Estate of Langston Hughes. / "The Weary Blues," from *Collected Poems* by Langston Hughes. Copyright © 1994 by the Estate of Langston Hughes. / Reprinted by permission of Alfred A. Knopf, Inc.

Random House: "A Rose for Emily" by William Faulkner, from *The Collected Stories of William Faulkner.* Copyright © 1930 and renewed 1958 by William Faulkner. Reprinted by permission of Random House, Inc.

Scribner: "The End of Something," from *In Our Time* by Ernest Hemingway. Copyright 1925 by Charles Scribner's Sons, copyright renewed 1953 by Ernest Hemingway. Reprinted with the permission of Scribner, a division of Simon & Schuster.

Viking Penguin: Excerpt from *The Crucible* by Arthur Miller. Copyright © 1952, 1953, 1954, renewed © 1980, 1981, 1982 by Arthur Miller. Used by permission of Viking Penguin, a division of Penguin Putnam Inc.

Writers House: Excerpts from "Letter from Birmingham Jail" by Martin Luther King, Jr. Copyright © 1963 by Martin Luther King, Jr., renewed 1991 by the Estate of Martin Luther King. Reprinted by arrangement with the Heirs to the Estate of Martin Luther King, Jr., c/o Writers House, Inc., as agent for the proprietor.